Huddled T

CW01501369

50 Years of Hull University Drama Department

by former Drama students

edited and introduced by
J. Michael Walton

The Barbican Press

Published by The Barbican Press, 11 Rokel Court, Hull HU6 7TJ

First published February 2013.
Reprint, May 2013.

ISBN 978-0-9563364-7-7

Set in Perpetua

Acknowledgements

Thanks are due, in the first instance, to all 138 contributors to this Anniversary Volume who have accepted a disgraceful level of arm-twisting of one kind or another in the midst of demanding and successful careers. They have accepted the responsibility of representing all those former students of Hull Drama Department over the last 50 years, many of whom, even if they have not submitted an entry, have been instrumental in spreading the word about the book through contacts they have maintained. To these must be added another former Drama student, Fiona Meakin, tolerant, astute and inspired designer of the cover. But, for better or worse, every former student and every present and former member of the Drama staff has a share in creating the Department as it is now, and part of its history as here laid bare. Current staff and students represent its future.

At a more personal level, I have received consistent support and encouragement from the rest of the committee who have initiated and organised the anniversary celebrations, Paula Lambert, Tony Meech, Louise Peacock, Tim Skelly, Amy Skinner (a photo from whose production of Euripides' *The Trojan Women* forms part of the front cover), Richard Tall and Emma Wales; from the Head of the Department of Drama and Music, Alistair Borthwick; from numerous other members of the University's administrative and academic staff too numerous to mention; and from all those associated with the University and the city of Hull who for half a century have indulged the Department's occasional whims and tantrums.

Had it not been for Martin Goodman, Professor of Creative Writing at the University of Hull and founder of the Barbican Press, the whole publishing process would have been far more difficult: much appreciated.

My wife Susan has also lived through most of the 50 years of the Department. Her active assistance when my skills in preparing the manuscript proved inadequate has been invaluable. She also did sterling work in proofing the final copy, but I alone take responsibility for any errors of fact, fiction, taste or judgement.

JMW, Hull, 2013
www.jmichaelwalton.com

Huddled Together

Contents

Introduction

It seemed a good idea initially to introduce a book of recollections with some words from Samuel Beckett, the Burke and Hare of memory, who can provide a quotation for each and every aspect of living in Hull. Beckett is reputed to have said that 'Hell must be like... reminiscing about the good old days when we wished we were dead'. Second thoughts prevailed, partly because, though it sounded like Beckett's droll humour, there seemed no way of finding out where or when he is meant to have said it, and partly because there might be readers for whom this was all too apt a description of their salad days in Hull (too many slugs in the lettuce). So the vote went instead to that later rummager through the past, dramatic pathologist Harold Pinter.

In *Old Times* (a production of which by Tony Meech went on a German tour just before Christmas in 1977), Anna says to Deeley at one point, 'There are some things one remembers even though they may never have happened. There are things I remember which may never have happened but as I recall them they take place'. This enigmatic proposition may better accord with the musings of contributors to this book.

The 138 who chose to reminisce here amount to little more than 6% of all the students who have studied in the Drama Department over the last 50 years. They have to represent the other 94% from all corners of the world whom we were either unable to contact, whose busy lives did not afford the luxury of wallowing in the past, or who preferred for a variety of reasons not to scratch and sniff their student experience in print. There are also, and most sadly, a number of former students who did not live long enough to have the choice. Some of these, along with three of the most fondly remembered members of staff no longer with us, are evoked in the accounts which follow: others we may not even know about. This inevitably slanted history is dedicated to all those former students who have or have not written here, not least for their help in contacting former confrères and consoeurs (is there such a word, Don?). It is equally for members of Drama Department staff, who, however disparate a set of individuals, have managed variously over half a century to provide an educational experience which gave most students someone or something to latch onto, as oracle, inspiration, mentor or simply friend.

As those who read this probably already know, the Drama Department was created in 1963 with a single member of staff, Donald Roy, an office in the Administration Building and the indispensable goodwill of the then Vice-Chancellor, Brynmor Jones, and his wife Dora. At the time there were independent Departments of Drama at only two British universities, Bristol and Manchester. Hull received positive impetus for the introduction of a dedicated Department of Drama from several senior academics, Professors of English and French, later abetted (less predictably, unless you knew he would soon become President of the Magic Circle), by the newly-appointed Professor of Biochemistry. At our lowest ebb in 1981 when the then government advocated Drama's closure, a huge proportion of the university staff, academic and administrative, proved to be just as supportive as those early advocates. That Drama was regarded as anything more than a source of irritation which occasionally added colour to the Cottingham Road culture – a sort of campus (or just camp) court jester – was something of a surprise and soon took on the appearance of an act of supreme altruism when it meant that other disciplines and individuals found themselves in the frame as the University faced successive rounds of huge cuts. The Careers Service offered major support providing figures to show that as many as 85% of those who had graduated with either the Joint or Single Honours degree were making use of their drama in their subsequent profession, giving the lie to one of the University Grants Committee's justifications for singling out Drama for the chop, namely that there were no jobs to which such graduates could graduate.

As it was, we managed to justify that faith when subsequently achieving a rare maximum rating in all areas of the Teaching Quality Assurance evaluations of the 1990s, the top rating of 5 in the then Research Assessment Exercise and the accolade of top place in one of the prominent Press League Tables for the subject. Significant numbers of our graduates were already making a national, and in many cases international, impact in their chosen careers. Such a reputation has continued to grow, to which many of those who have contributed here, as well as those who have not, bear abundant witness. This aspect of Drama at Hull is a success dependent as much on the students as on any efforts of the staff, but a combination of both is reflected in the time and dedication put into Admissions. For as long as it remained practicable, every member of staff was involved in the selection procedure which, aided by the input of current students, aimed to give an account in miniature of what an academic course in Drama involved in a department graced with technical facilities as good as in any educational establishment in Europe. A significant proportion of contributors recall their interview, even more the impact on them of first stepping inside the Gulbenkian Centre.

Our graduates who have become performers had worked backstage, in design and on front-of-house. The designers and technicians had acted in front of the public, some in lurid leotards they have never forgotten. The directors, writers, administrators and teachers had experienced something of every aspect of the theatre, enhanced by introductory practice in radio, television and film. The programme of stage performances, from full productions of the classics to experimental lunchtime performances – one manifestation of the HUDDLE (Hull University Drama Department Lunchtime Event), was exhaustive as well as exhausting. The course was underpinned by a rigorous study of theatre history and dramatic literature with a world, not just an anglophone, perspective. The real defining character of a degree in Drama from Hull may be breadth but is more probably stamina.

Perhaps this is the moment too to record, somewhat sheepishly, the tolerance of members of staff in other departments with whom we shared students for the lack of balance so many Joints applied to their two subjects, especially at times of major productions, when the pressure of drama schedules was severe; we were inclined to make few concessions to the demands of the more academic side of the degree courses, our own or anyone else's.

The Department's more formal history over those 50 years is recorded elsewhere, if more briefly than it may deserve.[1] Such accounts may be said to come from the prompt corner. In contrast, these in the following pages are from the stage, the control-rooms, the wardrobe, scene-dock and dressing rooms, tours, parties, GAFTAS (our version of the BAFTAS) and cricket matches: on occasion, from the classroom too. To change the metaphor, what

---

[1] Roy, Donald, *Hull University Drama Department, 21ˢᵗ Birthday*, printed within the Drama Department, 1984.
Walton, J. Michael, 'The Drama Department, University of Hull, 1962-92', reprinted by Hull University Press from Chapter 2 of Dellar, Pamela (ed.), *People Make Plays: Aspects of Community Theatre in Hull Since 1955*, Beverley: Highgate Publications, 1992, pp. 18-35. See also, Walton, *Recollections of Hull Drama Department 1965-2003*, privately printed for the Hull University Archives in the Hull History Centre, 2009.

are recorded here are messages from the coalface, many of which proved a surprise to me, usually a pleasant one. There are tales of occasions and embarrassments, triumphs and disasters, life-changing moments and life-affirming encounters, Guest HUDDLEs and First Nights, but, above all, an abiding sense of affection for the years spent moving from callowness to confidence. My own children always claimed they could recognise Drama Department students in the street, less because they had seen them onstage than for the aura they seemed to carry with them. Of course this could be a result of the plumbing in many of the famous and infamous houses that were handed down from Drama generation to Drama generation. From initial interview to current profession, the memories have flooded in, including some 'which may not have happened but as I recall them they take place'.

The decision to organise the material chronologically rather than by subject-matter or degree was easy enough to make. The first entry is from 'the oldest known survivor', one of that very first set of Ancillary students. Happily, Alwyn Humphries was not only among that first small group with Donald Roy in 1963/4, but re-merges in the University records, following an MBE, with the award in 2006 of an Honorary D Mus, for his outstanding contribution to composition and musical education.

The final entry is from Abbi Greenland who graduated with Single Honours Drama in 2009. Abbi's memoir is preceded by, but linked to, that of her mother, Penny Greenland (MBE 2001, for her work as Director of JABADAO, the National Centre for Movement, Learning and Health), who also read Single Honours Drama at Hull, graduating in 1976. Penny's own mother completed a degree in History at Hull in 1946. The link is serendipitous but revealing.

Between, are the trailblazers, from Ancillary or Subsidiary years to the first Joint Honours and the first Special (Single Honours) students who from the 1990s have outnumbered the Joints. This is reflected in the fact that none of the contributions since 1996 is from a Joint student, though most of those from before that date are. That those graduating from the early years should have supplied such a large proportion of all contributors can best be accounted for, I imagine, from a pioneering spirit informed by an intake and staff-student ratio small enough to afford opportunities to all. Sheer numbers have made this harder to maintain. Subsequent generations, especially the women who have always outnumbered the men despite the relative number of entries here, had to learn how to hustle (? standing for Hull University Study of Theatre with Limpet Endurance). Though for some this may have proved training for the professional world outside, there were many whose potential was not cultivated until after they left. Perhaps that is how it should be and there are numbers of examples here of how people discovered areas of interest and expertise previously unexpected from the range of experience to which the course and the productions in the Gulbenkian gave initial access.

As it is, every graduation year from 1969 (the first Joint Drama degrees) to 2006 is represented. Recent years have offered fewer. The lack of responses from students I never came across because I had by then retired (2003), deprives me of the complete picture, but is perhaps explained by there being none among them I could so shamelessly browbeat, bully and blackmail into submission. The authors have not been hand-picked. They are simply those who chose to contribute: and no entries have been rejected. In the first rubric, I sent out dire warnings about my definition of Editor. Some pieces have had to be tailored to avoid overlap of anecdotes, or condensed to what is more obviously Department rather than personal history; others shamelessly to fit available space. The virtue is that all have demonstrated a flair for conjuring up the past which should prove interesting even to those who have never met or heard of the authors. The prevailing vice is excessive modesty about their own achievements since graduation, but together they blend into a truer portrait of the Department, warts and all, than any single author could ever have offered.

Probably the older we get the more retrospective we become. University experience has changed out of all recognition in 50 years. Nonetheless, whatever frustrations, disappointments or anxieties the present generations of students face, at least a significant proportion of Drama graduates will, I trust, be able to agree with Hannah Miller, who writes of the various professional Drama 'Mafias' and entitles her piece 'You Never Leave Hull University Drama Department'. Or, as Miss Julie had it (in the 'Strined – burge' play to those taught by the treasured Harry Thompson, with his cunning perception that cultivated eccentricity is the hallmark of the memorable teacher), 'No matter how far we travel, the memories will follow in the baggage car'.

J. Michael Walton, HUDD 1965-2003, Emeritus Professor of Drama 2003 –

The Oldest Known Survivor

Alwyn Humphreys, MBE. Single Honours Music, 1966; Ancillary Drama, 1964; Hon D Mus, 2006
TV presenter and conductor

I've been called a few things in my time but never in my wildest dreams did I imagine that one day I'd be referred to as 'the oldest known survivor' – it's a phrase that conjures up visions of the Boer War or Chelsea Pensioners. However, the founding of a Department of Drama at Hull in 1963 was, for me, an answer to a prayer. My original intention had been to read Welsh at Bangor, with its thriving drama society led by the then greatest living Welsh playwright, John Gwilym Jones. However, after I'd filled the application forms my Headmaster sent for me: 'Music's your subject boy – change it!'. So I looked in prospectuses for a Music course where I could do Drama too. Enter the University of Hull, a brand new Drama course and Donald Roy.

My recollections of those early days are of being more of a full-time performer than a student. Every week there were rehearsals, concerts and plays, and academic work seemed incidental. The drama productions were performed with the barest of props at the far end of the Assembly Hall. This meant being on the stage all the time, even if you weren't part of the action. In one play I sat at the back reading a newspaper until it was time to make my entrance: Eliot's *Sweeney Agonistes,* I think, which I recall clearly for another reason. I had to snog a prostitute. I don't remember the name of the student actress – Tina? – but I vividly recall her bright red hair and an extremely tarty look. My snogging was not convincing enough for Don, who directed me to fondle her buttocks. I'd never touched a girl's bum. It's the truth. Doing it in public was a serious challenge bringing squeals of laughter from my Music colleagues in the audience, one of whom I was specially trying to impress. She would have nothing to do with me afterwards. I was shop-soiled. Thanks Don.

Yes, happy days certainly, but the drama course was also hugely beneficial in developing self-confidence which I sadly lacked at the time. In later years the fact that I'd done Drama at Hull was extremely useful, especially when I diverted my music career into television producing and directing at the BBC. People were impressed by the fact that I'd been there. And they continue to be, because, believe me, there's still some life in the 'oldest known survivor'.

Drama by the Back Door

Michael Theodorou. Joint French and Spanish, 1967; (Hon. Drama Ancillary because he could act)
Actor, director, writer

The odd thing about the past is that it has a way of finding you in unusual ways. On a recent holiday I came across a history lecturer who had been my contemporary at Hull in the mid-'60s. The following year while on holiday I met a nuclear physicist who had been a student at Hull in the mid-'50s. A few months later I chanced to look at the Hull University website and was delighted to see that Mike Walton was listed under Drama Department staff as Emeritus Professor of Drama. After some hesitation I decided to drop him an email and almost by return I had a communication in which he named the play and the role I'd played for him in 1966.

I wasn't officially a member of the Drama Department as I was supposed to be studying French and Spanish, but Mike had seen me in a Dram Soc production of Camus' *Caligula* and came up afterwards saying something like 'It was a terrible production, but you were the best thing in it. I'd like you to play Tolen in Ann Jellicoe's *The Knack* with the Drama Department'.

Drama's performance space was an old gym which seemed an odd venue for performing plays, but there was a full lighting rig and a stage at one end with a box set for *The Knack*. I remember two other of Mike's productions and a Brecht play done in Czech by a company from Brno. I was quickly smitten by the acting bug and felt very much at home within the Drama Department who also seemed to have the best parties. I was summoned to the Head of French shortly after my appearance in *The Knack* who told me in no uncertain terms that I was at Hull to study languages and not to 'act in plays'.

There was also at that period of time, I seem to recall, a gentleman in the library called Philip Larkin who I was told was a poet.

These reminiscences come 45 years after the events described so they may be a bit hazy, but I recall my association with the Drama Department as being a key to my future development as actor, director and writer for which I shall always be grateful.

Plays and Players

Richard Grayson. Single Honours English, 1970; Drama Ancillary, 1968
Actor and Teacher

Chris Hitchens and I were in the first Department play produced in the Theatre Lab, David Campton's one-act *Out of the Flying-Pan*. Rehearsed and directed by Donald Roy in a few lunchtime breaks, it suited the only-just-finished sparsely-equipped ex-gym, wall bars still glowing from topcoat black matt. It had a set comprising two chairs and a small table, not challenging the stage crew.

A very different enterprise followed a few weeks later when all the Ancillary [*3-term*] and Subsidiary [*5-term course, mainly for those studying languages*] Drama students took part in Dylan Thomas's *Under Milk Wood*.

A couple of memories of this: an all-day Sunday dress rehearsal when the massed forces (a cast of over 40) muddled through, finally finishing at 10.00pm. At the end of a harrowing notes session JMW, directing, said, 'So, as it's clearly not yet ready, we'll run the whole thing again in 10 minutes'. I recall cycling home through the snow nearly three hours later, wondering if I shouldn't change courses to Applied Astrophysics.

And, in performance a couple of days later, the sound techie slipped up. The tape wasn't faultless and the 'swashing in the dark' peeing of PC Attila Rees into his helmet was far too quiet. For it to be heard by the audience the volume had to be turned up to max. On this night the sound operator omitted to turn it down afterwards. The next sound cue came before the First Voice confided that 'the owls are hunting' and when it came the audience leapt in their seats at the hoots, imagining owls overhead the size of the Flying Scotsman.

The academic year ended with a play very much of its time and with a great jazz score specially composed and played live on-stage. It was Ann Jellicoe's four-hander, *The Knack*. Once again acting with Chris Hitchens, I played the no-hoper (Michael Crawford in the indifferent Richard Lester film) and some genius thought it would be good publicity for the production if the beauties in the Department sat suggestively in swimwear on a truck in the Rag Day

Parade. I was to chase behind them desperately, like a damned soul, never quite catching up. OK, but the route was from the University, down Beverley Road and throughout the town. I suppose I was fitter then and it mercifully wasn't a hot day, but even so … and I had a performance of the Rag Revue that night. We revived the production in October for next year's incoming students, but in the absence of Chris Hitchens his part was played by the director. I felt my own contribution was being weighed up at close quarters.

Mike also directed James Saunders' haunting *A Scent of Flowers* in which I played the darkly comic Scrivens, the undertaker – 'Funereal decorum is my business'. After one rehearsal Mike and I were at the bar in the Queen's on Queen's Road. We struck up a conversation with a morose fellow standing next to us. He was miserable today, he said, because he had just finished with a 'princess'. This apparently was the title he gave to young girls who had been cut down in their prime, requiring a coffin make-over. Yes, he was an undertaker. Looking back, it seems callous that we encouraged him to talk of his undertaking experiences. Orton, writing *Loot* round about then, would, I'm sure, have capitalised on the conversation's treasures. He informed us that he had a sideline in selling second-hand (transit) coffins to yacht-owners at Bridlington to use as dinghies. I decided to base none of my characterisation on him.

The Hull University Drama Department Lunchtime Event – acronym HUDDLE – gave us plenty of entertainment. Sir Donald Wolfit, appearing at the New Theatre in *Dear Screwtape*, took time off to come and address us. I had never been as close to such a famous person and clearly held him in much awe. His manner was regal and relentlessly intimidating as he spoke down to us lengthily about loyalty, hard work and commitment, chain-smoking all the time. He was so impressive that when he had departed I took one of his butts out of the full ashtray as a souvenir (Sad).

Almost as impressive were Micheál MacLiammóir and Harry H. Corbett. The first took a distinct shine to Dave Edwards (our butch stage technician) and publicly referred to Mike, his dresser, as his 'bearded French maid'; and the second, a week or two later, sat in front of us, dressed in what looked like one of Archie Rice's castoffs [*Osborne's* The Entertainer] and in a sour mood, silently challenging anyone to ask him why he should waste his vast talent appearing in another series of *Steptoe and Son*. There was a lengthy and awkward silence. Then one of our brighter first-years [*Paul Roylance*] asked the great man 'Where on earth did you buy that suit?' It was a pertinent, but risky question. A moment's silence, then Harry H laughed and talked for an hour non-stop, mainly about working with Joan Littlewood, exactly what we had come to hear.

The British première of *The Sunday Walk* by Georges Michel celebrated the final year of the first generation of Joint Honours students' graduation. The production toured to York Arts Centre and, for two weeks, the West End, at the Little (very little) Theatre, Garrick Yard (off St Martin's Lane, no less). A set suggesting locations in a French town and fit for touring had to be constructed. An ingenious vertical scroll, about seven feet tall and hand-cranked between two rollers was the solution.

Sadly, it never really worked reliably. It kept unwinding at one end, but not managing to rewind at the other; a bit like trying to roll back toilet tissue. Entrances and exits were delayed when the door openings failed to appear in the canvas backing and sometimes the whole construction seemed near collapse as stage-management struggled. On bad days we took to using the wings for entrances and exits, leaving the audience to puzzle over the purpose of the static backdrop.

But the author came and seemed happy, and we did attract the attention of French Theatre specialist and Sunday Times critic, Sir Harold Hobson, who struggled up the umpteen stairs, stayed to the end and didn't write us off completely in his review.

Remembering the Theatre Lab

Deirdre Barber (Kinkaid). Joint Drama and English 1969; Ph D, Drama, 2001
Retired after a patchy career including professional acting

The Theatre Laboratory, the Drama Department's rehearsal, performance, partying and hanging-out space, was my home for four years. I came to Hull in 1965 to read English with Ancillary Drama, and then changed to the new Joint Honours course the next year, so I was there for nearly all its early life.

The campus was smaller in those days and the Theatre Lab was tucked behind the Chemistry building and facing the Arts Block [*now the Larkin Building*], where the lecturers had their offices. It was newly converted in 1965; it had been a gym and the wall bars were still in place, with a badminton court marked out on the floor. Raw new rostra and a few double-sided flats had been provided and the wall bars covered with hessian curtains. The latter didn't last long, if I remember rightly; one of the first things I was to learn as an unsophisticated 18-year-old was that theatres are scruffy places subject to continual revision. As the late great Harry Thompson said, 'No good theatre ever came off a drawing-board, ladies and gentlemen'.

Some of the equipment was quaint by modern standards. Opposite what was usually, but not always, the stage end was a gantry, reached by a ladder, with a closed lighting and sound box at one side. The lighting was regulated by Strand Junior 8s, mechanical resistance dimmers which could overheat and stick when the levels were low for any length of time. I remember David Edwards, the first Department technician, taking one apart and reassembling it in mid-performance. To dim all the lights at once, you placed a batten across all the knobs and pushed them down. Computers? What are those?

Scenery was painted the traditional way, with pigments mixed with size. This glue came as crystals, which were put in water and melted over heat, then added to the diluted pigment to make a paint that didn't rub off the scenery. I'll never forget the smell of size being heated – wonderfully atmospheric.

There was no wardrobe-mistress back then, so the students made costumes unsupervised. I remember going into town looking for some white cotton material and being shown some piqué by the saleslady, who pronounced it 'peaky'. I nearly said, 'I hope it feels better soon'.

As well as preparing scenery and costumes there, we also hung out in the Theatre Lab's two dressing rooms, taking it in turns to buy big jars of instant coffee. I remember washing coffee mugs with a scene-painting brush. Backstage there were also showers which no one used, left over from the gym days, and eventually a loo you couldn't use during performances, as the flush would be heard in the auditorium. The Lab was great for after-show parties too, atmosphere courtesy of a few coloured gels and vinyl records booming over the sound system.

With the rostra, staging could be flexible. Mike Walton's 1969 production of *him* by e.e. cummings used a stage at one end, a circular space in the middle of the auditorium, mirror plastic and projections: multi-media before there was a word for it. It hit the late '60s zeitgeist: though the tickets were free, a black market developed in the students union as word spread.

The Gulbenkian Centre was still a building site the year I graduated. I believe that after it opened, the Theatre Lab was kept on for a while, but, returning a few years later, I found it demolished and its grave a flower bed. There had been worries that the Gulbenkian would turn out to be a restricting, 'official' space like the Middleton Hall and that there would be an end to the experiments and the making-it-up-as-you-go-along freedom, that were typical of the scruffy, friendly Theatre Lab. But no: at one of the Drama Department's anniversary celebrations I was at a party in the Gulbenkian and for one moment thought I was in the Theatre Lab, so similar was the atmosphere. *Plus ça change, plus ça* – luckily in this case – *la même chose*.

In Joint

Graham Cowley. Joint Drama and French, 1969
Theatre Producer

The 1960s hadn't really started in Salisbury by 1966. I suspect that was true of other provincial towns too, as it was in a class of rather neat, well-behaved 18-year-olds that I sat beside that October for the first lecture of the first Hull University Joint Drama degree group. We listened respectfully to Don Roy as he explained his definition of theatre as an exciting event that took place before an audience. The example he gave was the difference between watching a striptease act in a club and watching the same strip in the privacy of your bedroom. Impressed with this racy introduction to the academic study of Drama, I lost no time in engaging with the traditional student pursuits of getting drunk and falling in love. For me, the '60s had finally started.

Our first lecturers were three very distinct personalities. Don Roy, ingrained with all things French, offered loucheness and chain-smoked Gauloises. I was in his production of *A Yorkshire Tragedy* and was overjoyed when, after the last night, he gave me my costume, a scarlet velvet tunic with embossed sleeves.

Harry Thompson was a true eccentric. He looked like an elderly sergeant-major in his loudly-checked sports jacket, but was genuinely fond of us, especially the boys, for whom he would cook curries from time to time. His weird pronunciation of words like 'Elizabetthan' and 'Veeking', and his reminiscences of working as Bernard Miles's house-manager at the Mermaid, ensured full attendance at his lectures. We adored him. He got me my first job when I left Hull, as an Acting ASM at Derby Playhouse.

Mike Walton, only a little older than the students, was a martinet about handing essays in on time, but a professional director, slyly funny in rehearsal. After graduation he brought our production of *The Sunday Walk* to York, then London (to the Little Theatre, Garrick Yard). He also linked several of us for life (Fred Steadman-Jones, Gary Penny, Gareth Armstrong) in playing a very camp group of fairies in *him* by e.e. cummings.

To be honest, I struggled with the academic course. I liked reading plays, but at the time I had only a passing interest in theatre history (though the seeds planted then grew into a consuming passion in subsequent years). But what I loved beyond all measure was acting in the plays in the Theatre Lab. The Lab was the former University gym. It was painted black. It was cold and the roof leaked. It was magical. I cherish the memory of Fred Steadman-Jones, our one mature student, directing rehearsals of *Reynard the Fox* perched at the top of the wall bars, while the rest of us impersonated forest animals, choreographed by the dancer Ansel Wong. Geoff Rowe has never quite shrugged off the persona of Brun the Bear and Richard Saunders is still known by some of us as Wolf. I played the Fox, and later became a theatre producer ...

As the Department acquired a second year's worth of students, then a third, more members of staff arrived. Nick Hern, himself only a recent graduate from Bristol, spoke to us of German drama. Our lives have intertwined ever since. As a publisher of plays, first at Methuen then under his own imprint, Nick Hern Books, he has promoted the careers of most of the playwrights I have worked with at the Royal Court and other new-play companies, Joint Stock and Out of Joint.

My own progress through the three years was marked mainly by the differing lengths of my hair. To my joy Don Roy encouraged me to grow out the neat haircut from my arrival and cover my ears, so I could play an Elizabethan gentleman. My parents were dismayed, but that was as nothing to how they felt at the end of my second year when my hair nearly reached my shoulders, for *Dr Faustus*. Compromising in my third year, I cut my hair but grew a beard, though that soon shrank to a moustache to play the Son in *Six Characters in Search of an Author*.

Did it all prepare us for life in the professional theatre? Yes and no. As drama students, going from show to show and being whisked into *The Mysteries* in Derby we were of course insulated from the need to earn a living (or indeed get into debt). But one HUDDLE, where actors visiting from the New Theatre talked to us about their, lives made an impression – the actor who said 'I've done pretty well – I've been in work most of the time' brought the chill wind of reality briefly into our lives. But whatever else, Drama was viewed as being slightly suspect, but a bit glamorous, by the rest of the University. We were the first degree-year at Hull. It was fantastically exciting for a provincial boy to be part of this new thing.

We Weren't Big, But We Were Clever

Liz Gill. Joint Drama and English, 1969
Journalist

We were an average of three Bs clever, in fact. Grade inflation makes that sound an easy entry requirement, but back in 1966 it would have been the equivalent of four A*s today. The reason the bar was set so high was that the fledgling Drama Department was desperate to prove its academic worth to the University's doubters. The law of unintended consequences, however, meant that since girls tended to be better at exams there were twice as many of us. 16 females to 8 males didn't matter for most things, but it did make finding plays to perform pretty difficult and ingenious solutions were thought up. Our summer-school production of the Scottish play, for instance, had two Lady Macbeths and nine witches.

Practical theatre skills were a relatively small part of our term-time studies, confined in our first year to a three-hour workshop on Saturday mornings. At a time when every other self-respecting student was hours away from even waking up, we would be sashaying around in our rehearsal skirts in the ramshackle old Theatre Lab trying to please an extraordinary woman called Honor Matthews. Honor was, I think, genuinely old, not just old-to-a-young-person-old, tall and angular with prominent teeth and an apparent disdain for any kind of adornment or artifice. She was also magnetic, motivating and inspiring. She travelled up to Hull every week from the Central School of Speech and Drama], where she no doubt taught actors of dazzling talent, to teach a group who were on the whole decidedly undazzling, but she never, ever, made us feel like the poor relations. On the contrary she made us feel nothing was impossible: Ibsen, Wilde, Shakespeare, the Ancient Greeks. We could understand them, we could give them our best shot.

As well as insights into great plays she taught us practical skills, some of which have proved enduringly helpful. I've used her relaxation techniques to beat sleeplessness and her voice projection tips to bawl from the kitchen to the kids' bedrooms. And for years I could do a stage fall as a great party piece before I'd even had a drink. I'm sorry now that I didn't know more about her: when she finished the class she'd go off to the station and we'd go for coffee and post-workshop analysis.

She was the exception to the rule because, being such a small department, we all knew each other pretty well and we knew our lecturers, and usually their wives or girlfriends too, often socialising at parties and 'Theatre Lab' events. It was unusual then – it didn't seem to happen in other departments – and must, given the size of student populations today, be almost unknown now.

So we were small, we were intimate – in some cases literally (you know who you are), and we were amateur. The people who educated us and who also directed the shows we put on were obviously not amateur: they were professionals with a wide range of skills. Even among us students there were those with considerable gifts and experience as well as people like me who had done a couple of school plays and thought it might be a lark to do something different at university. And of course in the following years the Department grew in confidence and stature and gained state-of-the-art facilities and probably students to match.

Many of the Class of '69 did go on to carve out successful careers in the theatre or allied occupations, but my memory of those pioneering three years is that there was a sense of doing something for love, for fun, for experimentation, regardless of whether it led to a proper job at the end. But then it was the '60s.

I never had the inclination, never mind the talent, to go into the theatre, but I have had a reasonable working life as a journalist. And I've had, as all hacks have, someone say to me at a party 'I thought of being a journalist. I was very good at English at school'. No, no, being good at English is well down the abilities list: colleagues can help with a snappy intro, sub-editors can iron out stylistic errors. Before you write the story you have to get it and for that you need to be able to adapt yourself to a situation, to be able to read the character you are interviewing who may be toff one minute, a tough market trader the next. You need in effect to be able to play a role. So Drama has been much more use to me than my other joint honours subject of English.

Thanks, Hull.

'You are all Yorkshiremen now'

Geoffrey Rowe. Joint Drama and English, 1969
Administrator, Crucible Theatre Sheffield; Finance Director, Welsh National
Opera; currently Chief Executive, Everyman Theatre, Cheltenham

My earliest memory of Hull is inevitably the train journey to Paragon Station,
never having been further north than Essex. 'The London boy goes North' –
to misty, damp, end-of-the-line Hull, the city with a cinema called Cecil. To
get to Hull (or indeed any university) was something of a last minute surprise
to me, so I had no idea what to expect of the course or the city.

As the train strained through Hessle and Haltemprice and sensibly bypassed
Goole, I had a fantasy moment that it would be just like the film of *Saturday
Night and Sunday Morning*. I appreciate the film is set in Nottingham but it was
all 'the North' to me at the time. In an early scene Billie Whitelaw served
Albert Finney fish and chips across a counter and her eyes glinted, hinting at
more than merely salt and vinegar. You did end up eating a lot of fish and
chips in Hull, but I cannot recall my 'haddock and six' leading to romance.

I was originally going to study just English, but arrived to discover that there
was a great deal of Anglo-Saxon in the course. However, the Drama
Department had landed a large percentage of women from the UCCA lottery.
Were they condemned to present endless productions of the *House of Bernarda
Alba*? So, in a deft move from disaster I transferred to joint Drama and English,
increased the men to 8 out of 24 and had a really happy and interesting time
for three years. I count myself extremely fortunate to have spent time
studying plays and theatre history and then work in the theatre ever since.

With only 24 of us in the year we had close contact with the lecturers and
good opportunities to act and direct. We were made to feel special as the first
Joint Honours and we were a tight knit group spending many hours in each
other's company. Some of the lecturers, I now realise, like Mike Walton and
David Edwards, were not that much older than the undergraduates. Were
they frantically reading the texts each evening to keep just ahead of the
students? I recall the Theatre Lab – a former gymnasium with a fantastic
atmosphere. It had limited staging possibilities – no flying, no wings – and
therefore you could do anything fairly cheaply. A great place for parties, and

with a live phone which all and sundry used to call home on Sundays. I remember odd aspects of the plays I acted in. Changing a bike tyre on stage in *A Scent of Flowers* – more difficult than it sounds, believe me, if you have to finish by the time you say the line 'there, it's all done; wearing a pink tutu in an e.e. cummings play – clearly Mike Walton's revenge for some transgression; playing a bear in a children's play in the monolithic Middleton Hall; cast as a boring father (I was good at those) in *The Sunday Walk* which we toured to a garret in London after Finals. I also recall practical lessons every Saturday morning with an elderly lady called Honor and the shock of being told that we had to buy a pair of tights and wear them.

And, of course, H.L.B. Thompson – Harry, with his great certainty about everything dramatic and theatrical, often conveyed with wilful eccentricity: his curious pronunciation of certain words, his tales of old India and his army career. As with all great teachers, it was possible to feel great affection for Harry, to laugh at his curious ways and still to have great respect. He persuaded me out of a career as an actor ('You are very good, Geoffrey, but you will starve until you are 40 and then play everybody's Dad'), into management and found me my first job.

It was a time of student protest and the occupation of the University administration block. I can recall standing on the main road watching my fellow students gather to march into town and a housemate shouted to me to join in the march. 'Sorry', I replied, 'have a rehearsal'.

'What did you do in the student demos Daddy?'

So we came to Finals and the graduation ceremony, and suddenly the 24 were dispersed – to teaching mainly, I believe, and a few to the theatre. I went with another Hull graduate, Graham Cowley, to Derby Playhouse. He was an Acting ASM and I was both House Manager and Publicity Manager. We shared a flat, appropriately, in Macklin Street. The distinguished Chancellor presiding at the Graduation said that all we graduates could consider ourselves forever connected to this great County – 'You are all Yorkshiremen now'.

And so we are.

Ugly Parsimony and Bacon Sarnies

Richard Saunders. Joint Honours Drama and Swedish, 1969
Ageing Adman

Harry Thompson stands beside the overhead projector in the lecture theatre. His subject is the Italian Masque. On the screen behind him, a quotation appears. With a slow, metronomic, trademark wag of his finger, Harry declaims, *'The more money that is spent on enterprises of this nature, the more they are to be praised – being thus associated with kings and princes to whom ugly parsimony is an evil strange'.*

These are the words (allegedly, and approximately) of Renaissance theatre designer Nicola Sabbatini. Or was it Sebastiano Serlio? I should have been paying attention.

Anyway, whichever it was, he was explaining why the lavish sets and ingenious mechanisms he designed for these Masques – and, for that matter, the playhouses in which they were performed – had such eye-watering budgets: 'Because they made the Client look good'.

We class of '69 learned a lot from Harry. We learned that *Three Sisters* is a play about 'not going to Moscow'. We learned that Melodrama is 'a thing upon thing thing' and that outdoor productions are 'whimsicult in the wet'. We learned that 'when they stay away, they stay away in droves'. And we learned how to conjure up truly evil sweat-inducing curries from tinned meat that harboured vain aspirations to being out-takes from the manufacture of Pedigree Chum.

Yet, of all the things I learned from Harry (and Mike, and Don – the blame should be spread equally) the one that, bizarrely, has come to resonate down through the years is that obscure quote from that equally obscure lecture on the Italian Masque.

It's like this. When I graduated at the end of three utterly unforgettable, mind-blowingly enjoyable and – how could they not be? – formative years, it was pretty clear that the Swedish half of my degree wasn't going to get me any further than a (hypothetical) edge over my mates in chatting up blondes

24

who were fluent in English anyway. And so it fell to the Drama half to kick open the door to a career that has, for the most part, involved persuading people to spend obscene amounts of money on ideas I'd had in the bath.

I think it was around the time that a high-ranking RAF officer happily OK'd the production of a recruitment commercial I'd written, on the grounds that shooting it wouldn't cost any more than shooting off a couple of Sidewinder missiles, that an agency suit was heard to remark, 'Saunders doesn't get out of bed for less than half a million'.

OK, there were the low-budget family sagas revolving around stock-cubes too. But where's the fun in suffering for your art in the smoky confines of a sound stage in Park Royal when you could be hearing the magic words, 'Doors to automatic and cross-check', as the flying circus leaves town for yet another sun-soaked location extravaganza?

After all, Saunders had a high-maintenance reputation to maintain. So there were bound to be moments. Moments where I'd find myself standing at sparrow's fart in the middle of the desert/beach/mountains/wherever, scoffing my bacon sarnie and looking around at all those camera cranes and grip trucks and catering vans and tracking vehicles and helicopter rigs and honey wagons and all those utterly indispensable highly-talented highly-paid people and thinking, 'Fuggin' Ada, that was an expensive bath'.

And there, too, would be the Client – tasked with watching where all his company's hard-earned money was going, counting all those trucks and helicopters and people and counting up the air fares and hotel bills and *per diems* and realising, 'Christ, this is an expensive bacon sarnie'.

That would be the moment when 'What I Learned From Harry' would come to my rescue. That would be the moment to stroll over to the Client and murmur reassuringly into his ear, 'Don't worry, guv. In the words of Nicola Sabbatini, "the more money that is spent on enterprises of this nature…"'

The Paper It's Written On

Gareth Armstrong. Pass Drama, 1970
Theatre Practitioner

Early in 2012 I was required to produce documentary proof of my Bachelor of Arts Degree from Hull University. I had no idea where it was. Having not attended the degree ceremony, the certificate had arrived by post and that was the last I remember of it. The piece of paper, when I eventually tracked it down to an old tin box, was slightly foxed and, like its owner, showing signs of age. When I presented it to prove my qualification part-time job on the fringes of academe I put my thumb over the line that classified my BA, 'Pass'. Well, I never wanted a degree in the first place. And I very nearly didn't get one. A sympathetic exam board and External spared me the indignity of a fail.

Arrogance and ingratitude are not the monopoly of the young, but the late '60s was a fertile period for those of us inclined that way. If you were born in 1948, you took almost everything for granted; free orange juice, free milk, free healthcare, free schooling and free higher education. My local authority paid for everything, and with a penurious clergyman for a father I qualified for the most generous grant. At the end of every term I even managed to save a tenner (not much short of £150 in today's money). Student militancy characterised those years, but being as politically unengaged as I was academically indifferent, the frequent campus sit-ins gave me the opportunity to escape to plays in London at the Royal Court, the RSC or the National.

An indulgent lecturer told me when I showed some shame at my Finals performance that, though I had hardly enhanced the Department's academic reputation, I hadn't wasted anybody's time, except occasionally my own. I could, he told me, take some pride in the breadth of practical work we had tackled together. And though, like everything else, I took for granted the opportunity to perform some very rare repertoire, play well outside my range and fail honourably, this was something I'd only ever have got at a university. I didn't need much convincing, but I left knowing that all I wanted to do was make theatre. Which is how I've happily spent the last four and a half decades. I'm going to laminate my degree certificate now, though I doubt if anyone will ever want to see it again.

Memories of My Time

Lynne Gledhill (Barrow). Joint Drama and French, 1970
Semi-retired teacher; hospital, community broadcaster

The autumn of 1967 was one of the most beautiful I can remember, and the golden leaves on Cottingham Road would not have disgraced New England. There could have been no better time to start my new adventure as a Drama student at Hull.

I was thrilled to work in the Theatre Lab, which oozed 'Drama' from every pore. Its black walls enveloped us like a cocoon, where we belonged and felt safe. It was just grubby enough to feel truly theatrical, yet just clean enough to be civilised. Theatre Lab parties went on long into the night, and involved lots of Dancing: 'Fire' and anything by Cream, bring back those days immediately (both now regularly on BBC Radio 2, by the way).

Saturday mornings saw us, unlike students from other departments, up bright and early to attend classes with our visiting tutors from London, Honor and Tom, always searching for our hidden talents, 'It's in there. And if it's in there, we'll find it. We must!'

Those of us on Joint degrees felt a constant two-way pull, and Drama usually won. I myself refused to go to France for a year because I did not want to lose touch with 'my' Drama year group.

Our Lecturers were memorable – all different and all unique. They all contributed in their own way to our development, but for me the shining star was Harry Thompson (Hari Thompson, Hari Hari' …) Harry taught us the realities of putting on a show, and that 'Bums on Seats' are the main factor. Also, following his advice to: 'give them a water show, Ladies and Gentlemen', I did much later include dry ice in one show of my own, and he was right – they loved it.

Whenever anyone mentions 'Real Tennis' I immediately remember Harry telling us about '*Jeu de Paume*, Ladies and Gentlemen'.

I recall setting my hair on fire in the Theatre Lab while stage-managing a production requiring candles – my staunch actors fortunately beat me about the head until I no longer posed a Fire Risk, (thanks, Guys).

I recall our Summer course in London, when I attended the Old Vic for the first time, in the standing room of course, and when we also attended a performance of 'Hair', dancing on the stage at the end (actually more of a slide, with the extreme rake of the acting area).

I also recall our lunchtime 'HUDDLE' meetings, which offered us the opportunity to meet Famous People It never occurred to me at the time how difficult these may have been to set up – thanks to those who arranged them for us all.

Finally, there was the time I broke my foot by jumping (atypically) enthusiastically from the Theatre Lab stage while in rehearsal for a Greek Play in which the Chorus wore masks, and which the BBC came to film. I was the one clumping around with my foot in plaster. What a Pro!

My time at Hull gave me so much, but it was only some years afterwards when I fully realised this. We learned teamwork and tolerance, and were given the space to experiment and sometimes make mistakes.

I look back fondly to those days and am always grateful.

Beginners, Please!

Dorothy (Dot) Clague. Joint Honours English and Drama, 1970
Retired Drama and English Teacher

So there I was, in my first ever seminar with my new Tutor, fresh from my sheltered country grammar school, somewhat bewildered and very nervous (Am I clever enough? Will anyone like me? Why does everyone else exude sophistication and confidence?). He has told us we can call him by his first name. We can call all the lecturers by their first names – a new and slightly disconcerting experience. He is talking about Greek Drama and at the end requires one of us to produce a seminar paper for next week on Aristotle's *Poetics*. His sharp, bright eyes flash round and we hastily all look down. Then I hear, 'We'll go in alphabetical order, so that's you …', he consults his list …, 'Dot Clague'. Oh, God!

Off I go and pore over my black Penguin Classic (*Aristotle, Horace, Longinus: Classical Literary Criticism* – I have it still). I make copious notes. I try and work out what it means and what I think. I find out as much as I can about Aristotle himself (Oh, lovely, lovely *Oxford Classical Dictionary*). I don't really know what a 'seminar paper' is, but am too worried about seeming stupid to go and ask him *now* what's expected or how long it should be.

Inexorably, the next seminar arrives. The Tutor calls on me to begin. My heart is pounding. I am virtually struck dumb with uncertainty about what I've prepared – can it possibly be right? I manage to croak out a few disjointed sentences before drying up completely. There is a heavy silence. Everyone looks away in embarrassment apart from the Tutor, who fixes me with a very beady stare and somehow the foxy beard takes on an aggressive thrust. He says 'Humph', or something very like it, and then. 'Not really what we mean by a seminar paper'. I am crushed.

He sweeps on, thank God, expounding on Aristotle and everyone scribbles notes. My face burns. Not only will he think I'm stupid, but lazy and disorganised too. I might as well leave now, this minute, and go back home. I'll end up having to get a job at Broughton Road Co-op. Oh, God, the embarrassment.

I sink down in my chair and keep very quiet. Then I hear him ask a question about bloody Aristotle, whom I now hate. No-one says anything. There is another long silence. I suddenly realise I know this and breathlessly give the answer he is looking for, consulting my pages and pages of notes. He looks over his specs in surprise. 'Why didn't you say all this before? He doesn't look quite so fierce. The others don't look quite so terrifying. Perhaps I'll stay after all.

It was good being there in the early days of HUDD. It felt as if we were pioneering something exciting, with the Theatre Lab part-cultural outpost, part-womb (great post-production parties). I remember a palpable enthusiasm and it felt increasingly comfortable working in a Department where one didn't feel anonymous and where staff and students worked closely and informally together on productions.

Looking back, I realise how broadening the Drama course was in its range and variety and how successfully it planted seeds for the future. I'm sure that all the practical work we did instilled confidence and, in my case, equipped me with all the acting skills needed to survive a career in the bizarre world of the comprehensive classroom. Thank God for all the breathing exercises and the voice work. I never had any difficulty filling the diaphragm and projecting to the back of the Hall when necessary. And my voice survived all the wear and tear of the hurly-burly.

We can all probably trace the on-going pleasures of life back to HUDD. My love for Medieval and Renaissance painting, I know, comes from Harry Thompson's copiously illustrated lectures. So many plays and playwrights are now part of my DNA. (*Waiting for Godot*, Ibsen, Pinter, O'Casey) – that goes back to Hull. The familiar frisson of pleasure and anticipation when theatre or cinema lights go down – that too. And oddly enough, after my inauspicious start with Aristotle, I have become a serious classics groupie and will travel many a mile to take in a Greek tragedy. How will they do the Chorus? What kind of costumes? Music? Masks? Will I get my fix of pity and fear?

So – thanks, HUDD. – and thank God I stayed.

'Time Flies Like an Arrow; Fruit Flies Like a Banana'

Tony Hill. Joint Drama and American Studies, 1970
Building Manager

Three years at Hull in the late '60s in 300-1200 words? Easy, because, as a child of the '60s, I've forgotten most of it. Strangely, the buildings most immediately spring to mind, the Department's temporary headquarters in Salmon Grove – not exactly King's College quad was it?

The Theatre Lab, memorable for Practical Drama on a Saturday morning (who's idea was that?), post-production parties, and a dimly-recalled 'Happening'.

Sitting in my room in Loten Hall watching the Gulbenkian change from a hole in the ground, brick-by-brick into, well, the Gulbenkian.

Centres of extra-mural education – 730 Beverley Road, 5A Salisbury Street, 66 Cranbrook Avenue and the Queens Hotel on Queens Road (Notice on Cocktail Lounge door: No dogs or students).

And people: Harry Thompson, whose presence and memory still looms large, gently waking me at the end of a 9.15 seminar through which I had slept, with the words 'The sleep was probably of more value for you than my words of wisdom on Aeschylus'.

Mike Walton in a 9.15 lecture, heroically attempting to get us interested in Euripides. The pacing became more frantic, and the head scratching more urgent, as he realised we weren't with him in spirit.

Nick Hern – energy and enthusiasm personified, agreeing with everything you said, 'Fantastic idea', 'Great take on that play', 'Brilliant thinking'. Essay returned and marked C– –.

Honor Matthews – near-orgasmic in her praise and excitement at my ability to breathe without falling over. Hands in prayer to her mouth, and a big intake of air 'Ooh yes, Darling'. Not so enthusiastic about me falling asleep (again) during a relaxation exercise.

Don Roy, beard-stroking and ruminating, postulating the theory of Godot or godillots (you see, I was listening some of the time).

And David Edwards, calmness and control personified, that whimsical half-smile as he explained to me in the Theatre Lab, immediately after registration on my first day, when I enquired what school he'd been to, that he was a member of staff, not another fresher. Incidentally, is David Edwards the hairiest man in the world, or is that just a rumour?

And the HUDDLEs. Harry H. Corbett telling an eager audience that the worst thing possible for anyone pursuing a career in the theatre was unwanted or unplanned children. There followed a diatribe about responsible sex, casual relationships, and so on. We'd never heard of STDs or AIDS or anything like that, and VD was something you caught from glasses in the Buttery, or off the seats of public lavatories.

I remember most of my fellow students with warmth and affection. Why did I never keep in touch with any of them? Something to do with growing up and maturing. I wonder when that will happen to me.

Some years ago, when my sons and their friends asked about whether or not they should go to university, I told them to go, because, if they did it right, these would be the best three years of their lives. I added that they were for me, prompting some heated exchanges between me and my wife. I say it now: they *were* the best three years of my life, but only made so by the fact that I was a member of the Drama Department – Oh God, if this gets published I'm in deep trouble.

So that's my summary of three brilliant years (1967-70) in the Drama Department. There is an editor that shapes our ends, rough hew them how we will. Feel free to ignore, censor, or correct any or all of this memoir.

Acting My Socks Off

Nigel Jeffcoat. Joint Drama and American Studies, 1970
Therapist in the Child and Adolescent Mental Health Service, Alder Hey
Childrens' Hospital, Liverpool

I went up to Hull in October 1967; but the 'summer of love' which went before was such a busy and exciting time for me, that I had not given this big change in my life more than a passing thought before I got on the train at King's Cross that autumn.

I had been living in a large, airy bed-sit not far from Gloucester Road tube station in London. I had a day job at the City and Guilds of London Institute and in the evenings I worked in the flies at the Theatre Royal, Drury Lane, for the hit musical *Hello Dolly*.

Rehearsals for my third season with the National Youth Theatre were about to begin. After *Coriolanus* at the Queens Theatre on Shaftesbury Avenue and *Anthony and Cleopatra* at the Old Vic in 1965 and 1966, Michael Croft now commissioned a new play, *Zigger Zagger*, from Peter Terson, about the power and influence of football on an impressionable teenager. A successful London season at the Jeanetta Cochrane ended in late August, but there were still another busy few weeks with the NYT. During a week in Sunderland I learnt that another member of the company, Gareth Armstrong, was also about to join the Drama Department at Hull. 'See you in Hull', we exchanged breezily as we parted – both feeling a little apprehensive about what might lie ahead.

We need not have worried. My abiding memory of my three years in Hull is the opportunity it gave me to act my socks off in a wide variety of plays – plays by Lorca, e.e. cummings, Beckett, Aeschylus, Shaffer, Planché, Frisch, Halliwell; and, of course, I made important friendships and relationships, some of which continue today. I may not have done myself justice academically, but I have made up for that in later years. I am happy with the choices I made at the time.

In October 1967, the Gulbenkian Centre was little more than a muddy hole in the ground; but my cohort were fortunate to be among those who would present the opening productions in 1969/70. Until then, our home was the

Theatre Lab, a glorified Nissen hut which had been the University's gym. It was here that I discovered the satisfaction of making an audience laugh, in David Halliwell's *Little Malcolm and his Struggle Against the Eunuchs*. I played the nerdy fantasist Dennis Nipple who's fevered soliloquy ends with the climactic ''Uddersfield dissolves!'

The intimate space of the Theatre Lab was perfect for establishing a rapport with the audience. Other parts I particularly enjoyed playing there were Estragon in *Waiting for Godot* and Harold Gorringe, the waspish antiques-collector, in Peter Shaffer's farce, *Black Comedy*, in which the audience can see when the actors can't and vice-versa.

We returned to Hull earlier than usual in the autumn of 1969 to work on the very first productions in the brand-new Gulbenkian Centre, a double-bill of Greek tragedies, one by Aeschylus and one by Euripides. I played Orestes in Aeschylus' *Choephori*, which we presented using powerful masks and a spare, gestural and physical acting style. Then, in the spring term of 1970, the official opening of the Gulbenkian was celebrated with a reconstruction of a playbill from Hull Theatre Royal in 1820; this consisted of three plays to exploit the full machine-stage, a melodrama and two shorter comedies. The centrepiece was J.R. Planché's *The Vampire: or The Bride of the Isles*. My first appearance as the vampire was to rise ghoulishly from a coffin in Fingal's Cave, to the accompaniment of the strains of organ music played from the pit – and at the finale, I vanished from view down a trap-door in a cloud of smoke and with a bang loud enough to awaken the Mayor of Hull in the front row.

I left Hull in the summer of 1970 and in October began my first professional job in the theatre, as an ASM at Hampstead Theatre Club. I continued to work in the profession for 10 years, getting work reasonably regularly and having some memorable moments along the way. But priorities changed. Other interests bubbled up and I decided to call it a day around 1980/81. Certainly, the opportunities given me at Hull had built enough of the confidence necessary to give a challenging profession my best shot.

Back Then

Don Knibb. Pass Drama, 1970
Retired Managing Director, Careers/Connexions Service Company

I'm afraid this article may have more than a touch of 'back then' and 'in my day' about it, before bemoaning the universal truth that 'fings, indeed, 'ain't what they used to be'. But the thing is, back then in 1967 when I first arrived in Hull (scarcely knowing where it was) to form part of the second Joint 1 intake. The Department's creative home was a much-abused but extraordinarily tolerant hut known as the Theatre Lab. To describe the Theatre Lab as 'quite basic' would be like describing St. Mark's Basilica as 'quite pretty', or the Pyramids as 'getting on a bit.' It gloried in being basic.

It was a low single-storey hut with a raised area at one end which housed the control room. At the other end was a double changing area that would have struggled to justify the name ' dressing rooms'. In between was a compact – but highly adaptable – performance area and auditorium. Nowadays it wouldn't be within hailing distance of Health and Safety regulations, but now is now and then was then.

We loved it, and took enormous pride in the sheer quality of some of some of the work produced in what seemed at first sight to be such an unprepossessing building. From the British première of Frisch's *Don Juan or the Love of Geometry,* favourably reviewed in both the *Times* and the *Guardian*, through the almost overwhelming intensity of *Yerma,* to my own improbable appearance as Six Hundred Pounds of Passionate Pulchritude in e.e. cummings' *him* – said to be unstageable (although that didn't stop Mike Walton), the Theatre Lab had a way of coping with pretty much anything that was thrown at it. It positively encouraged original thinking and resourcefulness, and was a magnet for performers and non-performers alike. It housed the formidable Honor Matthews' Saturday morning practical classes, which signally failed to prepare me for the peculiar demands of playing Six Hundred Ps of PP, but did at least make me grateful for being male since we escaped the chastisement routinely handed out to the women for 'failure to handle a skirt nicely'. It also provided a backdrop for a remarkable HUDDLE with the film star Veronica Lake, who arrived complete with bottle of gin and left with the contents but not the bottle. And whenever there was a performance taking place, you would be likely to find Harry Thompson lurking in the shadows, making sure he kept everyone's feet firmly on the ground. 'Oh God, they're emoting all over the stage out there. Look, Donald, don't forget that you've simply got to allow the punters time to get at the bar during the interval'.

There was also a workshop where I spent many happy hours hammering and sawing under the benign and gentle guidance of David Edwards. On one occasion, when we were running particularly short of time even by our standards, I volunteered to remain behind after rehearsal one evening to spend most of the night by myself re-building and re-assembling parts of the set. By about 6.00 in the morning I'd had enough and, since it was far too late to go home, decided to catch a bit of sleep on an old chaise longue that was kept in one of the dressing rooms. All went well until the cleaner let herself in a couple of hours later and recoiled in terror thinking she'd found a dead body. There was, I believe, screaming, which didn't abate much when the body stirred into what passed for life at that time in the morning.

Towards the end of my time in the Department we moved into the brand new Gulbenkian Centre, with what to us was its cavernous auditorium, its space-age equipment and its unrivalled facilities. As an aide to producing good theatre and enabling actors and directors to get the most from a script, it knocked the old Theatre Lab into a cocked hat. But to many of us it never really matched the intimacy, intensity and raw passion that the Theatre Lab could generate, and couldn't produce quite the same thrill and excitement.

Some 40 years on something similar has happened on the professional stage in Hull, with the move of Hull Truck from its old premises in Spring Street to its more luxurious new home in Ferensway. The new theatre is more accessible, has much better facilities and meets modern standards far better than its predecessor. But to me it will never have quite the same compelling charisma as Spring Street nor attract the same affectionate loyalty.

If only they'd asked Joint 1 when they designed it.

From Hong Kong to Hull

Patrick Lau. Joint Drama and American Studies, 1970
Theatre and Television Director

Looking at the photograph of this naïve, fresh-faced and bespectacled Chinese boy in a shiny suit, clutching a big formal overcoat and a guitar at the old airport lounge in Hong Kong, with his tearful mother seated next to him, I really would have liked to reassure him that in the next three years, in a place called Hull, he would be able to send to his anxious parents photographs of himself as a Spanish courtier with a big moustache wounded by Don Juan; the dead Greek step-father of Electra; and, less schizophrenically, a Chinese coolie being given a hard time by a Brechtian soldier. Little would he know that after three enthralling years in the cold damp city where the air always had the faint whiff of fish, he would be in black leather from top to bottom posing as a reckless adventurer into the profession of theatre director.

The first sight of the Theatre Lab was, especially under monochrome skies, like the set of one of those black and white British war movies. Any minute you would expect to see either Dickie Attenborough or Trevor Howard striding out from the back door in uniform. The Nissen hut was cold and dark. It still had wooden wall bars from its earlier life as a gymnasium, on which we used to hang, pretending to be martyrs in torment or Orestes chased by the Furies while dear old Honor [*Matthews*], our eccentric and passionate visiting practical tutor, would be entranced by our suffering. That dilapidated interior freed us from all restraints and conventions; it made us fearless and extraordinary. Even in those heady days of the late '60s, it was quite unusual to see skimpily-dressed girls performing an orgy with a tall nearly naked minotaur in Lorca's *Yerma*, entirely by candle light (Health and Safety, what's that?). I gradually lost sight of that little anxious Chinese boy from Hong Kong.

When Harry Thompson lit his joss-sticks in my first tutorial with him, medieval drama rituals came alive. His ever-present sense of humour, his ready chuckles, his formal attire, his owl-like spectacles all made him look like an escapee from P.G. Wodehouse. His wagging finger was never a gesture of reproach, but a beguiling prelude to a juicy story, starting with 'Well, my dears (chuckle, chuckle), I am so glad that Jackie has taken care of herself.'

What Jackie K's marriage to Aristotle Onassis had to do with Greek drama I can't recall.

We all thrived in the free and easy atmosphere given by the tutors. Don Roy, waving his French cigarette between his long manicured fingers and breaking into French at the first opportunity; my wise mentor, Mike Walton, the tutor who had directed and acted in the professional theatre, dazzling us with insights into Greek drama; John Harris, oozing kindness and decency; Dave Edwards, the ever-calm technical guru and Nick Hern, only a few years older than us, giggling like a mad head-boy while teaching us Brecht. This wonderful bunch made learning scintillating and their spouses became good friends.

Unfortunately, Drama was not a Single Honours subject and we were there only as Joint degree students. Most, if not all of us, paid less attention to our other courses as Drama was just too alluring. And after all, that was the 1960s and good times were had by one and all. There was a deep sense of us being superior hippies in the university. Students a year ahead of us, the first ever Joint-degree Drama BA Hons brigade, were ancient as far as we were concerned. They usually played old folks in our drama productions, until in our second year, those young upstarts, Dame Jenni Murray (then Bailey) amongst them, stole the juvenile roles. There we were, young lions and lionesses, with trendy lecturers, smoking and drinking through many parties in that dark Theatre Lab thinking we were so cool talking about Judi Dench playing Sally Bowles and John Gielgud in Peter Brook's *Oedipus* at the National. We were so sure that we would be part of that profession as our time in the Department made us addicted to the joy and adventure of theatre.

I was also one of the lucky ones to have made a foray into that profession when our lecturers made arrangements with the Derby Playhouse to have some of us working as Acting ASMs in their *Mysteries* cycle during the vacation. There we were, in bare feet and sitting amongst pros in patchwork and floral jeans, hearts pounding with excitement on the first day of rehearsals. I was quite puzzled as to why all my fellow-students were cast as Angels and I, the Plague. Anyway, I managed to upstage them all banging a drum in my skull-mask. It was the adventure of living in digs in a strange town and finding the cheapest fish and chips after the show that informed the wiser ones amongst us that a career in the theatre might not be as glamorous as we had thought. And just around the corner would be the upheavals of the three-day-week and the looming figure of Margaret Thatcher with a huge pair of pruners for the subsidized arts.

In our final year we deserted our beloved Theatre Lab with hardly a backward glance and threw ourselves into the gleaming new Gulbenkian Centre. Suddenly the sense of 'mucking in' disappeared almost overnight. There was too much gleaming expensive kit, including Radio and TV Studios, to allow curious and ignorant hands to freely explore. Productions became more formalised in that space. Nevertheless, that was our last stand before being propelled from the Department into the outside world. I found myself challenged by it all, but comfortable in the role of a director and did some of my best work in the Gulbenkian.

In this mixture of anxiety and the anticipation of being flung back to Hong Kong by the UK Immigration Department, I was guided by Mike Walton and the other staff into entering a competition for the Theatre Directors' Training Scheme [*of which Trevor Nunn and Ken Loach, among others, were alumni*], sponsored by the Independent Television Authority (yes, how utterly bizarre that sounds now, but nothing unusual in the more culture-friendly environment then). The night when I came back from my final interview in London, (clad in black leather), having won a place in that scheme for two years, with my family of tutors and fellow students surrounding me with warmth and euphoria on the set of my production of *Les mariés de la tour Eiffel,* was the night that I realised how Hull Drama Department had changed my life. Hong Kong was no longer home.

Snaps and Seeds

Joan Mills. Joint Drama and American Studies, 1970
Fellow in Voice and Performance, Theatre Film and Television Television
Department, Aberystwyth University

I am on the phone to my mother. A real phone of course. Mobiles don't exist because it's October 1967. I keep on having to put money in the slot and I know I am going to run out of change any second. My mother is trying to reassure me that life in Hull will get better. I am trying to explain what's wrong between sobs and sniffles: 'It's really flat, and ... and ... it smells'.

I have just taken a walk outside Cottingham, where I was resident at the new, not even quite complete halls: The Lawns. All around were flat winter-desolate fields of rotting cabbage and sprouts. 'It's just going to take a little time to settle in; you'll soon make friends ...', says my distressed mother.
'No, I won't, I don't know *anyone* and ...' peep, peep, peep: the pips. No more change. Silence apart from the relentless East coast wind which cuts you in two.

So that's the first snapshot from Joan's HUDD album: a sad, totally homesick, wet-behind-the-ears, 19-year-old in a white phonebox.

I really thought studying Drama at university was going to be glamorous and fun. But I was hopelessly parochial and had travelled from the wilds of the West Midlands to this Mecca for the Drama-keen. I was straight out of school, from a very ordinary conservative, working-class family and everything, but everything, in this new environment shocked me. I blushed to the roots of my hair when, travelling back on the bus with my new best buddies, Marilyn, Nigel, Gareth and Kath, I heard someone say 'Piss off!'. Worse was to come: I died a thousand deaths when I found myself in a lecture on the Greek Theatre and Mike Walton began to discuss the use of the phallus in Greek comedy, and I realised *what* he was actually talking about and, even more shockingly, he was now showing slides of *them*.

So snap two: Joan with eyes popping, attempting to look unconcerned and as if she looks at giant willies all the time.

Here are a few more: Joan watching rehearsals for Max Frisch's *Don Juan or The Love of Geometry*. Having failed to be cast in the play I am given a dual role – Production Assistant and Assistant to the Lighting Designer (a horribly competent boy in the year above me). Why is this significant? I am realising something. I am not sure what being 'Production Assistant' means, but it is giving me the opportunity to see the whole picture. I had been so disappointed when I wasn't cast, but acting, I now understand, does not allow a wider viewpoint. I am enjoying this new perspective. It is the start of something I will explore over the next 40 years, the moment I realised that being involved in theatre was not just about acting. It is why a university Drama Department was the right place for me rather than the limited horizon of a drama school.

Two more quick snaps: David Edwards, the Department's Production and Technical Manager at HUDD quietly inserting a screwdriver into one of the failing, ancient 16 channel resisters of the Theatre Lab board whilst I was operating it during the show, to persuade it to work: sparks flying, lots of little shorting noises. It was an insulated screwdriver... but even so. What did I take away from this? His calm, his lack of panic, the fact that we expected to keep going through impending disaster. How well this example has served me, not the scary electrics bit, but the attitude. Oh, and the love of the technical things that make live theatre a somatic experience ... and the overcoming of fear. Like the moment when, having foolishly volunteered to work on the rig for a *son et lumière* performance of *The Play of Daniel* in Beverley Minster, David asked me to take a reel of cable up to the clerestory. Cable over my shoulder, I set off up the spiral staircase to discover that the 'balcony' I had seen from below was actually a two-foot wide ledge walkway with the occasional buttress that might, just might, stop you falling to instant death 97 feet below. Quite a good snap this one: the moment of decision, captured as I stepped onto that ledge. 20 minutes later I was quite at home in the angelic regions of the beautiful Minster, enjoying the thrill of viewing the place from a privileged position, relishing danger in the service of art.

Much of the course was more scholarly than these 'snaps' might imply. We did attend classes and had seminars: we even read books sometimes. In Harry Thompson's lectures I was delighted by, and the manner in which, his scholarship juxtaposed with his Buddhist belief allowed him to connect ideas and events across disciplines, cultures and time, igniting a curiosity in me which continues to burn some 40 years on. We loved Harry; we loved his mix of the anarchic and erudite. And he, like most of the lecturers there then, seemed to like us. They spent time, they engaged with us and made us feel worth the trouble. Even after we graduated they followed our developments with apparent interest. When I was a fledgling director at the Royal Court, Harry would turn up and take me out for a pub lunch (on my miserable salary quite a significant treat). This continued contact as we launched our selves into the scary real world meant a great deal.

In my year at Hull there were 8 men and 27 women, all on Joint degrees. We were so lucky to be a relatively small group of Drama students, treated as individuals, nurtured and encouraged. So, did Hull influence what I was to become? Certainly: the whole possibility of directing opened up for me. The range of other skills I had a chance to explore, in design, making, sound and light. I became a director who loves the whole technical process of theatre and relishes the problem-solving. I was never daunted by the kind of technicians who attempted to fool a young female director (at a time when they were very rare): 'Sorry love can't be done ... needs a Fresnel and there's none left, darlin' (Ms Little Dim Brain). 'Really? Well fancy that, because I can see at least two and in any case you could use a Profile there couldn't you... I notice we have six of those...? The course awakened a curiosity about the whole process and I am sure this is why my career has been so varied. I have worked in traditional theatre spaces, but also staged work in village halls, churches, schools, pubs; I have directed plays, but also devised, made performances and worked on site-specific events.

My final 'snap' is an actual photograph, from the formal opening of the Gulbenkian theatre, recreating an 1820 bill from Hull Theatre Royal. It is a scene from Planché's *The Vampire or The Bride of the Isles* with students from all three years involved. I know what happened to some: a few now lecture in universities; I recognise several professional actors; some directors; a writer or two; arts managers and administrators; a photographer. Sadly, at least one died young. Some, I have no idea what happened to. But caught in that moment, we are full of pride and promise, excited and open to the possibilities the world will offer, ready to take off.

Thanks to the Drama Department we were prepared.

A Degree of Practicality

Gil Osborne (Woodstrom). Pass Drama, 1970
Former Artistic Director, National Arts Centre, Canada

Well now, what can I say about the Drama Department? The most important three years of my life in so many ways other than getting a degree. Let's face it, I was a washout academically and I'm sure my long-suffering tutor will agree. After succeeding so well at school thanks to my parents and teachers forbidding me any involvement in theatre unless I managed three As and got into Hull, I lost all interest in academia and flung myself into what I really wanted to do – ACT.

And act I did. And I stage-managed and operated sound and worked in the paintshop and did FOH and observed directors and got involved in any and all productions that came my way. It was a magical time. Starting in the little black-box Theatre Lab and then shifting to the larger, more formal Gulbenkian Centre, I experienced in microcosm almost everything I later achieved in professional theatre. Guided by our lecturers (although I only realise that in retrospect), I received a total and professional grounding in the art of theatre. I too left the 1969 Sit-In left to go to rehearsal. Politics be damned, you are NEVER late for rehearsal.

I somehow managed to absorb more of the formal education than I ever realised, despite missed lectures and vamping through tutorials. Not much was in evidence in my disastrous Final exams, but I have since found it popping up all the time in my professional career. Shakespeare? Phooey! According to Harry Thompson the real hero of that era was Burbage. That one single lecture introduced a startling realisation – theatre is practical, theatre is human, theatre is not about idolising past gods. Theatre is about being professional. How much that has influenced my career in professional theatre, even if at times I wandered off into la-la land, just because…

I'm out of theatre – 30 years burned me out. But although I'm now in a completely other digital world, I still have that hankering to act again. And I still remember playing Donna Elvira in Frisch's *Don Juan or the Love of Geometry* with glandular fever and a temperature of god knows what, and never missing a show. You NEVER miss a show.

From the Ridiculous to the Sublime

Joan Snowball. Joint Drama and English, 1970
Retired Careers Adviser, teacher and wine-bar proprietor

It didn't start off too well, our Departmental Drama Course in the summer of 1968. I was a hick from the sticks, unused to London Transport, and had got off the train a stop too soon for the hostel where we were to stay. On realising my mistake, I made a dash for the now departing train. With right foot on the running-board and left hand yanking open the door, I leapt to get inside – to find my suitcase was blocking the doorway with me left dangling outside the moving train. By now, people on the platform were screaming, whistles were blowing – but the commuters on the train had eyes only for their newspapers and it took my desperate squeak of 'Could somebody help me, please?' to prompt one of them to rush forward, grab me and my suitcase, and haul me aboard. With a severe admonition, 'Never do that again if you value your life, my girl'. My saviour returned to his *Times* and I, shaken and shaking, reached for a calming cigarette. Unfortunately, my trembling fingers couldn't hold the match steady; the flickering flame set light to my fashionably long curtain of hair, and went on to singe both eyebrow and eyelashes before burning itself out, filling the compartment with an acrid stench in the process. The commuters, however, continued to stare fixedly at their papers, studiously avoiding my gaze. They clearly had me down as a complete attention-seeker, if not some communist/Buddhist anti-Vietnam protester (well, it was the summer of '68).

From the ridiculous to the sublime, however – for the course itself was truly inspirational. As a South Shields schoolgirl, I hadn't seen much professional theatre – just a few touring productions taking Shakespeare to the provinces; now I was exposed to the best that London Theatre had to offer, in all its glorious range and variety, from popular comedies like *There's a Girl in my Soup* to classics such as Shaw's *You Never Can Tell*, with a stellar performance from Ralph Richardson. Young egotist that I was, I'd long felt the pull of performing, but that course introduced me to the delights of being in the audience; it marked the start to a lifetime of theatre-going, a habit which has brought much pleasure, and to which I've introduced both my husband, Roger, and, passing it on to the next generation, my son, Jonathan. For the latter, though a mathematician by education, and a trainee actuary by profession, theatre-going is an intrinsic part of life. Had a bad day at the office? Cheer yourself up by going to the theatre (*Noises Off* at the Old Vic did the trick on that occasion). Celebrating a pay-rise? Go to Stratford and take in a matinee of *Taming of the Shrew*. How to entertain the visiting parents? Get tickets for the new production of *What the Butler Saw*.

Over the years (and the world), I've seen a huge range of theatre – great plays, great productions, great performances, in London, at Stratford, in New York and Athens: and at Malvern, our local theatre, touring productions of *The Birthday Party* and *Waiting for Godot* so good they almost converted my husband to Pinter and Beckett.

It wasn't only professional performances that I appreciated on that summer course; during our own workshops, I started to realise just how talented were my peers. I can still recall, word for word, Dot Clague's magnificent rendition of 'I am Sixty, going on Seventy' – a Mermanesque parody of *The Sound of Music*'s 'I am Sixteen going on Seventeen', penned, I think, by Chris Johnstone (another talent). I can also recall many other great performances, by staff and students, from my time at Hull. Gil Osborne as Yerma acted with an emotional depth and maturity beyond her years. The play's director, Nick Worrall, coolly handled a cast teeming with stroppy women (what drama queens we were.). Other memorable productions included Jarry's *Ubu Roi*, Pinter's *The Room* and Shaffer's *Black Comedy*.

I recall one of our lecturers saying that the Department wasn't just about training people for a theatre career, but educating appreciative audiences of the future. They certainly succeeded with me.

Hull Trucking

Linda (Rachel) Bell. Joint Drama and American Studies, 1971
Actor/Teacher

I arrived in Hull in 1968, fresh from a Girls' Grammar School in York and very proud to be the first of my family to make it to University – to be what was spoken of as part of the 'top two per cent'.

The Drama Department was everything I hoped it would be, a glorious mixture of scary and exciting and, above all, completely absorbing. It was never a case of attend lecture, go away, live REALLY exciting student life. My whole University life was consumed by the Department. I fear American Studies saw very little of me, but my only regret is that it was not yet possible to do Single Honours Drama .

I have much for which to thank a fellow student, Mike Lynch. Somewhere during my first year he cast me as Mary Tyrone in Eugene O'Neill's *Long Day's Journey into Night*. After that, I never looked back and seemed to be constantly learning lines for something, *The Crucible*, *Black Comedy* and *Three Sisters* with particular pleasure, but there were many more. During this time the Gulbenkian was completed and we (rather sadly) left our old drama hut, but I enjoyed the truly professional facilities, despite the lack of a bar (to Harry Thompson's disgust).

As my course came to an end and the horrors of the real world loomed, another fellow student, Mike Walker, who had become the Director of the Hull Arts Centre, gave me a job as an ASM and my career began, utterly seamlessly. Whilst there I met Mike Bradwell and joined the original Hull Truck Theatre Company. In fact it occurs to me that my life has been informed by a whole series of Mikes. I married Mike O'Neill and I will always give credit to Mike Walton of the Drama Department for encouraging me to believe I was a decent actor. It gave me the guts to actually DO it, and that shaped my whole future life.

'Errors You Can't Erase'

Michael Butt. Joint Drama and American Studies, 1971
Writer

1968. The hippy was working the coach, going from seat to seat, asking us if we wanted to join a demo against the Vietnam War. I stared out the window, trying to make my confusion look like decisiveness. I'd just had a photo taken of myself in a booth at the Station in which I looked like a seven-year-old on his way to his First Holy Communion. And now I was going somewhere where inexperience was the only sin. What was that smell that accompanied us? Fish? It was like being abroad, somewhere Nordic perhaps. Or Russia. I didn't think, because I didn't then know, that Chekhov's body was returned to his homeland in a refrigeration car designed for fish. Whatever, my stomach pains told me, a catastrophe was unfolding: I'd left home for university.

An inaugural talk. The two men on the broad stage wore markedly different styles: one was in corduroys, and bearded; the other, plum-faced, in a grey suit. I knew from my programme that one of them was Philip Larkin, the poet, and head of the University library. But which? I guessed the corduroy. Wrongly. It was the bank manager from the 50's who'd penned the line I relished: 'They fuck you up, your mum and dad'.

We spent the first few Drama practical weeks in leotards, handing each others' unknown bodies over our heads. A shared embarrassment that bonded us. If I could only get my teeth fully into the mockery I might find a purchase against the waves of nausea that otherwise would drown me.

And then I began to write, because there was a place for it, and I was allowed to: sketches, scenes, a play. Voices I could hide behind and luxuriate in, with time and freedom. Thank you, dear tutors, Don, Harry, Mike, John and David.

It would have been nice to have abandoned my Catholicism before I'd arrived at the fish docks, but then you never know who you are until you're gone.

How Hull Became Hollywood

Reg Farrier. Joint Drama and American Studies, 1971

Now unemployed (due to ill health), but once a professional actor, graphic artist, advertising copywriter, and Business Development Manager in I.T. company

In 1970, some members of the Department ventured into film-making. Shot in Super 8, the first film was a tribute to the Spaghetti Western genre (and the films of Sam Peckinpah) entitled *Vamanos Gringos!*, co-written and directed by Dave Kent and myself, camera by John Saxby; and featuring selected Joint Drama students.

Having gathered a motley collection of imitation six-guns and rifles, we began filming one Sunday morning in late February in a field near The Lawns in Cottingham – the day after the snow had melted. The field, along with a shed, a horse and a handful of chickens was to stand as a Mexican village.

Barefoot and clad in a pair of off-white pyjamas, I (El Indio) survived hypothermia and the unit moved to the next location. This was the famous Theatre Lab (The Bank of El Paso) and surrounding buildings. Here a congregation of townsfolk got caught up in a bank robbery, a shootout between bandits and bounty hunters and much carnage. Who can forget Chas Griffin's stunt fall onto concrete, shot down as he made a getaway? The final scene started with bandit El Indio running across a railway line before climbing up a hill outside Hull (Sad Hill) cemetery where the two bounty hunters were waiting in ambush. There followed a Sergio Leone-style La Resa del Conte trio face-off and all were shot by one another. The bags of swag taken from the bank were seen to contain nothing but Players No. 6 coupons (hence the film sub-title *A Fistful of Coupons*). There was no verbal soundtrack, sadly, but the music of Ennio Morricone and Jerry Goldsmith plus the dubbed gunshots brought it all to life.

Anyhow, we all had great fun making it.

More films followed in the next year:

The Perils of Polly, a Victorian melodrama, again directed by Dave Kent, camera by Chas Griffin.

Vag, a 30's romp directed by Steve Hare.

Rotation, a '60s' homage to TV's *The Prisoner*, directed by Terry Ellacott, camera, Pete Oliver. I do not know if any more films were made post-1972, but all those involved in the cinematic birth of The Drama Department are proud of their self-financed achievement. Oh for today's video camera and sound technology – just think what could have been done with that.

As a matter of record here are the casts of the films mentioned.

Vamanos Gringos!, Dave Kent, Pete Edwards, Reg Farrier, Chris Jones, Martyn Auty, Steve Hare, Pete Draycott, Terry Ellacott, Chris Harding-Roberts, John Lee, Mick Butt, Kit Thacker, Chas Griffin, Mike Lynch, Don [*Malcolm*] Sinclair, Christine Llewellyn, Linda Garbett, Nick Wilmott, Sara Jennet, Linda [*Rachel*] Bell, Ken Allison, Sue Riley, Cathy Mackie, Val Jones, Sue Hyams, Dave Parry and Mary East.

The Perils of Polly: Don Sinclair, Annie Moore, John Lee, Roy Jarrett, Reg Farrier, Terry Ellacott, Mary East, Bryan Bishop, Steve Hare and Dave Kent.

Vag: Bob Carlton, Bobbie Wilcox, Nick Wilmott, Pete Oliver, a red car, plus others.

Rotation: Reg Farrier, Jackie Walker, Don Sinclair, Martyn Auty, Pete Wood, Dave Lumby, Jeremy Ancock, Sue Scott-Moncrieff, Dave Kent, Ray Smith, Annie Moore, Lynne Miller, Steve Hare, Bryan Bishop, Dave Griffiths and Jim Lambert.

Spirit of the Air

Valerie Jones. Joint Drama and English, 1971
BBC National News Correspondent (retired)

I played the part of Ariel, Spirit of the Air, in the Victorian melodrama, *The Vampire or The Bride of the Isles*, part of the triple bill which officially opened the then brand-new Gulbenkian Theatre in 1970. It was a play that made use of all the exciting stage-effects we now had, including a full fly-tower above the stage and a trap, through which the Vampire met his gruesome end.

It was such a change after the very basic hut we'd used for previous productions. I had to be flown in on a 'cloud' (made of wood) above the stage before the curtain opened, so I could descend, ethereally, to protect the heroine Lady Margaret from the clutches of the Vampire.

Not being too good at heights, I simply had to remember not to look down.

After Hull, I went into journalism, starting as a trainee reporter on a local evening newspaper and eventually became a national news correspondent with the BBC, for both radio and television. I was still, perhaps, using performance skills in front of the microphone and camera. It was a job that took me around the world.

I was in Kuwait for the Iraq invasion and a few months later in Baghdad. But I have never forgotten my three years in the Drama Department at Hull or lost my love of the theatre. Both paths of my experience came together when I played the role of a reporter in Hattie Naylor's Radio Four play, *The Siege of Masada*.

It's Not What You Know, It's Who You Taught

Ian Lancaster. Joint Drama and American Studies, 1971
Managing Director, Reconnaissance International Ltd

I co-founded Reconnaissance International and became the MD in 1990. Reconnaissance gathers, analyses and disseminates information on strategies and technologies to combat counterfeits – banknotes, passports and other government-issued documents, medicines, vehicle parts, cosmetics and all kinds of consumer goods. We publish specialist newsletters, reports, manuals and run conferences for a world-wide market. Reconnaissance followed from my previous five years making holograms through my first company (Third Dimension Ltd) and two years running the Museum of Holography in New York. I discovered holograms while I was Arts Director at the Gulbenkian Foundation.

And therein lies this tale…

I started as Director of Arts at the UK and Commonwealth Branch of the Calouste Gulbenkian Foundation (its full name) in 1977, my third job as an arts administrator, following a year as the Publicity and PR Manager at the Library Theatre in Manchester and four years as the Drama and Dance Officer at East Midlands Arts, the regional arts association.

Then in 1981, out of the blue, I was contacted by Mike Walton, then Acting Head of Drama at Hull (sitting in for Don Roy, who was on study leave). He notified the Foundation that the Gulbenkian Centre at the University, and the Drama Department itself, were under threat. With Margaret Thatcher's government cutting university funding and attacking support for the arts, the University was faced with around 20% funding cuts and the Universities' Funding Council (or whatever it was called) suggested that the Drama Department was superfluous and could easily be closed. As a major funder of the Centre, how would the Foundation respond to its closure?

For the first few years of HUDD's life students exercised, had workshopped, performed and partied in the Theatre Laboratory, a wooden hut beside the Chemistry Department. The 1971 graduates only worked in it for our first year – 1968/9 – but loved the very special atmosphere in the run-down, cramped, damp but inspiring Theatre Laboratory.

Over the summer of 1969 the Department decanted into the brand new Gulbenkian Centre, a building purpose-designed by Peter Moro, the designer of Nottingham Playhouse and the leading theatre architect of the period. Surely the Gulbenkian Centre was, and still is, one of the best drama and media teaching studios in the country? Credit must go to Don and his team who specified what was wanted, briefed Moro accordingly and then raised the funds to build it, which included a substantial grant from the Gulbenkian Foundation.

The Foundation – then, the single largest source of money for the arts in Britain outside government – had a policy at the time of supporting university arts activities, with a particular focus on the dramatic arts and capital projects which would have a long-term benefit on students' exposure to, understanding of and practice in theatre arts. The Hull Centre was one of a handful of British university theatres and arts centres (others at Newcastle and Kent) which the Foundation made possible through significant capital grants, but this was the only one specifically intended as a resource for a Drama Department, rather than a venue for visiting and student productions.

So it was that Mike sent an SOS to the Foundation.

Needless to say the University promptly received a letter expressing the Foundation's concern at the proposed closure of the Centre (or at least the removal of its core function as a resource for, and home of, the Drama Department) barely 12 years after it had opened. A letter which, along with no doubt many other protests at this potential vandalism, was instrumental in helping the University to put its weight behind maintaining the Department and this unique teaching resource.

Probably the Foundation would have responded similarly whoever was in the Arts Director seat, but it certainly was not a bad thing that the incumbent at the time was a HUDD Drama graduate. It helps to have people you've taught in the right place at the right time.

And the Drama Department can take the credit for this becoming my career path. I arrived at Hull in 1968, set on becoming a great theatre director. My first student-directing project, Sartre's *Huis Clos*, disabused me of that aspiration. But in the meantime I'd somehow become the Department's theatre visits' organiser – the schmuck who took it upon himself to select plays at theatres within an evening's coach ride and to organise the tickets and the transport to those plays.

So it was that I discovered that my talent lay in organisation (also known as Admin). Someone else spotted it too, because the inestimable Harry Thompson took me under his wing. I only realised this a few years later, but he it was who guided me into Front-of-House management in that new Gulbenkian Centre and who arranged for me to spend a Christmas vacation at Derby Playhouse – panto time – where I did box-office, ushered, sold ice cream and had useful talks with the theatre manager (whom Harry had probably primed). And Harry it was who encouraged me to apply for the new Arts Council-sponsored Arts Administration course at the Polytechnic of Central London's (now Westminster University's) School of Management Studies. I was one of about 12 accepted on to this postgraduate course in only its second or third year.

And then my arts admin career took me to the Gulbenkian Foundation, then, followed and inspired by the 1976 Fantastic Light Exhibition at the Royal Academy, to holograms, with an invitation to run the Museum of Holography in New York. I did that for a couple of years, but then returned to England and became editor of *Holography News*.

Throughout, though, I have remembered my three years at Hull with pleasure and gratitude. It was there that my organisational skill was spotted and encouraged, there that I learnt to deliver a presentation with confidence; from there that I went on to an administration course which taught me the basics of business management that have underpinned my modest entrepreneurial success.

'The Passing Tribute of a Sigh'

Marilyn Le Conte (Edwards). Joint Drama and French, 1971
Senior Lecturer in Acting at RWCMD; actress, teacher, dialect consultant;
director and writer

I entered the Department in 1968 by default, largely as the result of an ongoing political spat between Drama and French, the latter being the Department who offered me a place on their 'Special' course. Previously, Harry Thompson had wisely and politely demurred following my interview for Joint Drama in which, when asked what a cyclorama was, I asked whether it was perhaps a round cinema? In my defence, as I mentioned at the time, had I known all the answers I wouldn't have needed to be on the course; and at least it showed my classics education allowed me a vaguely intelligent guess. But there we are, someone dropped out – imagine that – and I got in, (but I NEVER rid myself of that feeling of not being as good as the others).

Chucked in at the deep end, with a theatre-going history of *Boeing Boeing* in 1960 and a boy's school production of *Coriolanus* in 1966 (I grew up on a remote radar station in Scotland, so don't judge me), I remember clearly being dazzled by all that theatre could be, in the broadest sense, and I revelled in the exposure to a medium with a history, language, politics, protocol and brilliant array of visual and auditory possibilities, all of which were utterly new and intoxicating.

What I thought I knew about theatre (not much) was challenged by what was laid at my feet which was iconic and iconoclastic at the same time. I suddenly understood that stories could be told in whatever way worked, they didn't have to be literal or logical, end on, pros arch or even indoors...hell's bells, the writer didn't even have to *punctuate*. For a nice girl from a conventional middle-class family, with all the reserve that it implied in the late '60s, it was a culture shock of the first order to understand it was OK to break rules, it was even expected. So when I was cast in e.e. cummings (even now it's hard not to put in an apostrophe) *him*, my real education started.

It's ironic that when we had bestowed on us the wonderfully modern and well appointed 'Gulb', so many of us suffered pangs of remorse for the loss of the Theatre Lab in our lives, with its wall bars, dusty floor, cramped dressing-room and that ineradicable scent of gymnasium. With all its faults and constraints, we cut our show teeth in there, then danced ourselves silly at the end of show parties, fuelled by cheap British sherry from Jack Kay's on the corner of Ella Street [*who now has the path to Goddard Avenue named after him. Ed.*]. Talk about rites of passage.

We didn't know we were cutting edge, nor how history would see us in decades gone by, but nevertheless there was a strong sense of being in a golden age of our own and I suspect we were horribly smug, self-important and just a bit precious too. And why not? We'd waved good-bye to censorship and opened the door to anything goes. Personally, I was still bewildered by most things, but I had colleagues who were making their own spoof films, writing plays and helping to found Hull Truck, and I was in awe of them. Somehow I allowed myself to be persuaded to take part in a play of John Saxby's called *Green* (he didn't mind capitals), wherein I had the single unforgettable line 'I see trees as men, walking' and promptly had my rice paper blouse eaten off by Mick Butt. What was THAT about? I tell my current students about it, and they think I am cool.

I will never stop being grateful for the hand of fate that allowed me to be part of something so rarefied, nor for the encouragement of those on the staff who dared to give me a chance and who scared and inspired me in equal measures. Though based on nothing tangible, my instincts to pursue a career in drama eventually proved to be the right ones. I frequently consider how lucky I am to be surrounded by performance on every working day, and still to have many of those wonderful, crazy friends, like Dave Kent, for instance, who used to sleep on top of his wardrobe. We all grew up to be pretty conventional in the end, disappointingly, but that was never our intention.

These I Have Loved

Christine Llewellyn-Reeve. Joint Drama and English, 1971
Film and TV Floor Manager, Location Manager and Line Producer

Hull Drama Department – These I have loved:

Harry Thompson – The Noel Coward of the lecture theatre using drama to teach drama so we 'Never, ever, forgot': 'The Ruritanian Tradition'; 'The Pago, Pago Line'; 'Portside out, Starboard Home'; and why Macbeth's ghost appeared three times – 'Because, my dears, there were three trap doors at the Globe – if you've got it, use it!'. Stagecraft in one. The 'dark ages' were never dark with Harry.

The Theatre Lab where we could hammer in nails, rig lights, build sets, perform, be outrageous and take risks before H and S.

Cottingham, 1968. The Lawns' first intake of students – My first night away from home– sitting alone in empty award-winning architecture in a huge refectory eating a gourmet meal of turkey with black cherries – then talking all night with my University-chosen room-mate, soon to become soul-mate.

Politics – The sublime – Hull Drama Department giving a haven to persecuted creatives from Czechoslovakia the year the tanks rolled in, and the ridiculous, the year a monkey was elected to be President of the Student's Union, campaigned for by Cosi Fanny Tutti, hippy dropout in a many-coloured coat.

Don Roy's achievement and the pride of being part of a new Drama degree finally recognized as a legitimate academic subject even if not yet as Single Honours. We took on any Joint subject, sometimes from scratch, so we could do Drama, even Theology. We lived and ate drama 24/7. The camaraderie was paramount amongst us to prove we were not second- class students.

The Boulevard, Hessle Road, 1969-71, reputedly the second most working class street in the UK, and home to our creative gang, who wrote, ate, lived, performed and experienced life together, never to be forgotten, nor forgotten by the locals who regarded us as eccentric aliens – the sound of wooden clogs at dawn coming along the street for the shift at the fish factory and never opening our windows on a Wednesday when they burnt the fish oil which left black grease marks on all the curtains. The mouse footprints in the cold fat in the frying pan, breaking the ice in the bathroom sink – A wake-up call to some of us from more comfortable climes. The original 'Young Ones'.

Mike Walton: 'Reconstruct the Theatre of Epidaurus using the stones as illustrated' (three) – (first vacation essay challenge December 1968). I have yet to get to Epidaurus to see if I got it right, but 45 years later I finally make it to Delphi. True to form I become over-emotional at seeing the theory of Greek drama in reality in the sheer beauty of that mystical place. I never miss the opportunity to visit ancient dramatic ruins wherever I travel (all-too-aware that I am gradually becoming one myself). I can safely say that the Drama Department created this lifelong love of theatre history. I have photos of myself, standing in ancient theatres, declaiming to no audience (nothing changes).

And there was the dramatic tension between the outrageousness of us and the tolerance of him – the look on his face when an apparently sparsely-attended seminar on 'Happenings' became an actual Happening with the invasion by a figure in a flying-suit through the first-floor window, and the rest of us pouring in from the corridor to stage total disruption before leaving the same way.

Watching Buster Keaton, in *The General* in our own Gulbenkian theatre, for the first time.

Reg Farrier, fellow-student, Sergio Leone and film-studies fan, who fired us all up to re-create the latest Spaghetti Western in an unexpecting Hull – only to have the camera stolen and the film destroyed – the Bad and the Ugly did not win, as the Good remade the film, and we even got the extras back, on a budget of student allowances for one week – a co-operative finance solution that taught us a valuable lesson about the vagaries of the film industry. Distribution was not a problem however, as we premièred it, red carpet, tiaras and all, in the newly opened Gulbenkian Theatre to a rapturous reception, mainly from those who had made it.

Interludes: *Three Sisters* (or *Sisters Three*), Hull Drama Department Production – giving me the huge opportunity to be a Costume Designer and making me face up to my never becoming a famous actor – but appreciating some great performances from fellow-students who did become famous actors.

The Rite of Spring – Viv Bridson – Lecturer in Dance and Movement. Viv could get anyone to dance – despite those leotards. Inspiring, demanding. I have never been so fit before or since as we toured in the vacation to London – to the Cockpit Theatre – where I later worked in innovative Theatre-in-Education. – She lit a spark. 'Don't stand behind a sterile drawing-board – you must work with people and see the whites of their eyes'.

The Unforgettable: A session with Alan Plater on writing for TV and the stage in the new Gulbenkian TV Studio [*now the Minghella Studio, opened by Alan Plater on his last visit to Hull. Ed.*].

A shocking session of Hollywood truths for us innocents with former film-star, Veronica Lake, a Theatre Lab HUDDLE.

I have recently discovered some of my old notebooks and realise that Nick Hern's lectures on Film include everything it has taken me 35 years to learn in the film and TV industry through hands on experience.

The breadth of what we covered in three years, academic, creative and practical never ceases to amaze me, now that I have also been a lecturer myself in Media Departments of Universities. It broadened our minds to all possibilities, exposed us to the best in historic and contemporary drama, TV and film and never shied away from encouraging us to be critical and to be constantly aware of the latest developments. It allowed me and my colleagues to explore our creativity, make mistakes and create works to be proud of.

Hull, Land of Green Ginger, fond memories, dark and bright days and the start of everything.

Unpromising Places

Cathy Mackie (Warren). Joint Drama and English, 1971
Community Arts Worker

From Hull on Humberside [*then*] to Birkenhead on Merseyside, via Barnsley, Southend-on-Sea, Wigan and Battersea – a journey through, to the eyes of the world, some pretty unpromising places. For me, however, starting out on that journey in October 1968, on the platform of King's Cross station in London waiting to board the student train, nowhere could have seemed more promising than Hull.

I felt lucky in many ways. Lucky to have secured one of the prized few places to follow a Joint Honours degree course in Drama and English and lucky too that almost all the costs of my spending three years doing what I loved were going to be paid for by my local authority. We were also lucky, I think, that not every essay 'counted' in the sense of contributing to our final degree mark so we could have off-days or weeks or months in the hectic and emotional process of growing up, without long-term consequences. I was lucky to be one of just 30 studying Drama in our year group. I especially appreciated the mature students (about a fifth of the year) for their help and advice in those panic-filled hours before essay deadlines and exams. Also, the welcome I received into the homes of both students and staff with young families who trusted me to mind their children and allowed a breath of normality into the otherwise strange and intense student world.

But going back to the beginning. It's 11 o'clock at night on my first Saturday at university, with other equally nervous fellow-students I stand outside a somewhat dilapidated prefabricated building in the main campus. Music is blaring out into the night. We open the door and are hit by a wall of sound and visually assaulted by brilliant coloured lights and gyrating miniskirts and flares. I had arrived at the Drama Department and this was where it all happened – the Theatre Lab. In the days before schools had their own black box theatres and their pupils a wealth of youth-theatre experience, this windowless, black-walled space offered a blank canvas which demanded creativity. Without wishing in any way to diminish the wonders of the Gulbenkian Centre, of whose fantastic equipment I was privileged to be in charge, stage-manager on its scary formal opening night, for me, the Theatre Lab was the special place.

It was very much the students' space – we could make a mess and experiment with ideas. There was always a group of students to be found in there, planning a production, improvising or just sitting about. It was in the Theatre Lab that I took my first and last role in a Drama Department production in the extraordinary *him* by e.e. cummings. At the time the realisation that my hopes of being a leading lady were not going to come to fruition was tough, but in retrospect everything I learned in stage crews and sitting beside directors, both staff and students, in the role of stage-manager gave me a wealth of experience which has found its way into my years as a drama teacher and a community arts worker.

It may be no coincidence that my professional life has been played out in numerous 'unpromising places' – dreary school halls, dismal outdoor spaces, youth centres and even worse, sports centres:

Morpeth Dock, Birkenhead, 1996 – once a thriving dockyard, now a wasteland on the edge of the River Mersey – The Invisible Cities project. Musicians, tightrope walkers, dancers, singers, installation and performance artists from all over the world join with local artists (myself included) to invite the people of Birkenhead to see their own 'city' through new eyes.

Birkenhead YMCA, 2000 – a grim hall in the old YMCA building. A group of men and women from a bail-hostel and a drugs rehab programme are introduced to drama by Max Stafford-Clark and two of his actors from their touring production of *A State Affair*.

Leasowe, Wirral, 2004 – an estate built on reclaimed marshland on the edge of the Wirral peninsula. Sunday morning, 10 o'clock, a carnival procession with eight-foot puppets to tell the legend of the *One Eyed City*.

So perhaps what I learned all those years ago in the Theatre Lab was that people, with their humour, their goodwill, their experiences – good and bad, their talents and their commitment, can create the magic we call theatre in the most unpromising of places.

Through a Glass Darkly

Heather Valentine (Rev. Heather Wilson). Joint Drama and Theology,
1971
Team Vicar/Religious Broadcaster

Memory, like an old familiar friend joyously welcomed, comes more frequently as the years pass, but often plays tricks: what I remember is an image, or a concept, sharpened by experience gained since the event I seem to remember first embedded itself in my mind.

Academic life never came naturally to me. It was a struggle. I envied those who seemed to party more, work less, get more deeply involved in productions and still come out with higher grades. But perhaps it was not all down to me. The workload for Joint Drama and Theology was enough to push anyone to the limit. Not only the extra practical requirements of the Drama course, but also New Testament Greek to satisfy Theology.

What do I remember? The Theatre Lab, HUDDLEs, 'Happenings', *The Rite of Spring*, the opening of the Gulbenkian Centre and a vast array of mainly mature students from more diverse backgrounds than I had ever previously imagined possible. It was a culture shock, but in a good way.

So what has proved useful in life after Hull? Wherever I travel abroad I seem to come across the obligatory basin of rubble that is, or was, a Greek or Roman Theatre. Some are more spectacular than others. Epidaurus I found breathtaking, Caesarea Maritima impressive with the Mediterranean Sea and ancient harbour as a backdrop. At Ephesus I was in my element drawing on resources from both the Drama and Theology departments. The faint yet sweet smell of wild rocket lingered like incense over Laodicea, one of the Seven Churches of Asia mentioned in the Book of Revelation. It has a wonderful theatre, mostly covered by grass but there were some signs of excavation on my last visit. At least when I have led pilgrimage groups amongst such ruins I have actually known what I've been talking about although many of the participants, I am sure, have been only politely impressed by my enthusiasm and knowledge of the theatre.

I little thought in those days at Hull that I would have a lengthy association with the *Oberammergau Passion Play*. 1990, 2000 and 2010 saw me combining work for the BBC, pilgrimage leadership and pleasure. It has also given me insights into how such dramas can have a lifelong spiritual effect on audiences, even today. I was privileged for all three productions to be able to interview the director and members of the cast. Privileged also, I believe, to have seen three wonderful, yet very different, productions. Yet I am fearful of a future where the demands of the Bavarian Tourist Board seem to be taking over from an oath made to God, for in my experience that can only lead to one outcome.

Mass Media – did we ever dream of the impact social media would have on our world? How all forms of audio-visual broadcasting would be demystified and available to anyone who can access the internet, indeed, did we ever dare to dream there would be such a thing as cyberspace and wifi? The Gulbenkian Centre should have given us a clue with its state of the art technology back in the '70s. But back then there was still an air of mystery surrounding broadcasting and technology. The only mystery today stems from a lack of ability to keep up with the speed and cost of change.

Ministerial training gave me two options: revisit areas already covered in the Theology part of my first degree, or attempt an MA. I went for the latter, never dreaming that my time in the Drama Department would stand me in such good stead, particularly when it came to the module on hermeneutics and my final submission on Spirituality and Broadcasting.

A university friend back in those days at Hull was reading Psychology. We used to work together and it always seemed to me that those of us studying Drama had a much better idea of what it is that makes people 'tick'. Being able to get inside the head of a character, trying to see where they are coming from and what it is that they are actually saying is a useful life-skill. Seeing life unravelling as a plot in play or film is beneficial, but it is, after all, only a reflection of life and, as in life, what is said is not always what is heard and what is observed is not always what is seen. Over the years I have found that real events and living people have overtaken my life and that I visit the theatre less. In life as it is lived I have at times written the script, played many of the roles, directed the action all with varying degrees of success. Always with the knowledge that there is a greater drama being acted out in which I have now become both participant and spectator. Looking back over the years I can see how my life has been scripted, directed, rehearsed with minute attention to detail and incredible sensitivity, for God is a great producer. The broadcasting awards I have won bear witness to His creativity and His sense of humour. My time at Hull was a crucial Act in a play He is still producing.

What didn't it prepare me for? Nothing adequately prepares you for meeting the needs of a young couple who have lost a child 23 weeks into a pregnancy. Or the grieving partner of someone who has died. Only life can do that and a strong faith. But what becomes more clear to me as the years pass is the human need for ritual to take the place of unspoken words, something to give substance to feelings which cannot be adequately articulated and acknowledges the pain of life-changing situations. Liturgy and ritual are the everyday drama which people still crave on such occasions, but it is a drama now cut off from its roots if unrelated to any form of belief system.

What would I like to do if I am lucky enough to have a long and healthy retirement? John Harris had a theory that the 'N' Town Mystery Plays originated in our home town of Northampton. Having discovered that an ancestor of mine back in the 14th century was a signatory of the Corpus Christi Charter for the building of a chapel attached to All Hallows Church (later rebuilt and renamed All Saints), research in that area is appealing.

I would also love to spend more time looking for possible links between the language of the New Testament writings and the dramas performed in the many theatres of the 1st century AD. Something so much a part of the society of the day must be reflected in the language of the early church, particularly the Pauline writings. Reading the *Book of Revelation*, with its visionary images, seems to me like a script for a cosmic drama of mammoth proportions in the Greek style. And perhaps that's what it is: the final act of a drama still to be played out.

Hooray for Hullywood

Martyn Auty. Joint Drama and French, 1972
Film and TV Producer

Only last weekend I was talking to a student from Hull. She was living in Cranbrook Avenue and she was young enough to be my grand-daughter. The conversation eased me back nostalgically until she mentioned that the Brynmor Jones Library has just had a multi-million-pound refurbishment. I was shocked: 'But it's only just been opened' I thought, 'We christened it with a sit-in. Oh, right, that was in 1969, wasn't it?'

Then I remembered that we hadn't had much use for it after the sit-in. When the first essays were posted on the Gulbenkian wall we duly trotted off to the library to look for the listed books only to find the mature students had got there first and taken them all out. The trick was then to ingratiate yourself with the older ones to try and borrow the books from them before the essay deadline. Occasionally, just to test if we were awake, Harry would add a few joke titles to the book list – learned works in Norwegian – which even the Brynmor Jones didn't stock. But Harry could be charmingly laid back too. I recall once in his tutorial he looked round the room, blinking, and noted that neither of the twins was there. 'Go and find me a missing twin' he told me. 'Which one, Mary or Jane?' 'Does it matter?' he shrugged.

As an antidote to all the scholarly study, the Drama Department required students to attend a Saturday morning class with a more physical bias. Even those of us who had done similar classes at school or the National Youth Theatre, were thrown for a loop by having to wear tights when you should still be in bed. The two tutors were such a stark contrast to each other: Honor stood there tall, legs and arms akimbo, like a Capital 'A' whereas Viv was contorted into an 'infinity' shape from which I can't recall her ever uncoiling.

Something to do with cinema was just beginning to dawn on me, inspired by the heroic writing and directing endeavours of Reg Farrier, Dave Kent, Steve Hare and Terry Ellacott, and by Nick Hern's film screenings in the Gulbenkian Theatre. Then, out of the blue, Hollywood showed up in the Theatre Lab in the once-shapely shape of Veronica Lake. This was easily the most memorable HUDDLE of my three years. A real movie star was on tour in a crap play at Hull's New Theatre and she was lured to the campus on the promise of a large vodka, it seemed, to spill her memoirs: 'The first time I set eyes on Joel McCrea, I gotta tell you, I creamed my jeans'. It went on in this vein – spellbinding. Years later, in the company of several veteran Hollywood agents, I mentioned Veronica's 'lecture'. Each of them vied with the other to boast how they'd sacked her as a client. Knowing that scene as I do now, I'm sure some of them were sacked by her.

More seriously, more poignantly, a true movie-maker, Anthony Minghella, worked and played amongst us for some years. He was the real deal. Even Harvey Weinstein, who once physically threw me out of his New York office, respected and loved Anthony. We all did. When I heard of his death I was on location in the Yorkshire Wolds shooting *A Touch of Frost*. I stopped in my tracks. I wanted to emulate Harry Thompson who, when he heard Noel Coward had died, was about to conduct a tutorial. 'Ladies and Gentlemen' he announced with a quivering lip, 'the Master is dead. I'm going home. I may be gone for some time'.

Indian Summer

Steve Hare. Pass Drama, 1972
Writer and author, Ph D student on the design history of Penguin Books

Early October 1969 I arrived at Hull for the first time in the midst of a glorious Indian Summer. Deceptively blissful. By November the fog was so thick you couldn't see the kerb, let alone the road ahead and by January packed snow was a permanent fixture. To start with, though, the weather was kind of wonderful and unique – and so was Hull.

I was fresh out of a particularly repressive school, at a time when we felt repression particularly keenly. Almost all my friends had been expelled. I had barely survived. School had done nothing to prepare me for university; and Drama at Hull was something that nothing could have prepared you for. And here I was, feeling (deceptively, of course) somehow special and privileged. Definitely privileged, though, in hindsight, with our student grants and brand-new first-year halls at the Lawns and flats for next to nothing thereafter. One house I lived in was for sale for £500. I could probably have raked up a deposit for it, but all such houses at the time were condemned, as the local authority set about demolishing huge swathes of perfectly serviceable Victorian terraces; rehousing people (usually minus most of their furniture which would not fit in the lifts), in tower blocks out in Orchard Park. Thus Hull became briefly the antiques capital of Europe.

All the same, Hull was an island, remote from the rest of Britain in 1969 before the bridge was built. And Hull University was an island, remote from the rest of the city; and the Drama Department a tiny atoll of exclusivity, remote from the rest of the campus. It would be difficult to get much further from real life. And yet we somehow felt ourselves at the very centre of things. When you did venture into the city you encountered a different world: the Land of Green Ginger – pre-war telephone boxes in cream and green, a slowly dying fishing industry and port, and real poverty and hardship. It smelt of the sea and the tannery and coal fires. Different from anything this protected little jumped-up southerner had ever experienced.

I had no pretensions to act, and eventually found my niche sourcing props for any and all productions. It led me to explore every corner of the city: into jumble sales, backstreet junkshops, antique shops and auction rooms. And we all loved the cinema and film, and were regulars at all the functioning cinemas – the Dorchester, Cecil and Tower – and also another 35 or so buildings around the city that had once been cinemas, now bingo halls, supermarkets, car showrooms, or just boarded up. We found our way into every one.

Hull also provided the perfect setting for the films we made; Victorian melodrama; film noir; even a western. We haunted the cemeteries, markets, docks, railway yards and the desolate wastelands of demolished terraces – being drama students; making art.

The course was everything I could possibly have wished I was ready for: intellectually challenging, endlessly fascinating, in the company of real eccentrics and occasionally real genius. It was the greatest fun and an endless challenge. But like school, it did little to prepare me for what came next. What came next, of course, was being sensible, working, career ladders. Instead we all signed on as film directors, pretty safe in the knowledge that whatever job the Hull dole office might turn up, it was unlikely to meet our particular requirements. In the meantime, and to keep ourselves occupied, fellow Drama graduate Dave Kent and I opened our own antique and junk shop on the Hessle Road, called, with a nod to our privileged education, 'BA Sales'. We'd discuss our relative business ventures in the queue with most of the newly formed Hull Truck.

Of course I was not ready for real life in 1972 any more than I was ready for university in 1969; I doubt that many of us ever were. Who was it said that education is wasted on the young? I have felt ready for it since, and now, in my early 60s, am off back to university to do some research. We shall see if university is ready for me now.

Stocking My Mind

Jenni Bailey (Dame Jenni Murray). Joint Drama and French, 1972
Broadcast journalist

1968, the year of student unrest, occupation of the administration block, Tariq Ali rousing the troops to action and a naïve, innocent, vaguely left-wing 18-year-old from Barnsley brought one suitcase on the train from Leeds, gasped in amazement at the beauty of Paragon station and made her way to a tiny student house ready to embrace whatever thrills and spills the late '60s had to offer. The house was populated by third-years from the Theology Department and Amanda, long, thin, posh, from Harpenden in Hertfordshire, also destined for religion, and my room-mate. We hated each other on sight. An inauspicious start. I thought, seriously, about turning back.

I stuck it out for Weekend One when we were summoned to attend at the Drama Department. The Gulbenkian Centre had yet to be completed. We had a glorified shed, the Theatre Lab, for our performances, but that first weekend wasn't spent there. I have only a vague memory of the venue. I do, though, clearly recall two days of the most brutal physical induction imaginable as we stretched, bent and danced our way to the beginnings of fitness. I was barely able to walk at the end of it, but thrilled that the practical would be every bit as valued as the academic. Things had looked up at once.

The Theatre Lab was a wonderful space for experimenting with performance. I can still feel the suffocation of spending long hours sitting in a cardboard urn, face whited out, eyes fixed blankly on a chink of light at the back of the room, intoning the part of the 'other woman' in Samuel Becket's *Play*. And it was in that small, intimate shed of a place that I almost managed to pull off Martha in *Who's Afraid of Virginia Woolf?* I was 20 – I guess around 20 or 30 years too young to take her on. The audience invariably tittered as I announced 'What a dump!' in my best attempt at a gin-soaked American accent. It took a while to realise they were laughing not at me, but the rather appropriate reference to the Theatre Lab.

The Gulbenkian opened in my second year and almost seemed to restrict our willingness to experiment. It was 'state of the art' and a bit scary, although it gave us a chance to have a go at TV and radio. And there it happened. That sense of coming home and knowing what you want to do with your life. Not the theatre, after all, although I still love it from the perspective of an audience-member, but my performance space would be the wireless – maybe I never recovered from the quiet intimacy of that urn.

I thank the Drama Department for three of the most entertaining and productive years of my life. The 'stocking' of my mind, the introduction of mad friends who could perform the whole of *The Magnificent Seven* from memory and the inimitable Harry Thompson's wagging finger and a line I've never forgotten, 'The thing about Chekhov, my dears; Russia, it's big'. I've watched many a production of *The Three Sisters* or *The Cherry Orchard* and never quite managed to wipe him from my mind. I hear myself telling them, silently, of course, 'Oh, for God's sake, get on the bloody train'.

Thanks, Harry.

Forty Years On

Malcolm (Donald) Sinclair. Joint Drama and Theology, 1972
Actor and re-elected President of Equity

Well, here you are ...

1969-1972, which are my dates, seem not that long ago to me. But I realise half my current friends weren't even born, and a lot of friends have died, and that's life, I suppose. I'm older than the Drama Department too.

As a youngster from the leafy South London suburbs, I found Hull startlingly foreign and instantly congenial. I must have travelled up the winter before for an interview in front of Donald Roy, John Harris and was Harry Thompson there? I remember little about the meeting in the Department's little suburban house in Salmon Grove, but I remember Mum and Dad picking me up at King's Cross off a long-delayed train because of heavy snow and finding that, far from tired and ragged after a horrendous journey, I was full of elation and excitement about the possibility of getting in. Thoughts of my other choices vanished entirely. And I was right, I had a wonderful time: it changed my life.

Hull was then still an industrial town, a fishing town, the smell of smoking fish often in the air. To a middle-class boy like me, it seemed satisfyingly working-class and therefore authentic in some bonkers way; people talked to you on buses, in the pub, or in the chippie. For the first year I was stuck up in Needler Hall, but life really started when I moved in with the David and Caroline Parry, Linda and Eddie in Victoria Avenue. I sort of became me in that house, despite David's bloody folk music drowning out my fabulous Benjamin Britten.

I was back recently talking to students, and one asked me what it was like revisiting; after a moment, all I could think of saying was 'Well, it all worked out, you see'. I wanted to act and I've managed to, for quite a long time now. And I owe a lot of that to my years in the Department. We acted in the new Gulbenkian, in the old Theatre Lab; I acted with the East Riding Youth Theatre, as did a number of us, as it was run by Paul [*Phillips*], a fellow-student. I played Jesus for them actually, and still have a picture of myself being scourged by some squaddies through the market alongside Holy Trinity on a busy Saturday, covered with blood. And there is a horrified young mother shielding her little girl's eyes from this ghastly vision ... What were we thinking of? Then we all went off to India with *The Tempest* for a month. There were great shows: the opening Victorian evening for the Gulbenkian, a marvellous *Three Sisters*; it still rankles with me that I didn't get Soliony ... I mean it! [*I didn't cast him because I knew he could do it. Ed.*]

Of the actual course, I remember quite a lot, at least, I think I do. It was chronological; we started at the Greeks and after three years we were up to postwar Angry Young Men and movies. Very good, and I wouldn't have had it any other way. I still remember Harry Thompson. His Ibsen lectures gave me a passion for his plays that I've never lost.

The course had its blind spots, though. I seem to remember Shaw was considered a bore, and the whole English comic tradition was undervalued. I say this mainly because a year after I'd finished, I did a post-grad course at the Bristol Old Vic School and their course was based on teaching us how to play comedy; because if you can play comedy, you can play anything. I believe that. As Kean said, 'You can fool the town with Tragedy, but Comedy will find you out'. But, God, the ignorance of my fellow actors then about the history and repertoire of the profession they had decided to enter. I felt very smug then about what Hull had given me.

What else? I saw the very first Hull Truck show; in fact I reviewed it for the Department 'Green Sheet', I gave it a rave, I am relieved to see. We had visitors to the lunchtime HUDDLEs: a damaged Veronica Lake and a bumptious Simon Cadell. We did lots of movement classes, which is where I perhaps found the lack of humour a bit trying, but it freed me up in all sorts of ways. Then there were the post-'68 politics including the new Gay Liberation Movement, which I found very heady and exciting; Philip Larkin wandering about the place like a huge disapproving bank manager. And the friends.

I loved my second year best of all, but by the end of the third, I was ready to leave. The student world seemed gradually too constricting; I wanted to get going ... which, after a few false starts, I managed to do.

Onwards.

Well Worth the Detour

Nick Brimblecombe. Joint Drama and English, 1973
Proprietor of Le Logis de Paradis, near Cognac, France

For any soft young southerner in 1970, en route for his University interview, emerging from Hull Paragon station for the first time was a shock. Being cut in half by a bitter gust of Arctic wind was just a preliminary to being assailed visually by cream telephone boxes, culturally by shops stocking alien products and linguistically by a local accent that didn't fit any yet met.

So, all a bit of a surprise indeed, and in many other ways once confronted with the Drama Department in the Gulbenkian Centre and its cool modern architecture. The state-of-the-art teaching facilities (would they appear a bit quaint today? Certainly not then) were striking and positively made you want to be accepted here. Stating it like this is not being as flippant as it may seem now, because then everyone was pretty relaxed about what is presently known as your career path. Anything was apparently possible following the late '60s; we were always very chilled about the future, as I recall.

I don't really remember that interview and can't for the life of me comprehend why I *was* accepted – CV: expelled from my expensive school after 'O' levels and then sculling around swinging London in mixed company for a couple of years, having a great deal of fun, even making a bit of cash, wasn't any kind of obvious qualification. But, Gentlemen, I am most grateful you apparently saw something there nonetheless.

Taking up that degree course meant establishing a working relationship with the Drama Department somewhere between joining an exclusive Members Club, a zany recreation area where you needed to be tuned into the current vibe and a place to become a bit passionate from time to time about projects that were, in the jargon, going down. Meanwhile, without seeming to notice this process, you later realised how much you had learned about the subject.

I guess as you go along you appreciate increasingly that life is all about the quality of contact with fellow-travellers. The acid test of them is, as far as I am concerned, whether these people are stimulating and remain memorable. Generally, that was the case in the D/D and sometimes doubled in spades. Of course, if you are engaged in a production, then there is an extra intensity

72

about your interaction and you can often forge working relationships which, may well bind you, even if they sometimes explode instead.

In my first year I was amazed by the quality of the work, Chekhov, Ibsen, Miller etc. that I saw on stage, by such earlier-year students as Linda [*Rachel*] Bell, Mary East, Marilyn Le Conte, Kit Thacker and Michael Walker.

The person who taught me, who most transfixed me with his gift for creating memorable verbal images of the history of theatre (some are with me to this day), was the inimitable Harry Thompson. Even if you were never quite sure where it was Harry was coming from, or maybe where he was going with it all, it was always one hell of a journey.

1972, the year before mine contained memorable ravers. If memory serves in that year there were Martyn Auty, Jenni Bailey [*Murray*], Linda (Fizz) Fitzsimmons, David Oddie, David Parry, Cass Patton, Tana Wolf and who, if they had ever seen it, can forget Don [*Malcolm*] Sinclair's spectacular disco dancing at Drama Dept. parties?

The 1973 graduates, my year, contained some singular characters and I recall many others apart from the following who first come to mind: Lisa Daifuku who invited me to Paris to meet her gangster boyfriend (well he had a gun) and our visiting the open-air theatre at Vincennes in mid-winter; Tony Browne, the most revolutionary of Irishmen, cast in the stern mould of Samuel Beckett in *Krapp's Last Tape*; Dave Griffiths, a wiser head amongst us juveniles; John Fisher with a fondness for Wagner; Brian Lead, the prestidigitator; Steve Pinhay – whose 'oil slick' moment (you had to be there...) was unforgettable during one of Viv Bridson's early Saturday morning lunge and flick sessions; Bobbie Wilcox, a very chic chick, who married Mike Stock who himself left after two years and joined up with Matt Aitkin and Pete Waterman; Alistair Wilson, very droll.

Then in subsequent generations the serious talents, Stephen Gallagher, Anthony Minghella, Tim Reed, Jimmy Swan etc.

'Well worth the detour to the end of the line', as Monsieur Michelin might say.

My Debut on the London Stage

Marion Hudson. Joint Drama and English, 1973
Librarian (retired)

At the end of Year 1, our group all went to London for a practical course at Goldsmiths College, led by a guest tutor, whose name I have fortunately forgotten. Our work was to culminate in a public performance of Physical Theatre. A couple of days before opening night we still had no show, despite lots of improvisation about dreams and nightmares. We, therefore, like many harassed professionals before us, got together behind the tutor-director's back to try and knock something into shape from the better work we had done.

Had we been more experienced, we would probably have done this somewhat earlier. As it was, we had to do the performance without the benefit of a technical rehearsal, let alone a dress. The show, which was rather shambolic, was tentatively called *We Are Such Stuff as Dreams Are Made On*, although one wit suggested we should just call it *Stuff* and have done.

It was chaos backstage during the performance, with people enquiring of each other, 'What bit comes next?', followed by, 'Am I in it?'. One of the better moments was the beginning of the second half, when the audience was to hear from the darkness a male voice singing an arrangement of 'These are the forgeries of jealousy' from *A Midsummer Night's Dream*. Dave Griffiths, the singer, had not learnt the words, but was relying on reading them off-stage. Alas, when the auditorium and stage were plunged into darkness, so were the wings, and the audience was treated to a beautiful male voice floating towards them, yelping very audibly 'There's no fucking light'. The rest of us struck matches, by the light of which he was just about able to read his Shakespeare.

Many of the students had friends and relatives watching the show. Luckily, I was a northerner, so none of mine had made the journey. However, it was interesting conversing with other people's nearest and dearest afterwards as they struggled to find anything remotely complimentary or intelligent to say.

I do not feel that my debut on the London stage was particularly glorious and no agents approached me to request my name on their books. It ought to be added, though, that most of the plays we performed were better than this.

From the Doors of Perception

Malcolm Knight. FRSA. Joint Drama and Eng, 1973
Puppeteer and Mask-Maker; Founder and Executive Director, Scottish Mask
and Puppet Centre; President, The International Federation of Centres for
Puppetry Arts (IFCPA)

From St Francis of Assisi:

He who works with his hands is a labourer.

He who works with his hands and head is a craftsman.

He who works with his hands, head and his heart is an artist.

It is no exaggeration to state that the Gulbenkian Centre and the Drama
Department at the University of Hull were major catalysts in my professional
formation. With hindsight I can look back at connections made, friendships
forged and influences established – more than sufficient to energise an entire
life.

When I first arrived for interview I was searching for my way to bring hands,
head and heart together in a unity of purpose. Harry Thompson and John
Harris interviewed me and to my astonishment offered the young 19-year-old
an undergraduate place. The first year was a maelstrom of activities including
playing Soliony in a cover-cast production of *Three Sisters*, several student
productions, HUDDLEs, artistic and intellectual fireworks. Don Roy
launched into the connection between theatre and sport, leisure and
recreation. Mike Walton presented a critique of Greek theatre and social
organisation raising fundamental issues about architecture, the masked actor
and the audience. Harry Thompson assailed us with details about Medieval
and Shakespearean drama, down to production costs and expenditure for the
Corpus Christi Plays and the Globe Theatre, emphasising the importance of
developing 'the cash register mentality' because 'money is the lifeblood of the
theatre, my dear' (wagging finger). This was topped off by a rich diet of
Saturday morning movement and improvisation sessions to introduce us to
the delights of physical theatre, dance and mime.

After a summer break in 1971 spent baling hay with Portuguese peasants outside Paris, it was back to the grindstone. John Harris was teaching a practical Mask Option and I found myself licking and sticking a cardboard template, then making the masks, for a production of Ionesco's *Jacques or Obedience*. John opened up the world of masks for me, from tribal societies and ancient civilisations to great popular and serious theatre traditions, Eastern and Western. There was also a stunning guest performance in the Gulbenkian Theatre from German puppet master, Albrecht Roser of Stuttgart, with his marionettes. His technical virtuosity and professionalism did combine the 'hands, head and heart' that I had been looking for.

I was cast as God on crutches in a student production of Wolfgang Borchert's *The Man Outside*. This was followed by a small part in Synge's *The Well of Saints* alongside Donald Sinclair; and as a semi-naked *doppel-gänger* of John The Baptist in Peter Barnes' *Noonday Demons*. In addition I was stage- manager for Genet's *The Maids* at Hull Arts Centre directed by Lisa Daifuku.

In the autumn of 1973 Lisa came up with the idea of translating and producing a little known French play called *Akara* (the Hebrew word for 'secret') by Romain Weingarten that had first been performed in 1948. The author recorded in a note 'It is up to you to convey ...the simplicity, the savagery, the horror and the pity emerging from this "thing" that is a cry'. This surreal tale focuses on a lawyer (whose secret is that he is really a cat) in the pay of the aristocracy, whose real identity is betrayed to them. They consequently turn into wolves and hunt him down before tearing him to pieces, leaving the love of his life alone and abandoned. Lisa wanted the backcloth and floorcloth painted in swirls with the action taking place on swings and trapezes using a variety of masks and puppets. The cat was played by Chris Hall and the lead actress was Georgie Ramsayer. The music was devised and played live on electric piano by Anthony Minghella (who went on to teach me how to make home-made pizza). *Akara* was presented under the auspices of the Green Room Club as an English première in the Gulbenkian on the 15-17 February 1973.

At the same time I undertook my first professional mask-making commission for the Yvonne Arnaud Theatre in Guildford's production of Andre Obey's *Noah*. This was thanks entirely to a referral made by John Harris to a former student, Patrick Lau, who was directing the play. Charles Lewson reviewed the production in *The Times* on Wednesday 4th April: 'Andrew Cruikshank is riveting when he describes the drowning of the last creatures and the men's insistent will to live. He is touching when he exhorts the animals to greet God with a sweet sound. At this moment the actors in Malcolm Knight's angular masks raise their heads towards a russet light like creatures in a Douanier Rousseau'. These very same masks were used in my final practical assessment in Hull called *Examination in Progress?* where they came to the attention of external examiner, Professor James Arnott of the Glasgow University Drama Department. They formed my pathway to Scotland and postgraduate research into the mask.

Meanwhile Nick Hern was introducing us to a series of remarkable films and to the plays of Peter Handke. Tony Meech, the Germanist who replaced Nick on the staff, made us aware of Expressionist drama. And, 'imagine if yus will', a seminar on *Endgame* without a word spoken as Harry Thompson removed his shoe and threw it violently across the room: 'That's the essence of Beckett, my dears'.

The third year went by in a swirl of activity towards Finals. For my English exams I had to tackle the daunting question 'Was Blake a revolutionary poet?' This set my creative juices flowing and my response apparently split the assessors down the middle: the point of this anecdote being that 'the doors of perception' always need to be cleansed and subjected to built-in shock-proof crap-detection.

In these times when investment in, and valuation of, the human resource is all too scarce, it is an honour and a privilege to look back upon the total dedication, commitment and support offered by the staff of the Drama Department to their students. The generosity of spirit provided by Don, Harry, Mike, John, Nick, Tony and Viv enveloped us all in a cocoon of creative activity. They were names not ciphers. And what's in a name? This brings me back again to questions of individual identity and social role. In the humanity of their existence they kindled a light in the darkness of our being that has yet to be extinguished.

Jottings

Sheila Tonge (McAnulty). Joint Drama and English, 1973
Playwright, writing under the name of Aelish Michael

Like many other contributors, I suspect, I could write a whole book about my time as a student of HUDD. However, for the sake of brevity, I have restricted myself to a few random snapshot memories.

My first on-stage role on my 19th birthday as the 80-year-old housekeeper, Anfisa, (nicknamed Anfleabag by the rest of the cast) in Mike Walton's cover-cast production of Chekhov's *The Three Sisters*, where our company of first-year students did our best to inhabit for two additional performances the set and costumes of the splendid full Department show.

The great HUDDLEs we had on a regular basis in the Green Room, including one with legends Dulcie Gray and Michael Dennison.

Nick Hern's wonderfully imaginative production of Brecht's *The Tutor* when the Gulbenkian was transformed into a Big Top.

The gentle and gracious Harry Thompson's idiosyncratic pronunciations (particularly of that well-known Norwegian playwright Eeepsen), and his marvellous seminar on writing comedy.

Taking the lead in an experimental production of Anouilh's *Antigone* whilst suffering from raging toothache, eliciting some sympathy from the two guards in the show – played by Bob Carlton (*Return to the Forbidden Planet*) and Dave Gittins (Red Stripe of *The Flying Pickets*).

John Harris's amazing lecture on 'isms', an unforgettable master-class.

Saturday morning compulsory dance classes with Viv Bridson where we pranced about bleary-eyed in our black leotards and tights. Also the dance 'tour' to Bretton Hall where Tony Minghella, Mike Stock, Peter Markham and my future husband, Ian McAnulty, made up the live band.

Painting my face blue to complement the blue evening dress I was wearing to play the part of The River Elbe in Wolfang Borchert's *The Man Outside*, much to the bemusement of my parents on their first visit to Hull.

Playing opposite Don Roy (then Head of Department) and struggling to find his lips amongst a veritable nest of whiskers when I had to kiss him in a production of Giraudoux's *Apollo de Bellac*.

The fab after-show parties we had in the Theatre Lab and how sad we were when that facility was no longer available to us. (I seem to remember a protest when we tried to save it from demolition? – but then we were always protesting about something.)

A truly formative three years, a long time ago, that still impact on me on a daily basis.

Oranges, Bears and Liquorice Allsorts

Peter Winn. Joint Drama and English, 1973
Student of Archaeology

40 years on it may be possible to see my three years at Hull in perspective. I have attended other august institutions in the meantime and spent most of my career teaching theatre, particularly theatre history, but, after retiring in 2009, I am now a student again and studying Archaeology. Turning over the sods of time and trowelling the layers of memory I have dusted down three little 'finds' from the early '70s. First and most spectacular was the moment when magician Eddie Dawes, the Professor of Biochemistry invited by Don Roy to contribute to 'Crypto-drama' lectures, made an orange disappear. It was the simplest of sleights of hand but I *swear* I saw that orange disappear in mid air. It burnt on my retina then and it is still there today. *That* was theatre.

Second was the fear and trembling associated with providing intelligent answers in Mike Walton's first-year seminars. I had never put drama texts into their historical contexts before and 'How and why could Shakespeare have written *Exit pursued by a bear*?' (because the King's Men probably had access to a handy bear), surely set me on my subsequent frivolous path.

Finally, who could forget Harry Thompson's lectures on Ibsen? He warned us that we couldn't understand the playwright until we were in our 40s and his best shot at explaining himself was to tell an anecdote about a little boy asking for liquorice allsorts… or 'something like them'. With his inimitable finger-wag Harry asserted: 'There's nothing like liquorice allsorts. And, you know, it's the same with Ibsen'.

I'm now well past my 40s, but I still can't face a Coconut Roll without thinking of Pastor Manders. Tiny fragments like this are as fresh in my mind as ever while essays, exams, productions and all the joys and horrors of our privileged undergraduate life in the '70s have faded.

With such scraps archaeologists build a picture of Ancient Rome and they probably get it wrong. I could dig some more through it all, but we make of the past what we want to believe in the present and I am happy with oranges, bears and Bassett's best.

Conjuring, *Cothurni* and the *Quem Quaeriti*s

Brian Lead. Joint Drama and English, 1973; M.Phil. Drama, 1978
Retired teacher and Member of the Inner Magic Circle

I first became acquainted with Hull and its Drama Department in the autumn of 1969, when I faced Harry Thompson and Mike Walton across a desk with Buster Keaton peering over their shoulders. Harry rattled off a series of quick-fire questions which made the Spanish Inquisition seem like a pub quiz, but I guess I managed to field most of them and clinched the interview by mentioning my interest in magic and performing with a ventriloquial duck. It must have made an impression, for when I turned up to register virtually a year later the first question posed was 'Have you brought that duck with you?'

Conjuring clung to me like a shadow after that. The Chinese linking rings were introduced into a production of *The Masque of the Red Death* and prestidigitation inevitably turned up in a music-hall presentation in the Theatre Laboratory – a much-loved wooden erection with a corrugated roof which preceded the Gulbenkian Centre. The bill also included J. Michael Walton (appearing as Luke the inebriated gamekeeper in an excerpt from *Lady Audley's Secret*), Linda [*Rachel*] Bell as Marie Lloyd and Dean of Science Professor Eddie Dawes, who doubled as President of Hull Magicians' Circle, with which I soon became connected.

The act (including the duck) was later reprised at the Hull Arts Centre as part of a fund-raiser for the fledgling Hull Truck Theatre Company which had its origins in and around the Department.

As Michael Rosen has commented, you can't escape from memory. Our memories scurry about out of sight, sometimes popping up to surprise us.

Up pops Anthony (then just Tony) Minghella and his non-stop 24-hour piano playing marathon to finance the purchase of a piano for the Department which he would make use of in his first musical play, *Mobius the Stripper.* I declined the title role owing to the requirement for nudity (I don't think even Hull was ready for that.), and although someone else finally took it on [*Jimmy Swan – who else? Ed.*], Tony himself ended up in the part on the first night.

That recollection triggers off another – the image of Bob Carlton (later of *Return to the Forbidden Planet* fame) climbing naked into a cardboard box during the television course.

Harry Thompson follows closely behind, with his tour of Beverley Minster (where our grandson would be baptised a couple of generations later), his exposition on the *Quem Quaeritis?* trope and an anecdote about two old ladies who turned up at a performance of the mystery plays expecting a whodunit by Agatha Christie.

Out pop recollections of the HUDDLEs which attracted touring performers as disparate as Michael Denison and Jimmy Edwards, all of whom wowed us in their own ways. It was at one such event that someone had the idea of heating up tomato soup in the tea urn, with disastrous consequences.

Although it is *de rigueur* for students to boast about the number of lectures they failed to attend, I'm sure I am not the only Drama student to claim that I never missed anything, from Viv Bridson's movement classes on Saturday mornings, clad in leotard and tights, to John Harris's mask-making workshops and Don Roy's renditions of Molière in the lecture theatre. I still recall fascinating debates about whether the classical *cothurnus* had a high platform sole (as indeed was the contemporary fashion in Hull at that time) or whether this was simply the peg which slotted a statuette into its base.

My subsequent career, both as a teacher and examiner, has been firmly based upon those foundations laid some 40 years ago, and I still frequently have cause to reach for the notes taken at Hull. Conjuring, too, has remained part of my teaching life as an extra-curricular activity. In 2011, one of my sorcerer's apprentices, Ben Proos, was awarded the Magic Circle's highest Junior honour of Young Magician of the Year … and, although it has changed quite a bit from the original version which my mother made for me when I was eleven, I still perform with an animated duck.

The View from the Control Room

Cliff Dix. Pass Drama 1974
Variously Technical Manager, Stage Director, Technical and Stage Manager,
General Manager and now owner of a lighting and sound supply company

At the dawn of the seventies there was much publicity for the new studio theatre Peter Moro had designed. I wrote, as a schoolboy, and asked to look round. Jacmel Dent, who acted as tour-guide, (a role I fulfilled regularly during my time at the Gulb, as I was always hanging about), told me later that I'd seemed unimpressed. But I was keen enough to make my UCCA form show Hull in several places, a devious trick to ensure I got in. Don Roy seems to have taken the informal chat we had when I visited as an interview and I came straight from my summer job at Nottingham Playhouse (another Moro building) to the Drama Department with the intention of playing with the technology, rather than studying Drama as an academic subject.

Intake years before mine had spent at least some of their time in the Theatre Lab, with it's motley collection of Patt 23s and 123s, a pair of Junior 8s and incongruous wall bars hidden by tatty curtains. With the arrival of Special [*Single Honours*] Drama and the Gulb, the Lab was relegated to HUDDLEs (perhaps most memorably in those years Bob Carlton's production of *Leonardo's Last Supper*) and after-show parties at which we flashed the lanterns by flicking the switches on the Junior 8s and played taped music through the dexion-frame, wheeled, sound system Jim Lambert had built, colloquially known as the 'Landship'.

My whole approach to the degree was at odds with the Department's academicians. I had a big glittering technical toy to play with and, over three years, drove possibly more lighting or sound, built more sets, flew more shows and generally hung around with Jim Lambert, Ruth Stuckey, Dave Lumby and Dave Edwards (until he was succeeded by Charlie Wass, who followed me from Nottingham Playhouse) *et al* more than any other student. Adele Caley (as she then was) in her role as Departmental Secretary, retained a card index of each student's involvement with shows. Most students hardly filled one side of their card in three years. I filled both sides of three cards.

My opinion was then, and is now, that this flexible studio space was built to be used. OK, it's slightly mean in proportions (boasting the smallest control room door I've ever met) and design idiocy in its early days meant you couldn't use the paint bridge if Vivian Daniels' strange stand-offish blokes in what was then the TV studio were actually 'on air'.

I hugely regret the set up that gave great priority to the 'departmental production', which was invariably something tediously arty and worthy, and severely limited the number of student productions (only usually arty and worthy) and gave them derisory budgets.

Of course, I did work on nearly all of both of these types (I wrote a *Tabs* article on the candlelit performance of a Don Roy-directed production of *Le Malade Imaginaire*), but I never felt affection for the actual shows. I subscribe to the belief that 'Art Is Entertainment That You Don't Enjoy'. So I will be forever grateful that, in my view, there was not one real 'entertainment' show during all my time, so that, if nothing else, I was trained to accept working to high standards on shows with which I had no sympathy. It has stood me in good stead through the tedium of a number of arty venues since.

Jim Lambert's training, which on one occasion included his dismantling various bits of the SP80 during a show while I was driving it, presumably to test how I coped with a challenge (?), combined technical instruction with a wicked sense of humour. It made him arguably the best teacher on the staff, and was a style that I copied, unashamedly, in my first job after graduation, as Technical Manager of Aston University's Centre for the Arts. My trainees there, incidentally, went on to become Heads of Departments at The Shaw in London, The Birmingham Hippodrome, Scarborough, Bury Theatre Royal and on *Who Wants to be a Millionaire?* among others. So it's a technique that works.

It took me over two years to exhaust the permutations of the Gulb's technical equipment. It looks dated now. All lighting was Strand as Zero 88, CCT and ETC didn't even exist. There was no competition for Strand in lanterns and Thorn was the only other control worth consideration. The concept of sound was in an infancy of reel-to-reel tape and 100V line speakers. No DMX, no MP3, and live mic mixing was barely a concept, even for rock groups. The world still waited for moving lights. The Gulbenkian Centre gear was state-of-the-art for the time, but motion was limited to a follow spot and colour change to cutting into another sheet of Cinemoid. We did some great rigs (to blow my own trumpet); the one for *Johnny Noble* was competent, but Frank Hilton's for the rendition of Japanese verse which formed part of a double-bill was true excellence. Perhaps the nature of a training system is to make the output formulaic; much of the design surely was.

Once I started working at Leeds Grand at Christmas '73 as *de facto* Head Flyman I commuted between Hull and Leeds, taking a few days off for Finals exams. John Harris told me years later that the staff knew full well what was going on, but accepted that my interests lay in real theatre technical work, rather than the world of academia. It says much for the quality of the Department's then technical staff and their teaching that I could walk straight into that job, and subsequently go on to convert the former BBC Midland TV studios to the country's biggest studio theatre, armed with information absorbed by osmosis from the tech staff. Formal technical training classes were limited to a term or so of drape folding and some basic seating-moving, because, of course, the academic areas were considered much more important. Thus, while the early '70s students laboured their way through the 'great works', I was in Leeds entertaining people by doing things like running panto or flying Anita Harris as Peter Pan. And all due to the training skills of the unsung heroes of the Department, the tech staff. So let's hear it for the Department's techies who variously helped me at the start of my career.

Oh, and what do I consider the peak of that career? Stage Director for several years running cabaret at the Country's biggest Theatre Restaurant. That's entertainment… not art.

Hull is another country ...

Maralyn Sarrington. Joint Drama and American Studies, 1974
Actor to Stage Manager to Company Manager to General Manager to CEO of
Theatre

What made me want to come to Hull? There were some legitimate, laudable facts that influenced me, sure: a campus university, the new and wonderful Gulbenkian Centre and a good teaching reputation amongst the small group of universities offering Drama at degree level (only six then, if I remember rightly?). But for me, I confess, the main and overwhelming attraction was its geography. Being at the end of the train line, cut off from the rest of the east coast and with the Humber only crossable by ferry, it was my idea of heaven and signified freedom. This was indeed 'another country'. No expectation to visit parents at weekends, even better, no unexpected drop-in visits either. Rather, a painless way of asserting my newly adult independence without any parental disapproval over leaving home. On the contrary, I was to be congratulated for going to university.

And now I congratulate myself for being lucky enough to have gone to Hull and joined the fraternity of the Drama Department. Both those facts have shaped my life and continue, even now, to influence it. I made some friends for life, met my husband in my second term (Ray Smith, Drama and American Studies 1973) and since have made new friends of previously unknown alumni – HUDD being the glue that binds us and gives us instant rapport, regardless of age or generation. I also acquired in Freshers week my own 'university name': Maz, given to me, by Mick Stock (later of Stock, Aitken, Waterman fame). It offered me insight into my future (although I wasn't ready to accept it at the time. That came some eight years later). At the time I was sure that I wanted to act when John Harris suggested to me that I might be well suited to stage-management as a career path (a great tutor, vividly and visually remembered by me for being able to smoke a cigarette right down to the filter, ash intact, without removing it from his mouth or pausing from teaching – how glamorously bohemian to my unformed teenage, provincial mind). It offered me a little taster of what it might be like to be a Company Manager when I was part of the welcoming party for the late, great Jimmy Edwards, on tour to the New Theatre, Hull in a commercial farce with Eric Sykes. He arrived to be guest speaker at one of our regular HUDDLEs, tanked up on breakfast champagne and barking for more in that booming, unforgettable voice irrepressible and larger than life. I had never witnessed such good-natured, but over-the-top theatrical behaviour before and the spell was well and truly cast.

We mustn't forget the parties, those of us who were fortunate enough to be there in the legendary '70s – exhilarating departmental bashes in the Theatre Lab, pulsating with disco music and the flamboyant dancing of up to a hundred+ drama students and hangers-on. Viv Bridson (our movement teacher) taught us well – how we could 'feel the space'. If you subscribe to the sentiment that buildings absorb atmospheres then this must have been one of the most joyous on campus when loon flares were the dress-code of choice and platform shoes should have carried a health warning for sprained ankles.

It's not only the 2012 Olympics that have a monopoly over inspiring the young and creating a legacy either. As a result of attending an Alumni event at the House of Lords in May (to be recommended by the way) I met for the first time, Marilyn Le Conte – a legend during my time in the Department for being beautiful, blonde and talented (and still is). Marilyn had graduated the summer before I arrived, although my husband Ray knew and remembered her, being in the year above me. We instantly clicked, having far more in common than our shared name, and our regular on-going contact with each other started. Through her I learnt recently of the possibility of a last minute vacancy on the MA course for Acting for Stage Screen and Radio, starting that September at the Royal Welsh College of Music and Drama where she is now a lecturer. No, dear reader, I did not audition (alas, writing this has made me nostalgic for student days), but my son did, and successfully, and so will have his future shaped soon, if not by HUDD then by a HUDD alumna.

What a glorious happy thing for me it has been that HUDD has been such a part of my life and that Hull itself is where it is on the map. Happy 50th and

THANK YOU.

Memoirs of Fat Anxiety

Sheila Hart (Morrissey). Joint Drama and English, 1974 (actually graduated 1975)
Secondary school Drama teacher, teacher trainer at University of East London, now 'early retired'

Sometime in 1972, three directors were holding joint auditions so we weren't auditioning for a specific part. The 'task' was to improvise a dance version of a nursery rhyme, Jack and Jill I think it was, so somewhere in their distant memories several people have an image of a gawky and self-conscious 19-year-old galumphing around the Green Room with little sense of style, grace or imagination. If I say I was subsequently cast as Fat Anxiety in Picasso's *Desire Caught By The Tail* and, after rehearsals strongly influenced I suspect by LeCoq's work, I played the role as a nervous chicken, perhaps you can form your own picture. In later life, as a teacher casting school plays, I tried to avoid inflicting that depth of embarrassment on children (unless, of course, I really disliked them…).

Inspired to dig around in old folders, I found a review by James Booth of the English Department of two plays I was in. Writing about *Akara* by Romain Weingarten (the English première translated by Lisa Daifuku who also directed), James graciously tried to find some meaning in the play, but wryly ended 'Since Weingarten was 19 … we should perhaps not be too disconcerted if it seems somewhat half-baked'. I am sure I was not the only actor who was perpetually puzzled, as indeed were the characters – 'Why are we here?' 'What are we playing?, Quint and hazelnut?'. However, the production was praised warmly, the huge backdrop of a cat's face, the strange sequence on swings, the use of grotesque puppets – 'a great sense of poise and style in purely theatrical terms'. James also mentions the shortness of the play. There was a great deal of repetition of lines and one night one of the actors (sorry to out you on this one Patrick Murphy, but I think it was you) mistook a cue and skipped a huge section – it made no difference to any understanding of the play, but I wonder if that was the night James was there.

The Two Executioners by Fernando Arrabal, was a gruesome play in which I, as the Mother, had my cruel husband tortured, offstage with the sound of a drill, while praising myself to my two sons, played by Richard Williams and Don

Reed. We attempted to use Northern Irish accents, though how well-sustained I hate to think. The centre table was miked so that every touch or movement created a painful grating sound and the whole thing was played masked under ultra-violet light with costumes treated so that they glowed under the UV.

The only image I have seen was just a normal photo of the cast so to this day I have no idea how the play looked. However, James praised 'the stark distanced effect of a universal ritual ... the isolated white masks and the emphatically-posed static declamations were a lesson in how such stylisation should be executed'. Thank you, James.

Take It From There

Stephen Gallagher. Joint Drama and English, 1975
Screenwriter, novelist

Jimmy Edwards – yes, Jimmy Edwards – sat on a chair in the corner of the room, and we all sat around him like cubs at a campfire waiting to hear a story. I remember him being smaller than I'd expected; small feet and delicate hands. He was well-groomed and dapper, with the look of a man who'd spent part of the morning with his tailor and the rest of it in a barber's chair. His un-identified companion fussed a little too much, worrying about protecting him from some non-existent draught, until Edwards told him to stop. He was a familiar figure from my childhood; the blustering, cane-swishing headmaster of television's *Whack-O!*, the faux-disorganised, trombone-playing comedy turn of Variety shows. But here, in the Gulbenkian's Rehearsal Room, he dropped the persona and talked about craft.

He spoke of his early days as a stand-up act, filling in between nude tableaux at the Windmill Theatre; of walking offstage when a cocky co-star's practical joke made an audience feel uncertain and excluded ('You're the one who lost 'em. You get 'em back'); of the fan who buttonholed him and demanded to know what Kenneth Williams was like ('He must have thought that we all live together in a big house').

Why is this an hour that I remember so well? It's not as if the rest of my time in the Department was incident-free or less interesting. I don't recall the exact circumstance, but I'm guessing that Edwards was in a touring company with dates at the New Theatre and his visit to us was one of those ad hoc, opportunistic things arranged by a member of staff.

I suppose that, like most of us, I came to drama with some amateur acting behind me and only the vaguest sense of the history and infrastructure of the subject I'd signed up to study. In the end, those were the aspects that came to interest me most. A hidden world had been opened up for me, wider and more complicated than any I could ever have imagined. A world, created and populated entirely by social outsiders, that one might conceivably join. Let's be honest, could it get much cooler than that?

I think one of the reasons for the clarity of the memory is that Edwards' unaffected, professional chat was like a point of transition. I've been lucky enough to make a career in the business and there has to be some point where observing begins to turn into belonging, even if you're not aware of it at the time.

Of similar retrospective weight and significance – at least for me – was the visit of actor John Franklyn-Robbins for the same kind of Rehearsal Room session. I believe he'd been invited by Mike Bowen [*Head of the University AV Centre*] and he didn't come alone, but was accompanied by an assistant producer from the BBC whose name I'm ashamed to have forgotten, since her contribution was of no less value. They spoke with thrilling honesty of the crapness of BBC bureaucracy and about the obstacles to creative enterprise in television drama. Then, as now, it wasn't sunny anecdotes that people wanted to hear. Professional horror stories are always the ones that entertain and instruct the most.

Franklyn-Robbins was rarely a headliner, but his career as a rock-solid character player was a formidable one. His was an unshowy professionalism that compelled respect and his stories came from direct experience. When someone asked a final question about the future of television drama, he and his companion both indicated the whole of the room and replied in unison, 'It's you' [*Considering who was probably present at the time, this was to a surprising extent true. Ed.*].

Roll forward (bloody hell) at least 37 years. Early in 2012 I took part in a week-long TV Drama Lab in Berlin, devoted to finding new pathways to international production. I was there because I've created, run, or written for shows in the US despite getting my training outside the Hollywood system, a training that started, I should say, as a student TV director with Mike Bowen in what was then the AV Centre at the back of the Gulb .

On the Thursday afternoon there was a public session in which I sat on a panel with two American writer-producers and we talked about the showrunning experience on both sides of the Atlantic. It was the usual rollercoaster mix of stories of terrible odds, breathtaking setbacks and executive short-sightedness. The crowd was receptive and the energy in the room was palpable.

In the Q and A I was surprised to hear some obvious British voices putting questions from the back. As the crowd broke up and I moved toward the next event, I took a couple of minutes to seek them out; it was a party of young British actors and they'd driven all the way to Berlin, fifteen hours in a van, just to attend the session. Their spirits were up and their enthusiasm was high. Which was just as well, as they were driving back that same evening.

And as we spoke, I found myself thinking, 'I know you. Because I've been you'. I offered some further encouragement and we swapped cards.

Meanwhile, my Australian cousin is always asking me what Hugh Grant's doing. I've never met Hugh Grant. We're in different parts of the business. She must think that we all live together in a big house.

Thank you, Jimmy. Thank you, John.

Thank you, all.

Per Ardua ad HUDD

Frank Hilton. Joint Drama and American Studies, 1975
Retired International Negotiations Trainer

An unusually warm spring day in Hull 1972 found me at the University in an interview with one of the Drama Department Admissions Officers, Harry Thompson. A very late letter (I was an RAF officer whose resignation had just been approved) to several Drama institutions had elicited a response only from Hull.

Harry seemed as determined as I was for me to obtain a Joint Honours place, and touted me round several departments to find a suitable joint subject that would take me. After some hours we finally succeeded with American Studies. Typical of Harry, he would not be beaten, certainly not by the less forceful mortals inhabiting the various departments we visited.

An early memory of the Department was of the high-tech nature of lecturing in the early 1970s. Our first lecture was given by Mike Walton (away in America for the year). He had made a video to be used whilst he was abroad. We thought at the time, if this catches on, lecturers would never need to turn up for work. I guess this first implanted the idea of lecturing in my mind for the future. Nevertheless, in the early '80s, Manchester University did not possess such farsightedness and my lectureship there was decidedly hands-on.

The theatre has a strong tradition of being strapped for cash. The student-run Green Room Club of the Drama Department was no exception. However, it was with great pleasure that I was able in 1974 (as GRC President) to turn down the annual departmental handout to the club. My time running various amateur dramatic societies in the RAF had at least taught me how to make money: primarily by supplying food and beverages to audiences after fixing deals with local suppliers. Not all my time in the Forces was wasted.

Having decided very early that I was no match for the acting talent in the class of '75, I turned my hand to production, specifically lighting. Here I was exceptionally lucky to come under the guidance of the Departmental Technician, Jim Lambert, an incredibly patient man with a very wicked sense of humour, as well as an exceptionally skilled technician. I will never forget our sojourn together with Viv Bridson's dance troupe which we took on tour. From large Yorkshire theatres to a classroom in Barnsley – we met every challenge. Laughter punctuated every day, memorably when Jim, with his accustomed forthrightness, announced in one student ablution block: 'I think someone's died in here', and immediately there followed a toilet flush – presumably at the hands of the 'corpse'.

I always thought that academic stress would only be generated by exams – how wrong I was. In 1975 I directed a small television piece as part of the course, a two-hander which I had to transcribe for TV. Apart from outside rehearsals we only had one hour of studio time in which to go through technical and dress rehearsals, as well as recording. The time was precise and if we were still recording after the hour was up, plugs would be pulled. The AVC Studio Manager was from the old school of 'live' TV and made life more hectic by counting down aloud the minutes remaining. We reached recording with 15 minutes left – only one full take was possible. All went well until my lovely cast jumped a page, leaving us all wondering where they were and with the cameras out of position for the rest of the recording. The Studio Manager kept on counting down in my ear as the production crew and floor staff went into overdrive. Thanks to them, we caught up and made the recording, with no obvious sign of a problem. Nevertheless, the stress was as great as I felt when flying in extremely bad weather. You live every second when you're flying; the same is true in theatre and in live TV.

What did I learn from HUDD that I took with me into the future? An understanding of the diversity and importance of good communication in all its forms. My later work evolved into training (mainly business people, but others as well) all over the world in personal interaction, latterly specialising in cross-cultural negotiations where poor communication quickly leads to misunderstandings and total breakdowns. The zenith of my career came when I was invited to be the first outside consultant to run workshops at the World Economic Forum in Davos; even people at the top are prone to the most unbelievable gaffs and pratfalls. There is no doubt that without my time in HUDD such a profession would never even have crossed my mind.

Swansong

Don Reed (Donald McBride). Joint Drama and English, 1975
Actor

When my friend Jimmy Swan died in October 2007 I wrote a memoir 'Swansong' or 'Ee, Betty, is it me?', which I believe still floats about somewhere in cyberspace; however I make bold to repeat some of its contents here and to throw in a few other memories.

I had gone to Ruth Stuckey's Wardrobe to work on my costume for 'The Chicken-Wire' *Changeling*. The director, Peter Winn, had acquired from somewhere a job-lot of chicken-wire and the costumes were to be made from this with a lining sewn inside. I thought I'd try to minimise the inevitable cuts and scrapes by doing it myself. From behind a full-length wedding dress with seed-pearls and a cascade of white organza appeared the round and hugely be-spectacled face of Jimmy who enquired:

'Ee, Betty, is it me?'
'Ee, Aa'm thinkin' ye'd be better with a veil.'
'Ee, Where do you come from?'
'Ee, Chester-le-Street way.'
'Don't be ashamed', the blushing bride declaimed, 'just because you come from Chester-le-Street'.

I'd never encountered the like of Jimmy before, and I don't think anyone else had either, or heard the like, or smelt the like. The waft of strawberry aftershave which followed him as he sashayed tappy-lappy in his four-inch heels and extra-wide flares a-flapping was palpable.

Jimmy-Speak was also unique, being a mixture of Old Palare and made-up Camperama, as in 'Moon-Child of my Loin! Viddy, Viddy Vadar the Bi-Jax Omey!' ('My dear, observe the gentleman to my right.'). Between the zhushing of his bits, the grolling of his Ria and the feely-faxing of his Bopling-Box, Jimmy found time to play the leads in *Le Malade Imaginaire* and *The Way of the World*, but Maria in *Twelfth Night* was his triumph.

Anthony Minghella made a most winsome Viola (cross-dressing was the theme; Viv Bridson wanted to stretch her actors). So relieved was Anthony at having got through his first scene with Olivia (the statuesque Tim Reed) that he forgot he had to go on again. Cue Jimmy, extemporising furiously in mock-Shakespeare – 'Fie on him Madam, I will hie me hence and see where he hath went'. Viola was in the dressing room having a fag and sucking a boiled sweet (Harry Thompson had presented the company with a large bag of 'Pick 'n' Mix'). The moon-round face of Maria appeared round the door and hissed – 'Gerron that f - - - - in' stage before Aa strangle ye'.

Wearing his 'Betty-Director's hat', Jimmy directed *Straight Up* by Sid Cheatle. I recall my friend Ian McAnulty holding aloft a pair of condoms and enquiring of Jonathan Kydd:

'What are these, son?'
'I dunno.'
'These would appear to be some kind of used contraceptive device. Can you explain what they're doing in my shrubbery?'
'Maybe they're from them Tower Blocks.'
'Them Tower Blocks is three miles away, son. I can't think what fit of communal abandon could have propelled 'em this far.'

Ian also appeared in *Twelfth Night* as Orsino and in *Mobius the Stripper* (Jimmy in title role), Anthony Minghella's first musical play.

I must here say a word or two in praise of Ian McAnulty, who throughout my time at Hull and in all the years to follow until his sad demise in 2000, was an excellent and reliable friend. If I was feeling low, Ian's solution was never to analyse or judge, but to offer practical support. He made me go and sing at The Round (university folk club); he sent me home with his old record player and a sheaf of traditional LPs; he came down to Devon to direct my one-man show; on request he would rifle through his collection of folk-music to make up a tape to restore my flagging spirits. Such friends are rare.

Back on Planet Jimmy . . .

After Hull, he became Front-of-House manager at Oxford Playhouse and I went down there hoping somehow to get into the company (some hope). The

State Visit to our flat in Summertown of Jimmy's Mam, sister Pat and redoubtable 84-year old Grandma (swathed in black astrakhan coat with enormous whistling hearing-aid), is branded on my memory. 'Wor Jim' had made himself scarce ('Ee, Betty, Aa cannet do with it'); so it was down to me to accompany them to Blenheim Palace, where we viewed with due reverence the small ante-chamber where Churchill was born. The respectful hush was pierced by Grandma, who enquired:

'Is that Aad Churchill's bed? Aa've hoyed better ones oot!'

Back home in Newcastle, Jimmy became a Theatre Administrator, Drama Teacher, Bon Viveur, Raconteur and Holder of Court in the Strawberry, the Three Bull's Heads and the Blue Coyote. Generations of his 'bairns' came there to do obeisance and be elected as 'Moon Child of my Loins'.

At Live Theatre, Lee Mattison had written a two-hander called *Swan Song*. I played a drag-queen (gold lamé frock and a blond beehive wig), looking back at her life and singing, the full version of 'There's No Business Like Show Business'. We heard of Jimmy's passing while we were still in rehearsal. I dedicated the show to him and thought 'Ee, Betty, it's definitely you'.

The West Road Crematorium was a packed house, the funeral lasted a full hour, and somebody said: 'Ee! I've never laughed so much at a funeral!'

Ee, Betty, we miss you.

How to end? A last memory demands to be recorded.

Ian McAnulty, Jimmy and others, elected in an improvisation session, to present *Oedipus* as a puppet-show. Jimmy as Jocasta delivered the closing soliloquy (in full afro-wig) thus:

'Woe is me wot have I done? I've gorn an' married me bleedin' son. So I deserve to be well-hung'.

Ee, man, Betty man. There'll never be another.

Hans Christian Andersen Lived Here

Hans Christian ('Hasse') Andersen. Ancillary Drama 1976; Ph D 1987
Senior Lecturer in Cultural Tourism and freelance political commentator on
Danish National Radio.

My time at Hull University – and specifically in the Drama Department – has
had a lasting and positive effect on my life and career.

I was entirely innocent of anything to do with Hull or its University in the
autumn of 1974, when I put in an application at Copenhagen University for a
grant from a fund called the 'Students' Awards for Independent Study Travel'.
I was a student of English at the time, but Copenhagen University did not
require you to spend any time in the country whose language you were
studying. Only by accident did I discover there might be some money
available to go to Britain to devote a year to specialising in British theatre.

The office dealing with the application told me that the place at Bristol
University had already gone, that Oxbridge was available at a cost, but that
the English Department had a new contact at Hull University. Would I like to
go there? 'Of course,' was my prompt response and I went down to see the
Librarian at the British Council in Copenhagen for some more information.

'I'm hoping to spend a year in Hull to study modern British drama', I said.
He looked, briefly, as if he had gone into 'sleep' mode, then said: 'I'm not
sure we have anything'. But from a shelf at the back of the small, dark library
he brought out a blue-cloth volume on *British Regions* and handed it to me. In
it, the author wrote: 'With its broad entrance roads and low skyline, Hull
reminds me of nothing so much as those modern cities you find in Siberia'.
This was when the Cold War was at its coldest: nobody compared anything
with Siberia in order to *sell* it. Undeterred, I handed in my application, took
some exams in the spring, sublet my room in central Copenhagen and set off
on my great adventure in early October 1975.

I was really an Occasional Student of English at Hull and I should pay homage
to the many excellent lectures I went to in English literature that year. It was
a rare opportunity to concentrate on creative writing at university level, at a

time when young Danish academics had their focus on Marxism and on the 'usefulness' of academic study, something that has now come to dominate.

But now to the central matter: Hull's Drama Department. I was told by the English Department to go to the Sports Centre on Registration Day and ask if I could attend some of their classes. Behind the desk sat two men, Donald H. Roy, as yet without a building named after him, and Robert Cheesmond, Drama lecturer, photographer and the only academic I have yet known with the courage to have his hair permanently waved. Don said that they would be very happy for me to follow something called the 'Drama Ancillary Course'. I was on Cloud Nine, I was so happy to be let in. The sun was shining outside, I was 25 years old, the world was my oyster. I was, very nearly, a Drama student at Hull.

I took some classes in English Literature, probably many more than in Drama, but the Ancillary Course was a great introduction to drama generally. It was, perhaps, a little 'experimental' in one sense: the Department had decided to let a young research student from the Isle of Wight loose on the Ancillary students. He was very enthusiastic, a little haphazard in his approach to pedagogics, didn't actually finish his Ph D in the end, but was endlessly charming. His understanding of theatre was genuinely comprehensive and clearly genuinely personal. And, although he did not finish his graduate dissertation, 22 years later the Department and the University gave Anthony Minghella an honorary doctorate.

When I returned to Hull in 1979 to write my Ph D in Drama, Anthony was a lecturer in the Department and immediately ready to help the new Danish research student. I was his lodger as well as friend in my final year, becoming his assistant when he worked on his break-through play, *Whale Music*. Being so close to a man of such infinite talent and yet so modest about his own abilities was something special. His early death was a great loss at every level.

I finished my first year at Hull full of enthusiasm for theatre: I had come to see the theatre as a practical art form; had, in just one academic year, been shown how to set modern British drama in the context of European and world theatre; had dabbled in stage make-up and production techniques, even acted under the direction of David Hill who has since become a great name in arts management.

Hull University generously offered me a three-year award to research into 1960s' and 1970s' British drama, under the supervision of Don Roy. Eventually I was allowed to take on some teaching and my three years in the Drama Department became a watershed in my profession. Drama and Theatre were to become constant parts of my academic career in Scandinavian Studies, Travel and Tourism. Everything I have later relied on, I learned in Hull's Drama Department. It was small with just a handful of full-time academic staff, most with backgrounds from outside the academic discipline of Drama. The result was that, for students, the academics made up a miniature universe of approaches to drama and to teaching: no two were the same. All were passionate about their teaching and theatre practice; all devoted themselves to their work; all took on a range of jobs including working in and running the theatre. That is how the Department functioned and, hopefully, still does.

It was always challenging, in a positive way, and for a youngish academic there could be no better training ground than a Drama Department: you learn to stand on a stage, make a fool of yourself in front of an audience and – this is the really important bit of the lesson – *read* the audience, so that you notice when you are (in danger of) sending them to sleep. That is essential for any teacher. I was never bored in a lecture in the Drama Department, with the exception of one or two which I gave myself.

Don Roy's and Anthony Minghella's names are now part of the Department of Drama itself: nothing could be more appropriate. They were pioneers in a discipline where everybody was working on the frontier.

But this piece has to be in praise of all the staff and students I met in the Drama Department between 1975 and 1987, when I eventually graduated with my doctorate. I am not in the least surprised that it has thrived and survived. The Department has been willing both to steer itself forward and to adapt, in a very challenging period for British Universities, while the University in general has been prepared to stand up for the subject.

Floreat, Hull University Drama.

50 Random Memories from 3 years in the '70s

Tom Atkinson. Joint Drama and English, 1976
Television Producer/Director

1.   Auditioning for the first play staged in my first term and actually being cast – as a corpse.

2.   Seeing Nick Wilmott on *University Challenge* give the correct answer to the music starter *before* the music was played; the cameraman zoomed in on him but Nick took the vision mixer by surprise so we saw only the bottom half of his head while the other team still filled the top of the screen.

3.   Monica's chip shop on Newland Avenue.

4.   Witnessing Ian McKellen, Gandalf-to-be, brazenly cheering and starting the applause from behind the proscenium tower after a lunchtime performance in the Gulb by his Actors' Company.

5.   Having my glasses smashed while playing squash and being sent by the University medical centre for an urgent eye examination at Hull Royal Infirmary – by bus.

6.   A crash course in camp from Jimmy Swan.

7.   Living in my well-designed double room in Downs Hall, brilliantly sited directly opposite Reckitt, the women's hall. Finding Downs had more washing machines than telephones.

8.   Discovering that the university switchboard could be bypassed, and so free long-distance calls made, if you dialled '0' and pulled the dial back quickly; the force required eventually caused the extension in Wardrobe to become detached from the wall.

9.   Baked bean toasties in the old Union building.

10.   Meeting Tim Hubbard for the first time; still a good friend after nearly 40 years.

11.   Walking onto the floor of a TV studio for the first time, in the Audio Visual Centre at the back of the Gulb and feeling completely at home; my career was decided.

12.   Unflappable Department secretary Adele.

13.   Watching in an early lecture a newsreel of Churchill's funeral, shown as an example of 'crypto-dramatic spectacle'.

14.   Running the sound desk at a remarkable talk by the renowned Shakespeare Professor G. Wilson Knight which reached an unforgettable climax with the grand old man alone on the Gulb stage and, for reasons that were not clear to me, wearing only a gold jockstrap.

15.   The smell of size bubbling on a gas burner in Eric Case's scene dock.

16.   Being thrown an imaginary orange at my interview and being asked to demonstrate what I would do if I had never seen one before.

17.   Hearing the screams that echoed round the Gulb when eccentric puppeteer Max Alexander leapt out of the staircase toilet and attacked Fiona Kelly with a wet (but unused) loo brush which he was transforming into a character for his production of *Ubu Roi*.

18.   Patsy Newey's father generously giving me a bike.

19.   Witnessing Tony Minghella's transformation of the Theatre Lab into a night-club for his first play *Mobius the Stripper*.

20.   Empathising with talented designer Glenn Willoughby who burned his hands badly just before exams by failing to let go of the rope on a badly rigged counterweight.

21.   Marlowe's *Doctor Faustus* staged in the open air in a mediaeval courtyard in York.

22.   Entering a competition to design a logo for a Hull area students' group and being beaten by someone with the marvellous name of Derek Demontrousers.

23.   Having a *Psycho* moment when taking a shower in the Gulb coincided with a nosebleed; I passed out and came to, naked, covered in blood and stuck to the plastic curtain.

24.   Sam Smith's Old Brewery brown ale.

25.   Getting advice which would have been invaluable had I become an actor from an old stager who came with Hywel Bennett's company to talk at a HUDDLE: 'If you need to pull up your trousers on stage, always fasten the waist first before the flies, then you can move if you need to'.

26.   Making my first radio broadcast on BBC Radio Humberside's student programme.

27.   Emperor Rosko's Roadshow at the Lawns Centre.

28.   Realising that you could get a room of your own in the library by requesting an audio tape which could only be heard on a cassette player – no headphones in those days.

29.   Delighting in Gary Yershon's music, especially his self-parodying rehearsal song for the children's show, Yevgeny Schwartz's *The King's New Clothes*.

30.   Cliff Dix's remarkable construction of a replica Restoration theatre on the Gulb stage.

31.   Being given an impromptu masterclass by Harry Thompson one lunchtime in the Union on how best to serve customers in the interval in a theatre bar: 'Put the till *in* the counter and serve *over* the bar, *never* turn your back on 'em'.

32.   Sitting at the side of the open stage each night delighting in Sue Uebel and Richard Williams' electrifying performances in Mike Walton's full-on production of Dürrenmatt's *The Visit*.

33.   New boy Robert Cheesmond's colourful dress sense, alarming even for the'70s.

34.   Designing an ultra-stylish programme for a double bill of Brenton's *Christie in Love* and Handke's *Offending the Audience*.

35.   Directing a spirited company in Colin Welland's comedy *Say Goodnight to Grandma*. Pat Monks gave what is still one of the finest performances I have ever seen in a theatre.

36.   The word SKIFF at the bottom of the plastic glasses in the Union bar.

37.   Having my hair cut for the first time by a hairdresser rather than a barber, at Steiners in the Station Hotel.

38.   During a vacation course doing an 'alien' make-up (blue skin with latex shreds) then at the end of the day taking it all off but forgetting to do my ears.

39.   Windy fog.

40.   Sharing 6 Sharp Street for two years with unsurpassable David Pritchard and his clogs and the house's mercurial owner (the late) John Saunders.

41.   Seeing *Ride! Ride!* the unintentionally funny and unsurprisingly short-lived 'Methodist musical' at the New Theatre; try as I might, two numbers, 'Riding for the Lord' and 'Oh you can't make a living selling nuts', remain unforgettable.

42.   Grandways supermarket.

43.   Learning to edit audio tape by cutting and splicing it.

44.   Learning how to focus lights, a skill that came back from nowhere three decades later at a charity event when I suddenly had to light Janet Suzman, and did so to her satisfaction.

45.   Learning how to throw a cleat, a skill that I have so far never been called on to demonstrate.

46.   Frank Hilton's unfailing kindness.

47.   Finding, and then not breaking, a collection of tiny crystal animals while stage-managing John Elliott's production of *The Glass Menagerie*.

48.   Taking Finals in tremendous heat in the well-glazed Sports Hall at the start of what would become the long hot summer of '76.

49.   The place at the Humber Ferry terminal that sold huge Toblerones, like a duty free shop.

50.   Hearing the squeals of delight in the rehearsal room from a student who, even before the end of our final term, had landed a job helping to launch Manchester's Royal Exchange Theatre; Alison wasn't a Drama student, but I have been married to her for 35 years.

Let's Get One Thing Straight!

Penny Greenland, MBE. Single Honours Drama, 1976
Director. JABADAO - Movement Play company

Let's get one thing straight.

Neither of us meant to do this family thing. Neither of us meant to go to Hull. Just as our mother/grandmother (History, 1946) never meant to go; and our cousin (Psychology, 2012.) never meant to go either. We all had other first choices, but something sucks the women in our family towards Hull. Good job. We have had the best of times …

cont.at **Abbi Greenland**, 2009 (p. 280).

'Dear (Hull) Diary' – extracts 1973-1976

Tim Hubbard. Joint Drama and English, 1976
After 25 years with the BBC, freelance broadcaster, lecturer, writer

13 May 1973: To Hull for an interview in the Drama Department. A man called Harry Thompson asked what impact 'sur-ray-alist' imagery in *Singing In The Rain* had had on me. I was expecting questions along the lines of 'Why did you only put us as your third choice on your UCCA form?'

20 September 1973: First day at Needler Hall. Cottingham seems nice enough. Introduce myself to a Japanese guy in the room next door whom I never see again until the day before I leave.

21 September 1973: Into the University. The English Department is really good. Met someone called Tom Atkinson, as we hovered outside a tutorial room, who's on exactly the same course as me. To the Gulbenkian Centre; some strange people. But interesting.

5 October 1973: Hadn't realised that the Drama Department would host shows too. Oliver Ford Davies, Zoe Wanamaker, Denis Lawson and Roger Rees (The Cambridge Theatre Company) in Ionesco's *Aunt Sally or the Triumph of Death*. *The Hull Daily Mail* calls it 'tremendous' and it is.

17 October 1973: And another one. Now The Actors' Company at the Gulbenkian. *Flow* and *Knots*. Sheila Reid, Edward Petherbridge, Caroline Blakiston, Ian McKellen, Robin Ellis, Paola Dionisotti. A lot of stuff about the actors 'voting' and 'talking freely' and 'gently sounding each other out' in rehearsals. They're doing *The Way of the World* at the New Theatre tonight. 'Sounding each other out' IS the way of the world for us at the moment.

10 November 1973: My tutor in the Drama Department is Tony Meech. He invites a group of students to his house for supper and he asks me to open a bottle of wine. I have never done this before in my life and try to force the corkscrew through the foil. I have to be taught how to do it. Embarrassing.

17 January 1974:   Getting to grips with how the Drama Department works. The lovely Adele (who will become the-lovely-Adele) chatted to me for ages today in between 'fern curls'. I almost understood everything she said.

2 February 1974:   Not so sure about the English Department now. It all seems a bit dull there. Spending more time in the Gulbenkian Centre.

17 March 1974:   Cycling along Inglemire Lane my trendy new cloak gets caught in the spokes of my back wheel. I am pulled off and almost throttled by yards of woollen fabric, but the bike survives (a good buy for £1 and the Dulux gloss black looks fine).

3 May 1974:   Can't think why I ever wanted to study English. The Gulb is my home now.

28 May 1974:   Going into the Brynmor Jones Library, Philip Larkin, gabardine raincoat flapping, taking the stairs to his office. Looks like a caricature of himself.

20 July 1974:   As an assorted devil in laddered black tights under a pageant wagon in a medieval York courtyard with *Dr Faustus*, nursing bruised and bleeding vertebrae where I catch my back every time I emerge from my hell-hole.

2 September 1974:   To a new home this year, Fitzroy Street with Chris Lilly, Carolyn Choa and others. The lavatory painted black. My father is horrified.

15 November 1974:   To see Sue Uebel as Wanda in *Rose-Marie* by the Hull Amateur Operatic Society. Was the ultra-violet paint on the Red Indian Braves' costumes in the Busby Berkley-esque 'Totem Tom-Tom' number *totally* authentic?

7 January 1975:   Atmospherically foggy around The Land of Green Ginger, but also teeth-numbingly cold, in town. 'Canned Ego' (you have to say it in a Hull accent) at Binns Department Store to have my hair cut.

12 March 1975: Totally spellbound by Sue Uebel and Richard Williams (as her former lover) in their two-hander scenes in Mike Walton's stunning

production of *The Visit* and watch, entranced, every night. I play her various husbands, but flounder alongside the two of them.

15 May 1975: To *Amy* – celebrating Hull heroine aviator Amy Johnson – at the New Theatre. 'My plane, bi-plane, there's nothing like flying. In air, up there, why not try out some flying? In my plane, bi-plane – gee what a sensation!' Camp, but charming; I even buy the cast album.

2 October 1975: Gary Yershon and I – kneeling on the floor in hessian robes and gold masks, musically accompany W.B. Yeats' *The Only Jealousy of Emer*. Gary is an accomplished musician, but I am not. He plays the flute beautifully while I try to hit a cymbal which I can just about see through one eye-slit if I tilt my head at a peculiar angle. 'A woman's beauty is like a white sea bird'.

4 December 1975: To Hull Truck's *Oh What!*. The programme says the second act is 'introducing the chromium-plated megaphone of destiny', but David Pritchard lit it so at least we could see something.

29 March 1976: *Ride! Ride!* – a musical about John Wesley at the New Theatre. 'We're riding, riding, riding ... riding for the Lord. Riding 'cross the country o'er mountain, hill and ford'. *Pyjama Tops* with Bob Grant from *On The Buses* next week. That's more like it.

5 May 1976: With Fiona Kelly, David Pritchard and Glen Willoughby traipsing around schools as part of a TIE project, *The Humber Ferry Show*. I am the swaggering, upstart captain. The kids hate me. Maybe they just hate the play.

1 June 1976: A pre-Finals drink and visit to the pictures, with Patsy Newey, Vanda Horvath *et al*; *The Way We Were* with Barbra Streisand and Robert Redford. 'So it's the laughter we will remember, whenever we remember the way we were'.

'The Best Toy a Boy Ever Had'

Tony Pearson. Joint Drama and Russian Studies, 1976; Postgraduate
Research Student 1976-1979
Retired, Lecturer Department of Theatre, Film & Television Studies,
University of Glasgow, 1979-2001

Orson Welles is famously supposed to have described a movie studio as 'the best toy a boy ever had'. That's how most of us (girls too) felt on encountering Hull's nearly new Gulbenkian Centre in 1973. We knew how privileged we were to have such a marvellous toy at our disposal and to be allowed to experiment with it so freely and inventively.

The Gulb is now over 40 years old; the Department celebrating its half-century. Many generations of undergraduates can now reflect fondly on its impact on their lives. Chances are, wherever their subsequent careers took them, they will rarely have encountered comparable facilities; or, if they did, will seldom have enjoyed such unrestrained access.

I have a fund of recollections – people, events, courses, productions – spanning most of the 1970s, so many that it is hard to know which to single out. I'll begin with dear old Harry Thompson and his obsession with fit-up stages, pageant-wagons, triumphal arches and mystery cycles. Best of all I remember his oft-repeated conviction that nobody could ever really understand 'Ib-berg' (his perverse composite for Ibsen and Strindberg) until they were past 40. I thought that idea eccentric, not to say preposterous, at the time, but the passing years amply succeeded in proving Harry's point.

Who could forget John Harris's lecture-demonstrations on conventional hand gesture and folding fan etiquette in Restoration Comedy? Not to mention his inspirational live impressions of the stock *Commedia dell'arte* characters? His methods, too, seemed eccentric, but how powerfully John got his material across. I vividly recall his splendid production of Congreve's *The Way Of The World*, with its sliding shutter scene-changes, lavish costumes and elaborate make-up. Academically sound in every detail, yet a wonderfully entertaining piece of theatre.

Later we had Mike Walton's atmospheric production of Durrenmatt's tragi-comedy *The Visit*, which employed inventive stage effects and moved audiences to tears. Mike's lectures on Chekhov, Stanislavsky, Meyerhold and company were to have a particular influence on my own subsequent teaching of Russian and Soviet culture. One special memory I have of Mike is his love of cricket and Staff v Students cricket matches. There was a notably dogged batting partnership one year between Don Roy and Murray Weston of the adjacent Audio-Visual Unit. I reminisced about that with Murray many years afterwards in one of my frequent dealings with him in his capacity as Director of the British Universities Film and Video Council.

Tony Meech's scheduling of regular Friday lunchtime screenings of classic films – many from the silent era – was significant for introducing us to cinema as a legitimate object of academic study at a time when it was only just becoming so. It also admirably augmented our study of theatre. Around 1976 he wowed audiences with his evocative production/translation of Brecht's *The Threepenny Opera*. Robert Cheesmond arrived in 1974, replacing David Edwards. I thank Robert especially for casting me as Eddy Carbone in *A View From The Bridge* in 1978 (even if I *was* the only auditioner not too young for the role), and also for that priceless line in his production of Yeats' *The Countess Cathleen*, 'I have seen a vision of hips and haws' (say it out loud).

Of the academic staff, I have left Don Roy until last as I have an extended Don anecdote to relate. I wonder whether he remembers beginning a formal lecture on Genet, delivered from the lectern to an audience of one – me. It was a 9am lecture, at year-end when attendances were often token. I wasn't really a 'goody two-shoes'; it's just that as a married student I had to drop my kids off at playgroup early on my way to university. My classmates, however, without such responsibility, blithely trusted that sufficient peers would turn up to mask their absences. No such luck. Don was understandably furious. He resolved to make examples of recalcitrant latecomers by pressing on with the lecture regardless, embarrassing them when they eventually sauntered in.

Other staff I remember with affection include Adele who ran the office so ably; Viv Bridson, all leotards and tights; Eric Case (workshop); Ruth Stuckey (wardrobe); and good old Jim Lambert (electrician).

I sincerely hope lunchtime HUDDLEs are still a regular fact of life in HUDD. In my day they led to a lot of highly innovative and entertaining performance work, affording chances to try out ideas by way of rough draft. I remember a sort of Happening in which the audience was led in procession beneath the stage by Max Alexander dressed as a clown and playing a saxophone. As for other student productions that come to mind, perhaps the most memorable is Anthony Minghella's musical extravaganza *Mobius The Stripper*, done in a cabaret setting in the old Theatre Lab wherein Anthony, Jimmy Swann and Ian McAnulty (all three sadly no longer with us) were part of a team parading their multiple talents to wide acclaim. In following Anthony's subsequent film career, I often found myself thinking of that seminal production.

The same three (along with Tim Reed, Sue Uebel, Joe Richards and Joan Hunter) were in a haunting production by Viv Bridson of Maeterlinck's *Peléas et Mélisande*. It's impossible to mention all those individuals with whom I worked and socialised; some are forgotten but Gary Yershon, Jonathan Kydd and Annie Whitehouse all variously looked me up in Glasgow when their careers took them there; Rupert Creed, Wyndham Perkins, Roger Wood, Jeremy Myerson, Fiona Kelly and Glenn Willoughby were a few of the members of a great team I had at my disposal on a production of Gogol's *Marriage* in 1975. Ian McAnulty, Frank Hilton, Don Reed and Bob Carlton, were all, like myself, a bit older than the average undergraduate and had done other things before university. The list could easily go on if there were space.

HUDD is a special place and its work must continually go forward. It has always promoted a climate of innovation and excellence, as well as a sense of ownership and shared mission. Its generous resources offer excellent opportunities for creative expression, suggesting that even the impossible might be achievable. In a lifetime of professional theatre-going I have on many occasions deemed the fare on offer to be less accomplished in artistic vision, production values and acting skills than many of the enterprising spectacles served up by eager students at Hull. Long may you thrive. Long may future generations discover the best toy a boy (or girl) ever had.

Building A Character

Gary Yershon. Joint Drama and Music, 1976
Composer

The year I arrived in Hull, work had recently begun on two massive building projects: the Humber Bridge and the easternmost section of the M62. On the campus, there were plans for a new students' union. We were under construction too, in the way that students always are.

I didn't fancy commuting from the halls in Cottingham, so the accommodation office found me a place in one of the university-owned houses. My roommate and I had little in common. We'd been put together because neither of us smoked. We shared the front room upstairs, overlooking Cranbrook Avenue.

With three other Drama students, I spent my second year in a large, dark house on De Grey St. I bagged the front room downstairs, which looked out onto the street, or would have done if I'd ever cleaned the windows. 12 months later, a group of us rolled the piano I'd bought in an auction (at least, I think that's how I acquired it) along De Grey St, turned right into Beverley Road, left into Fitzroy St, then heaved it over the threshold of No. 9, which was to be home till Finals were over. I bagged the front downstairs room again. I remember the house as a bright, airy place with a grassy garden. Perhaps my window-cleaning skills had improved.

We could be lured into central Hull by the prospect of a film or a play. I remember a touring production of *Who's Afraid of Virginia Woolf?* at the New Theatre. My friend, Chris Lilly, and I were part of a depressingly small matinée audience in that huge auditorium. The actors might understandably have walked through it, saving themselves up for the evening show. Instead they gave us everything they had, especially Miriam Karlin as Martha. Chris and I were so impressed we decided to thank them. We went to the stage-door, expecting to leave a note. To our surprise, Ms Karlin invited us up to her dressing room for tea. She couldn't have been more welcoming. 35 or so years later, I met her again, after a performance of the last stage play she appeared in, shortly before she died. I didn't expect her to remember me, of course, and sure enough she didn't. But she did remember that tour of Albee's play. And she remembered Hull and the New Theatre.

All sorts of stuff turned up there. An opera company – it might have been Glyndebourne or Sadler's Wells/ENO – brought *The Coronation of Poppea*. Jules Romaines' play *Dr Knock* arrived with Alfred Burke in the title role. Best of all was a local amateur society's new musical about the life of Hull heroine Amy Johnson. It was a tremendous achievement on one level and, accidentally, hysterically camp on another. The cast album is a collector's item. Another touring opera production, of *Carmen* this time, brought a few of us onstage as extras. There was hardly any rehearsal. They costumed us as soldiers, telling us not to worry about our journey from one side of the stage to the other – the chorus of tobacco-factory girls would make sure we'd get to where we had to go. That evening, looking tolerably dashing in uniform, we made our entrance at the appropriate musical moment. A tobacco girl flirted with me briefly, smiling, pouting, tossing the curls of her wig with abandon. Then she grabbed me unceremoniously and thrust me upon the woman next to her, who in turn whirled me on to her neighbour, who shoved me on to the next who propelled me on to the next until suddenly I found myself in the opposite wing, along with my fellow passed-parcels.

The month I left Hull, the easternmost section of the M62 had just been opened, the new Students' Union building was up and running, and on a clear day (with clean windows) the towers of the Humber Bridge were visible from the upper floors of the Brynmor Jones library. It seemed as if they'd always been there.

Next, Please!

Philip Dart. Joint Drama and Theology 1977
Theatre Director

When I started in the Drama Department in the autumn of 1974, I thought I might like to try a little bit of acting. Not because I had a burning desire to become an actor, but because I imagined it would be fun. How wrong I was.

I began my stage career playing a reporter in Mike Walton's production of Dürrenmatt's *The Visit*. I had three lines. Now, the lines themselves were not exactly challenging: 'Herr Ill? Herr Ill? Are you Herr Ill?' However, the reporter doesn't appear until the second act and by the time I reached the stage, nerves had got the better of me. My voice quavered, my hands shook uncontrollably and I managed to mess up the lines at every performance.

Things didn't improve: in my second year I was cast as a bright young thing in an early Coward play, *The Young Idea.* This was a more substantial part, but the action involved nonchalantly tossing a coin. Whatever I did, that coin would not land in my hand. I vividly remember my humiliation as the offending object rolled across the stage, forcing me to pursue it and pick it up before the play could continue.

Although instinct told me my acting career was likely to be short-lived, I was cautiously pleased when, in my third year, I landed the part of a Bridegroom in a Feydeau farce. The role sounded promising until I realised that I would be on stage for all of 20 seconds, with no lines. Obviously my lecturers had learned the art of damage limitation as far as I was concerned.

In retrospect these experiences, embarrassing as they were, helped me understand that my real love was directing. My various attempts to perform left me with the greatest respect for those who want to act (and have the talent to do so) and this realisation has served me well during my last 30 years working as a professional director.

The Turning Point

Jonathan Lunn. Joint Drama and English, 1977
Choreographer/Opera Director

I should have kept a diary, then this process of trawling through events from 1974 to 1977 would perhaps have been easier. But nearly 40 years on, I'm surprised how vivid the memories are.

A week in January 1976 changed my life. Half way through my second year, London Contemporary Dance Theatre came to Hull for a residency. The Company was spreading the gospel of modern dance and the teachings of American dance pioneer, Martha Graham. I had no clue about dance, confused Martha Graham with Eileen Fowler (who taught keep fit classes on TV in the '50s). I was told that LCDT was highly experimental and into physical contact. It sounded terrifying. Those of us doing the Improvisation Course were press-ganged into attending a week of technique classes, lecture demonstrations and performances that the Company was offering. I had no idea that I had a facility for dance. I couldn't put one foot in front of the other, but I found I could kind of make the shapes and was told I had 'potential'. The eight Company dancers seemed like perfect super-beings, expressive without saying a word, physically perfect in every way and committed to their cause, as though it were a religion and they its chief disciples. I just wanted to be one of them.

I thought training would transform me, ugly duckling style, into something, someone else. There I was, a non-athletic ex-public school boy who had repeatedly forged sick notes and locked himself in school toilets to avoid rugby, cricket, swimming and football lessons and who had until then only found his body useful for moving his head from the library to the dining hall. But almost overnight, I decided to become a dancer. I had to train that body. Suddenly I was up for 8.15am classes, sweating away, contorting, contracting, jumping and turning. Then more classes at lunchtime. Pa pa-pa pa, pa-pa pa pa-pa pa, bounce your head, contract your stomach, pa pa-pa pa, pa-pa pa pa-pa pa, 'Feel as if you're embryonic', our dance teacher, Viv Bridson would rhythmically intone. Good, Philip. Yes, Jim. Wake up, Carolyn. Be more masculine, Jonathan.

I listened to the voices inside and outside my head questioning my ability and my chances of making anything of being a dancer. It made me all the more determined, but I decided first to finish my degree. three years of training in London, joining LCDT for 10 years, dancing with my 'heroes', then pursuing a career as a choreographer and opera director, all lay ahead. But at that time my world was in Hull. I had a lot to learn and achieve, but I was happy living off a diet of cheese and onion toasties and marmalade crumble, when that was all we had in the house, and surviving on £7 a week. And being in the Drama Department felt like belonging to an elite club.

I occasionally left the Drama Department to go to the Union Building or the Library, for example. I remember getting stuck in the lift there when, heading back after a tea break to continue revising, we moaned about how totally boring revision was. We could always get stuck in the lift, one of us who shall remain nameless joked. It took only one heavy jump and the lift shuddered to a halt half way between the Classics and History floors. An hour later we were prized out, much to the bemusement of the engineer who couldn't explain why the lift, with only four people in it, had just stopped on its own.

Other things stand out, like the Friday afternoon screenings of film classics, and particularly watching *Brief Encounter*. Since childhood I had been a massive cry-baby at the pictures. I'd blubbed, aged six, through *Sleeping Beauty* (particularly the happy bits), *Born Free, Pollyanna, The Incredible Journey*. But I'd learned to suppress even a sniffle when puberty and boarding school set in. The peer pressure was too much – 'Lunn, we've decided that you're … dainty'. The fear of exposure by showing my feelings sent me into total emotional lockdown. But then came *Brief Encounter*. I found it excruciatingly upsetting, and snivelled the whole way through, ashamed and embarrassed by my inability to control myself. When it was over and we shuffled out of the theatre, I realised everyone else was also red-eyed and wet-nosed. The men were snivelling too. You mean we *are* allowed to show our emotions and cry? It was such a relief.

And then there were the inspirational productions that I witnessed or took part in – Mike Walton's *The Visit,* Anthony Minghella's cult *Mobius the Stripper,* Jimmy Swan's *The Maids,* Penny Greenland's *Coward Revue.* But it was simply the experience of being left to our own devices, entrusted to run rehearsals, put on productions and take responsibility for ourselves that was a revelation.

Whether working as an actor, dancer, stage-manager, costume-designer, make-up designer or choreographer, all the time I was waiting for someone to come in and tell us to stop. No one ever did.

I have alarmingly few memories of the lectures I attended, particularly those in the English Department (I still have nightmares that I am not allowed through immigration, or into a theatre until I have delivered my essay on Sylvia Plath). But I do vividly recall one of Don Roy's introductory sessions focusing on drama as ritual. We watched an early documentary about Bali, which came to a head, as it were, when we witnessed one ceremony with tribal elders passing a live chicken around a circle until the chief just took the chicken's head in his mouth and bit it off. Since that rather shocking introduction to the origins of Drama, I have subsequently strayed into many sacred rituals in Indonesia, India, China and among the Native American tribes in the US. I still haven't seen anyone bite the head off a living animal, but I never forget how captivated I was by the dangerous magic other worlds introduced to me back then.

In some ways my time at Hull opened my eyes to what I wasn't. I wasn't working class, and I didn't have a gruff and gritty Northern accent, much to my disappointment. I sounded like the public school toff from Surrey that I actually was. And I wasn't Jewish or Catholic either, which I regretted, as everyone around me seemed to be, and they all had an overbearing repressive culture to rebel against. I just had a wishy-washy Church of England upbringing, and understanding parents.

I don't think a day passed during my three years in Hull when I didn't set foot inside The Gulb. It was home, the place where it all happened, where everyone who was anyone – in my world-view at the time – would be. I still miss that.

'Oh Dear, Etta, I Am So Sorry ...'

Patsy Newey. Joint Honours Drama and French, 1977
Media Consultant after 30 years with the BBC

I couldn't have been more thrilled to receive the offer letter from Hull. Bristol had been my first choice on paper, with Hull joint second, but after my visit to The Gulbenkian, I knew this was where I wanted to be and felt I had wasted my train-fare going to Bristol after the Hull interview. In 1973 Peter Hall started his term as Director of The National Theatre to manage its move to the South Bank, but for me, 200 miles north was where it was all happening in Donald Roy's Gulbenkian Theatre and I was desperate to be part of it.

What a surprise then when a good neighbour and friend of my parents rang my Mum to say 'Oh dear, Etta, I am so sorry. I hear Patsy's going to study Drama. How awful for you!'. A definite case of 'Don't put your daughter on the stage, Mrs Worthington'.

Excitement built as reading lists arrived with dramatists I'd never heard of – Aeschylus, Sophocles and Euripides, followed by the list of gear we would need for our practical sessions. Was this a joke or a deliberate ice breaker, when we all – men and women – met each other for the first time on the stage of The Gulbenkian, wearing very bright and tight turquoise tights and black jazz pumps? What a diverse gathering we were anyway, without the entrapments of turquoise tights.

One of the first films we were shown was the recording of Winston Churchill's funeral and we discussed the inherent 'crypto-dramatic spectacle', a phrase I still love to use whenever I can. It applies to so many events and happenings.

Memorable productions – so many, but ones that stand out for me are Mike Walton's production of Durrenmatt's *The Visit* with Sue Uebel and Richard Williams. I was just delighted to be House Manager, and I watched mesmerised every night for seven nights (including the dress rehearsal) from Sunday, 2nd until Saturday, 8th March, 1975.

In June of the same year, the old Theatre Lab provided the perfect location for Anthony Minghella's first play *Mobius the Stripper*, which he wrote and directed as well as composing the music. What talent – he always seemed so much cleverer than all of us, as well as being such a kind and generous person. Our paths crossed a few times in London and I was very proud to be present at the same BAFTA awards in 1997. It was the last year that the TV and Film awards were presented together. Our table didn't win for Best Talk Show [*Esther Rantzen*], but I was able to bask in some of Anthony's glory at *The English Patient* winning no fewer than six awards. The BBC bosses were impressed by my contacts. His was the next table to ours.

I didn't get many acting parts at Hull, as there were too many students better than I was, but I do have a soft spot for my performance in Pinter's *The Lover* with Rupert Creed in May 1975. Disappointingly, 'the camera wasn't working', so I have no visual record of it.

Back from my year abroad in Paris, where I'd enjoyed lots of trips to the theatre, it was fun in my last year to direct Chris Jury in Ionesco's *La Cantatrice Chauve* (*The Bald Prima Donna*), bringing together both sides of my studies.

Other striking images and flashbacks:

in our first year, cycling every morning against the bitter Hull wind with Tom Atkinson, David Pritchard and Tim Hubbard from The Lawns to campus; how we longed to be able to afford the bus some days;

drinks at Nellies in Beverley where the old Nellies wouldn't let women buy a drink at the bar. Feminism seemed to be stuck in 1876 rather than 1976;

the joys of communal living, first in Dover Street, and then in De Grey Street. At the latter, we all – Heather Williams, Alison Stewart, Mike Scoblow, Jonathan Lunn and I decided to dye our hair red one day. I still have the photos of us all looking completely ridiculous, but very happy, our heads covered in tin foil. It was a one-off experiment; the generosity and kindness of our lecturers. Tony Meech was my tutor and supervisor and would often invite us round for a wholesome supper with his wife Liz.

35 years on and our son John has just finished his first year at Sussex University. I was so pleased when, as a very small child of five or six, he brought home his first and only self-portrait with the caption below 'I am happy when I go to the theatre'. It's framed and on his bedroom wall, a reminder to me that I too am happy when I go to the theatre. I would like to thank my lecturers and fellow alumni for enhancing that experience and, hopefully, enabling me to share the joys with family and friends.

As for our 'friend and neighbour', she really needn't have been so concerned. It was one of the best decisions I ever made.

Remoulded

Rupert Creed. Joint Honours Drama and German, 1978
Freelance writer; theatre director and broadcaster

I first came to Hull in February 1974 for an interview to study Drama and German. On the journey home the train pulled out through grim rows of back-to-back houses, smoke wafting into the night, just like on the start of *Coronation Street*. The time had already past when Hull fishwives would sit out in the street braiding nets, and they weren't ever so desperate or dim they'd be doing it outside on a wet-snow night in winter, but I didn't know that then. I just knew – like Arnie a decade or so later – that I'd be back. The Drama Department at the University of Hull was it – where I wanted to be. Friends back home were appalled and couldn't understand why I was keen to forsake the groovy delights of Brighton for a grim Northern city where the smell of greasepaint was smothered by the stink of fish. At that time it was. On low cloud days, the fishmeal factory on St Andrews Dock still gave out a pervading whiff. But on that day in February I'd seen the Gulbenkian Theatre and pictured myself strutting around the stage. I'd sat in a lecture hall and knew I'd be buying one of those Hull Uni scarves like the real students wore. I'd seen the Theatre Lab and even the name got me all excited. Yes, I'd be doing some experimenting of my own in there before long. Even if it did mean buying a pair of tights.

I started in October 1974, living in a student house on Cranbrook Avenue, and for the first term remember not being able to distinguish between staff and the fair number of mature students. In each year group there were only around six 'straight' [*Special or Single Honours, I hope. Ed.*] Drama students and about a 12-15 doing Joint Drama, so the student-staff ratio in tutorials was incredibly good. The course work started pretty much with Greek Theatre and moved chronologically through the centuries, getting as far in the final year as Osborne, Pinter and Beckett. The real attraction lay of course in being able to mount productions and get hands-on learning of all the various performance and technical elements. It felt we had almost unlimited access to the main stage, and to HUDDLEs in the Green Room. Life revolved around rehearsals, lectures, tutorials and drinking in the Student Union, which in 1974 was in what is now Staff House, before the new Union building opened a year or so later. Occasional forays were made into Hull – to the Bier Keller, (now Hitchcock's Restaurant) and to the Piper Club on Newland Avenue, whose dubious Sunday lunchtime delights included a live stripper. A common post-pub-closing ritual was queuing up to get an 'Arnett's fadge' in the small bakery at the bottom of Princes Avenue. Another was a night out at 'Nellies' in Beverley, whose main bar didn't even possess a bar-top: you were served by three elderly sisters, pulling pints from a pump in the wall onto glasses on a small table. It felt like a pre-Chekhovian experience and the three sisters, though unaware of the delights of Moscow, were adamant about forbidding women in the main bar.

Perhaps it's an age thing, but theatre in the '70s felt far more 'rock 'n' roll' than it does today. The small-scale touring movement was in full swing, there were feminist and political theatre groups in abundance and DIY theatre was everywhere. In the Department there were some weird and wonderful 'Happenings', regular Agit-Prop in the Union – often instigated by Stuart Cosgrove – and a climate of anything-goes experimentation. I remember a punk *Midsummer Night's Dream*, which seemed to get up the nose of the English Department and a production of Handke's *Offending the Audience*, which certainly did. The atmosphere was a heady mix of dramatic theory and practice, all fuelled by alcohol and the odd snort of snuff [*sic, Ed.*], courtesy of John Harris. Staff-student relations were wonderfully relaxed and I have a vivid memory of Harry Thompson's end of term Christmas tutorials which involved large spreads of mince pies and copious bottles of sherry.

In December 1977 the Department toured Pinter's *Old Times* to West Germany, sponsored by the British Council. Directed by Tony Meech, with a cast of Heather Williams, Pippa Thomas and Mike Walton, we set off on the Hull ferry to play a week of dates in the Teutonic heartland. Having spent the previous year at Kiel University, I was taken along to assist Ben Mulhuysen on stage-management and lighting, presumably because I spoke a bit of the lingo. Driving through Holland the next day we arrived at Bielefeld, did the get-in and went straight into the first performance that night. I remember a very portly German Fire Officer was required to sit through it all in the wings, keeping a beady eye out for any attempts by the Brits to fire-bomb the theatre. I don't think he followed much of the play, but he did get a bit excited at the lighting of a candle. At the end of the show, the cast were showered with bouquets and there was a standing ovation demanding numerous curtain calls. This was our first exposure, not only to the German practice of expressing audience approval by a commensurate period of sustained applause, but also to the very notion of a curtain-call. In the Drama Department at the time there was a tacit rule that students did not take a bow at the end of productions. If that was to stop us getting too much like Prima Donnas, it certainly backfired that night in Bielefeld. We were now seasoned pros and had the flowers to prove it. We also performed in Köln (twice), Wuppertal, Mönchengladbach and at Iserlohn where we were accommodated overnight in the British Army barracks. I still have a photograph of the cast and crew having breakfast in the Officers Mess [*of the Irish Rangers*], amidst a vast array of regimental silver.

At the end of it all I was lucky to get a job, only a week after Finals, as Stage-Manager with Hull Truck. Thus started a whole new learning curve, under the indomitable director, Mike Bradwell, with two years of national and international touring and a Wild West approach to the whole notion of what theatre could and should be like. I worked with Ken Campbell, Jim Broadbent, a young Frances Barber in her first professional role, as well as former student friends Pippa Thomas and Chris Jury. It also meant I stayed living in Hull and 35 years on it is pretty much my adopted city. I went on to start my own theatre company, Remould, which ran for 16 years, worked with the BBC in Hull and more recently have written plays for Hull Truck. My time at Hull University Drama Department gave me the confidence, enthusiasm and ambition to do theatre as a career. It also gave me a lot of friends. So, a big thanks to all fellow-students and staff. You didn't make me rich, but you certainly made me happy. And for better or worse, the city no longer smells of fish.

Thoughts from an MD

Kate Edgar. Joint Drama and Music, 1978
Musical Director

Here are a few thoughts from a graduate of the class of 1978.

I arrived as a rare Joint Drama and Music student, not knowing that there was such a thing as a Musical Director, then spent three years MDing many departmental shows and HUDDLEs, using my mates in the Music Department as the band.

I'm particularly proud of having got eight of them to dress in drag for Tony Meech's production of *The Threepenny Opera.*

The friendships I made at Hull shaped my professional career, including working with Gary Yershon on Phyllida Lloyd's Donmar production of *The Threepenny Opera* (almost as good as Tony's).

I'm now working, at the time of writing, with Rosi Hutt, who's directing the stage version of the CBeebies show, *Grandpa in my Pocket*, written by Mellie Buse. The Hull Mafia is alive and well and working at Nottingham Playhouse.

Lasting memory? – being tutored by Tony Minghella and being lucky enough to see the shows he wrote and directed at and for Hull.

Home, Sweet Home

Sarah Greene. Single Honours Drama, 1978
Actress and Broadcaster

The early experiences are clear and sharp in my memory.

On a very cold January day in 1975 with fog so thick you couldn't see the top of the Brynmor Jones, J Michael Walton patiently asked a nervous 17-year-old 'If we were to offer you a place in October would you take it?'. I couldn't quite believe it. As soon as I'd walked into the Gulb – with its wet puppy smell of size and its black womb-like theatre protecting and challenging at the same time – I was home. Yes, of course I'd take it.

The first night reverse-charge 'fern curl' experience, when the operator at Hull's very own exchange said before putting me through: 'Hermsick love? – Dern't worry, yer erl hermsick tonight'.

I auditioned immediately. For everything. Still 17, my first evening production was directed by third-year student, John Elliott, aged 34. Written by Peter Handke, the play was called *A Friend In The Audience*. At least, that's what I'd thought John had announced in the Green Room. It was actually called *Offending The Audience*. And it did. On the first night, I was forcibly ejected from the in-the-round stage by four very drunk zoology students – only to be rescued by the far more terrifying and supremely heroic Sue Lovett. She shoved me back into the fray saying 'give the fuckers hell'. OK then.

Baptism by fire didn't begin to describe the experience. But by now I knew no fear. Then again I was *still* 17 – just. So when the audition list went up for Tony Minghella's Humberside Theatre production of *Play* by Samuel Beckett, I put my name down before you could say 'torture in three large urns'. Surely, I thought, this would be less miserable than the Handke? It really wasn't. And I probably shouldn't have tried whisky for the first time just before the first performance. Thank god for Pippa Thomas getting me on the bus to the theatre and for Wyndham T. Perkins, an unlikely stage-manager, pouring black coffee down my throat before pouring *me* into my urn.

After that it was everything from Brecht to Vivian Ellis. We did not stop: writing, directing, performing, trying to dance, trying to act, design, light, create.

Just a few of the moments, images and lessons that have stayed with me:

Harry Thompson's extraordinary delivery, his eccentric pronunciation and his 'Three Most Important Rules of Theatre: NEVER build a thee-airter from wood – it will burn down. NEVER have a running-time longer than 90 minutes (oh, so bloody true). ALWAYS make sure there's a bar for every tier of the auditorium'. Inspired!

John Harris teaching me that Guinness and tomato juice was the most nutritious lunch on the planet;

trying to sing 'Home Sweet Home' as *East Lynne's* Lady Isobel Carlyle to the good people of East Riddlesden without falling off the front of our authentically-lit Victorian melodrama stage in a medieval barn;

we, the class of '78, attending our Finals exams in costume… that is, school uniform for TIE and full togas for Classical Drama;

the endless patience of Jim Lambert, Eric and Ruth.

I found the Drama Department and my soul mates and friends there to be all-absorbing. But there are myriad memories of experiences away from the building itself that would inform what happened inside it:

the weird smell of kapok hanging over Hull every Tuesday;

fadges from Arnett's bakery on the way home from a night out. Only ever wearing dead peoples' clothes bought either from *Granny's Treasures* or from 'Big Pauline' (Roland Gift's mum) in the union on a Friday;

our pet rabbit, Shitto, at 19 Auckland Ave – erstwhile star of Matthew Jacobs' production of *The Family* at the Humberside Theatre;

the courage of everyone in that play, especially my good friends (then and now), Liz Parker and Chris Jury;

white phone boxes;

endless union bar movie debates about a young upstart called Spielberg, about Woody Allen and line-dancing to 'Saturday Night Fever';

Matthew Jacobs and David Hanson looking like Teddy Boy gods after we'd all learned to jive at the Stevedore and Dockers Club for our 1950's production of *A Midsummer Night's Dream*. Why? 'Let's rock the ground whereon these sleepers be…'. And we did.

Looking back I realise the gifts Hull Drama Department gave me were the priceless opportunities to take risks, to make mistakes and to build confidence. Confidence to go out and audition. For everything. To start getting paid for working in theatre and television.

Another realisation came very quickly and I would add it to Harry Thompson's list of rules. Every Hull University Drama student lucky enough to use the Gulb should know that it's highly unlikely you will ever work in such a wonderfully well-equipped, elastic, warm and dry space again. Make it your home.

Political Theatre

David Hanson, MP. Single Honours Drama, 1978
Labour MP for Delyn since 1992; currently Shadow Police Minister, after
serving as a Minister in the Home, Justice, Northern Ireland, Wales and
Whips Offices and in No.10 Downing Street

I confess I'd not really heard of political theatre before I came to Hull – drama
was something that I aspired to do, enjoyed, or watched for entertainment,
mostly for me on TV. The fact that drama could also be a powerful tool for
change had not yet fully hit home.

That first changed for me when my interview for a precious place at Hull
University included studying a copy of *The Fire Raisers* by Max Frisch – a witty,
dark comic piece that talked of burning houses and innocent householders, of
standing by when others brought ruin.

I am forever grateful that in that interview I said – 'It's about the rise of the
Nazis isn't it?' – a moment of divine inspiration that I think to this day got me
my place on Special [*Single Honours*] Drama and changed the course of my life
forever.

Arrival in Hull can simply be described as 'Wow!' – homesick, undoubtedly,
in a far away city, yes, but ready to go with jump-leads attached to kick-start a
new life.

Single Honours Drama was a close knit group – in 1975 there were eight of us
– enough to put on a good play, but often needing the support of those who
did joint degrees, some of whom I quickly learned were really brilliant – and
some, like Chris Jury or Mellie Buse, have gone on to great things in their
own careers: Chris as an actor and director, and Mellie the brains behind great
children's shows such as *Charlie and Lola* and *Big Cook, Little Cook* – my kids are
impressed I know them.

We did a pub tour as a band of wandering minstrels – the Fergusson Fawsitt
in Walkington playing host to Chaucer's *The Millers Tale*.

We wrote our own Roman farce – akin, on reflection, to Frankie Howerd's *Up Pompeii,* but at the time a show in which we took considerable pride.

We, quite frankly, butchered Shakespeare's *A Midsummer Night's Dream,* set in a smelly fairground, full of rock and roll teddy boys and girls – with a 50s' dancing Puck entering to Dion's *The Wanderer* – oh Pippa Thomas, where are you now?

We spent a happy summer vacation course putting on a reproduction of the Samuel French 1870's prompt book for T.A. Palmer's version of *East Lynne* in the barn at East Riddlesden Hall, with the original music, and sponsored by the National Trust – rehearsing in Hull, building sets in the summer sun by the student union and then carrying it all to West Yorkshire in vans. Theatre by night – shopping, walks, pubs and pies by day. The audiences were enthusiastic and after the last night the director presented carnations to all the cast and crew, a touching gesture that helped us get over the 3am return to Hull after the strike, on the last evening of the show.

We put on a production of O'Neill's *The Great God Brown* in Leeds Playhouse. A real theatre and another paying audience.

I scripted a short play called *Friendly Enemies* about the American civil war, directed it in the TV Studio and felt a sense of real achievement. When I put in a stage direction *'soldier speaking from some bushes'* little did I think that Robert Cheesmond would cut down some real bushes for me.

But it was a production of Brecht's *The Threepenny Opera* that really cemented my life passion. I was on the gallery doing the flying for the set changes on that one (a none too subtle hint as to my acting prowess), watching and listening, inspired by the play, eyes most definitely opened. Sarah Greene, Colin Blumenau and Matthew Jacobs on stage below. I think the late Anthony Minghella wrote and played the music. Anthony's piano-playing in the darkness of the theatre was a feature of many Drama Department occasions. I could never work out if he was a student or a lecturer [*Both, over nine years, 1972-81. Ed.*]

It was Modern German Theatre and German Political Theatre with Tony Meech, who had translated and directed *The Threepenny Opera,* which really whetted my appetite. Reading *Mother Courage and her Children* and *The Resistible Rise of Arturo Ui* (Brecht's finest), broadened my mind and confirmed my emerging views.

I joined the Labour Party.

Once bitten, the chance to get involved in the Student Union was accidental, but proved irresistible.

In the dark days of South African oppression, the skills we had learned and honed in theatre transferred to an agitprop anti-Apartheid HUDDLE, my only starring role. It was set up and directed by Pippa Thomas and Stuart Cosgrave (undergraduate, then Ph D student in the Department, who would later become Commissioning Editor for Channel 4). Nothing too subtle, I confess, but on the steps of the Student Union, twice a day for over a week – Drama met Politics. A show with edge that made people who watched it laugh, cry and do a little bit towards changing the world.

We went to the Student Union for funding and started the Hull University Socialist Arts Group, reprising our agitprop play on demand.

For me at least that led to a wider involvement in the life on campus which sparked a journey and vocation I am still lucky to be engaged on to this day.

Helped by the support of students from the Department, who thought it would be fun to get a Drama guy elected, and with a guaranteed 50 vote start, I stood for Union Vice-President and won: a different stage that eventually would lead to the high theatre that is the House of Commons.

So thank you Hull University Drama Department – I was lucky to have the chances you gave me. I shall forever be in your debt.

All Gong and No Dinner

Mellie Buse (Franks). Joint Drama and Russian, 1978
Writer/Exec Producer, Children's TV

The year was 1977. It was our final year. We were living in De Grey Street in what was commonly known to be the coolest Drama Department house on the planet. Quite how we'd achieved this level of 'cool' is beyond me. But we had. So there we were, at the pinnacle of cool, planning our Gulbenkian swan songs in which we'd scale the heights of creative genius before launching our not insubstantial talents on the nation. And how enriched the nation would be.

The nation, however, was somewhat preoccupied. Because it was also the year of the Queen's Silver Jubilee. While the City of Hull was festooned with union flag bunting and while street party tables groaned with *quiche lorraine* and Double Diamond Party 7s, we students were not amused. A Royal shindig was the last thing we wanted. There was much Republican chit-chat in The Lord Nelson, a favourite haunt where we'd gather to change the world through the medium of beer. It was absolutely not cool to show any interest in The Royals. And we were cool, remember that.

As if things weren't grim enough, an edict was issued from on high saying that in honour of Her Majesty, all productions that took place in the Drama Department during her Jubilee Year must be BRITISH. *WHAT?* Not only that but they had to fall within the years of her reign. Were we *seriously* going to be denied any dreary Ibsen or table thumping Brecht? Were we *seriously* going to be prevented from mounting that seminal political work from Azerbaijan or that Early Australian Folk Tale told through mime and gesture with authentic aboriginal instruments? There was an instant uprising. The place became a hotbed of rage, dissent, ANARCHY!

Into this melée tripped J. Michael Walton who had the onerous task of directing the 'Departmental Production', which, in line with the edict, was a whimsical little British musical about Samuel Pepys – all frocks and wigs and finely-turned ankles. This was *And So To Bed* by Vivian Ellis, circa 1951. Mike may have briefly wondered if he would get any support at all from his students given the revolutionary atmosphere that prevailed. But he'd formulated a cunning plan. What if he asked the De Grey Street bunch to be the Production Team – music, design, choreography? What if he asked them to 'run' the show? Would they refuse? Would they hell!

J. Michael was totally wised up to the fact that we were complete suckers for a 17th century camp-up. Our Jubilee protestations were instantly silenced. It had all been hot air. We were all gong and no dinner.

So when the cool De Grey Street tarts succumbed to flattery, the rest of the Department had nowhere to go. Even Martin Franks, despite his railing at the Jubilee decree, couldn't quite bring himself to turn down the role of King Charles II and he boasts to this day that he played it with ALL HIS OWN HAIR – we did, however, have to pad his calves.

So Kate Edgar was on music, John Turnbull on costume, Tim Faulkner on set and Heather Williams and I were in charge of the hoofing – the latter being the ultimate proof that it was a political move by Mr Walton. We taught the company the uppy-downy limping dance that you see in all period drama and which appears to be a firm favourite with the RSC to this day. Oh yes. Heather and I were the Sarabande Queens.

It all went swimmingly until, to reward us for our labours, J. Michael and his dear wife Susan invited us all to Sunday dinner. We were chuffed and intimidated in equal measure by this invitation. Truth to tell we were actually terrified of Mike. He had a razor sharp intellect and beady eyes that could burn a hole in your soul [*Yeah, yeah. Get on with it. Ed.*]. So imagine our horror when half-way through the Sunday afternoon in question while we were still working out what to WEAR, our phone rang and it was J. Michael enquiring somewhat brusquely where we all were. The penny dropped with an echoing clang. Sunday dinner in Hull was LUNCH. We'd failed to turn up having planned to arrive at 7.30pm. For DINNER! Oh God! The ignominy. The social ineptitude. The shame We went crawling round to the Walton house the next day with flowers and chocolates and a gazillion apologies and I'll never forget the feeling of abject mortification when Susan opened the fridge to get the milk out to reveal mountains of cold roast potatoes, acres of Brussels sprouts, cauldrons of cauliflower and half a sheep.

We're permanently scarred. However, the legacy of Hull University Drama Department outweighs the Sunday Dinner/North/South-divide emotional baggage that we've carted around with us for over 30 years. Recently I've been lucky enough to work with Debbie O'Brien, Kate Edgar, Rosi Hutt, and Heather Williams. Colin Blumenau has employed my daughter. Philip Dart has employed my son-in-law. And I married Martin Franks who still has beautiful hair and dodgy calves.

So big thanks to HUDD. And to J. Michael Walton. And to Vivian Ellis. Oh, and to her Majesty The Queen. Obviously.

[All written, of course, by a top story-teller from La La La Land. Maybe 1977 was some sort of minor anniversary for the Queen, but here in East Yorkshire it was the Golden Jubilee (1927-77) of their only University. Somebody had the idea that the Drama Department should have a themed year staging a play from each decade. And So To Bed was a two-birds-with-one-stone job, none of my intellectual colleagues being much enthused by the '20s or the '50s. The J.B. Fagan play was first performed in 1926 (to accompany The Great Strike, doubtless). The Vivian Ellis musical was indeed from 1951. The half-sheep of the Dinner Debacle was probably themed cow (see one of the songs, 'A Chine of Beef'). De Grey Street, however, was indeed an idyllic hovel, inhabited by a bevy of Dresden shepherdesses and assorted swains (or lackeys). And you did all get good degrees whether you deserved them or not. Ed.]

These Foolish Things

Heather Williams (Straun). Joint Drama and English, 1978
Actor and director

Academically I wasn't the most successful student. In fact, when I turned up to do my first English Final (I was a joint student) they were shocked – they thought I had left the Department. Creatively, however, it was the time of my life.

Where else would I have had the opportunity to perform in Brecht, Gogol, Priestley, Coward, O'Neill, Pinter, Poliakov – let alone all the new plays and contemporary scripts? – probably not at drama school. High points have to be three projects that took place away from the University and the Gulbenkian, at least for the most part.

We toured to Germany with Tony Meech's production of *Old Times*. I was fascinated how we could turn up in a sleepy town and suddenly a huge audience would materialise, as if from nowhere, and delight in Pinter in English. It instilled in me a life-long love of touring theatre (and taught me never to over-indulge in Irish whisky when you have a 200 kilometre drive and a performance the next day).

Mike Walton's production of the T.A. Palmer version of *East Lynne* for The National Trust in the old barn at East Riddlesden Hall, complete with the original songs unearthed by Kate Edgar, was also a turning point for me and inspired me to produce site-specific plays throughout my career.

Finally, taking part in Anthony Minghella's first film, *A Little Like Drowning*, was an extraordinary experience. I took from that my love of producing new writing – and an unforgettable memory of driving around the Isle of Wight in the back of a van with Anthony and a coffin, unable to find a location. Above all, I remember at Hull being nurtured as an actor and practitioner.

I feel immensely privileged to have worked practically non-stop for 35 years in theatre as actor, director, practitioner and theatre educator. It is safe to say that all of my work has been informed one way or the other by my learning at Hull. I feel most grateful for the solid overview I gained of the history of theatre against a context of contemporary work. When I was Director of Youth Theatre at Bristol Old Vic for 12 years I based the learning framework on my degree course – even the five-year-olds moved seamlessly from Greeks to Medieval to *Sturm und Drang* – and they are now grown up, using that learning to work as artists, and passing it on to other children and young people.

Many of my fellow students have become life-long friends and/or work colleagues. I am now Artistic Director of Myrtle Theatre Company and in 2011 one of our shows toured to the new Hull Truck building. I was extremely moved to find one of my lecturers in the audience and was able to thank him in person – something I'm sure I never did in 1978.

I was, however, extremely disappointed to find Arnett's had stopped doing fadges all through the night on a Friday.

From a Gobby Shite

Christopher Jury. Joint Honours Drama and English. 1979
Actor, Writer, Director, Lecturer

For me the three years at Hull were undoubtedly life-defining.

I discovered and developed the politic perspective which is central to my personal identity, I decided upon my future career and I fell in love for the first time; and all this set against the gleaming spires of … sorry, the dingy back-streets of, Spring Bank.

In 1976 Hull, the town, not the University, was definitely a backwater; high-street fashion in Hull was a year or two behind where I came from, and that's saying something 'cos I'm from Coventry.

Indeed, for me, Hull in '76 was like 'another country' and I loved it. It was like a living museum to the novels of Sillitoe or the plays of Wesker. The terraced Victorian houses interspersed with WWII bomb-sites; the back-street pubs which had never thought to serve crisps let alone chicken-in-a-basket', the white telephone boxes and the strange food like patties and fadges: for middle-class students from the South, Hull was like an anti-Disneyland, a northern theme-park to wonder at patronisingly before high-tailing it back to Surrey. For me it was paradise.

But, of course, the Drama Department was a haven of bourgeois culture and metropolitan fashion and in my first year I hated it. I was saved because in the autumn of '76 Punk Rock broke across the UK and at last I had found my social niche. Suddenly, to be belligerently rebellious, foul-mouthed, aggressive and pissed was the ultimate in cool, and believe me I was the main man.

So I bought a donkey jacket and some Doc Martens, joined the Communist Party, started the Hull University Socialist Group, (along with Tayside rebel without a Ph D yet, Stuart Cosgrove), and occupied the Main House whenever the opportunity arose. However, my class-war aspirations were somewhat compromised when I fell in love with a girl from East Sheen of all places. I think I was her 'bit of rough' and because of her civilising influence, I was eventually tolerated by some of the more open-minded of the Drama Dept middle-class, Metro-set – although I suspect I was a bit like an exotic pet.

So, despite my best efforts at alienating myself from the Drama Dept, during my second year, I actually started to fit in. I also stopped going to lectures or tutorials – well only those I had to attend to avoid being thrown out. Despite this absence from formal classes I worked my butt off. In my three years at Hull I directed two HUDDLEs and a Main House show (a dismal failure), took a show to the Humberside Theatre, lit two shows, set-designed a show in the Main House, stage-managed numerous HUDDLEs and several Main House productions and performed in over 20 shows – all this as extra-curricular activity.

What an amazing time. And what fantastic support from the staff, the lovely Barbara in the office, Jim the grumpy but dedicated chief techy and all the teaching staff, Mike Walton, Robert Cheesmond, the two Tonys, Meech and Minghella, John Harris, Harry Thompson and of course the Capo De Capi himself, Don Roy.

As he was the Head Honcho, the representation of power, I was almost permanently at war with Don Roy, but today his generosity and tolerance for my anarchic presence have my utmost respect and gratitude. Professionally, I went on to work extensively with Tony Minghella as he started his career in UK TV and Tony Meech has remained a friend to this day.

I now teach in a University Drama Department and the model of production-based teaching and learning I encountered at Hull 30 years ago is still the model I use. I can also say without doubt that the level of out-of-hours teaching support, trust and autonomy we got from the all the staff at Hull '76-'79 would simply not be possible today. During this time the Department had a very close relationship with Hull Truck under the leadership of the company's founder, Mike Bradwell. Every year, in exchange for using the Gulbenkian Theatre to try out their Edinburgh shows, Mike would meet with graduating students looking for work. In my time in the Drama Dept, Rupert Creed had joined the Truck in stage-management and Pippa Thomas as an actress. Unfortunately in my graduating year none of us was offered a job with Hull Truck.

So I went off to Lincoln to join a TIE company, (playing Freddie Fluoride in *Desmond The Dentist*). Six months later Mike Bradwell called me out of the blue and offered me a part in the Hull Truck 1980 Edinburgh show, just like that, over the phone, a straight offer, no audition, no interview, no nothing. Amazing. And so I joined Hull Truck for the first time and, for the next ten years, my working relationship with my two Hull mentors, Mike Bradwell and Tony Minghella defined my career.

Many of the friends I made at Hull are still among my closest friends today: Liz Parker, Maurice Devlin, Barbara Mackie, Jeremy Myerson, Sarah Greene, Helen Jackson, Chris Stanton, Chris Keenan and Rupert Creed, to name but a few, are all still incredibly important to me in 2012. In the summer my own daughter graduated from Sheffield University.

And after all these years, Edward Bond's *Lear* directed by Tony Minghella, *The Family* directed by Matthew Jacobs and *Waiting For Godot* directed by Liz Parker count as the best work I have ever done.

'Something Appealing, Something Appalling'

Bren McGowan. Single Honour Drama, 1979
Policy Wonk (Local Government)

The words 'drama' and 'theatre' are used as interchangeable these days. Of course, they are not: drama is the action; theatre includes what surrounds it. That includes everything from creating prop jellies for a jelly fight (yes, I did that), to Front-of-House (and I did that as well). The Gulbenkian is special in so many ways. Its flexibility is legendary allowing for end-stage and proscenium arch on the same night. It's fairly unusual in that the actors are on the ground so that all of the audience looks down on them; literally as well as metaphorically. When we did *Toad of Toad Hall* for a vacation course production, the wild animals were under the seating blocks when the show started, coming out about 20 minutes into the play. One day, I fell asleep and woke as the other animals started scratching and howling. I sat up with a start, hit my head on the seating block above me and let out a very loud, pained 'Ow!'.

Much as the stage can be interesting, backstage and Front-of-House provides a whole new range of challenges and, if I'm honest, it's where I learned most. My first show in the Gulbenkian was *The Lion, The Witch and The Wardrobe*. This was, I think, the show where Pippa Thomas made a fortune on refreshments in Front-of-House that set a very high bar for future FoH Managers. I'm not entirely convinced that this wasn't achieved by watering down the coffee and reusing paper cups; it certainly showed very sound commercial sense.

The technical run for *The Lion, The Witch and The Wardrobe* would surely have reminded Lady Bracknell of the worst excesses of the French Revolution. It was such fun that it led to alcohol being banned entirely from the Gulbenkian. I seem to remember that John Turnbull played Mr Tumnus with a pot on his arm. I just avoided falling into the basement; somebody had lifted part of the floor and I only saw it at the last second. This may have also been the tech run when one of the lighting bars started to rise unexpectedly, everybody went to grab it, but there weren't enough people so up it went. Somebody, however, didn't let go at the same time as everybody else and nearly had a trip into the flies. We thought that was funny, but we were less amused by the alcohol ban for the building; in retrospect, I think I can see why it had to happen.

Front-of-house always seemed to be regarded as a bit of a punishment. I don't know why, as learning to work with the public is useful. I'm with Alan Ayckbourn who said 'Bad Front-of-House can sink a show quicker than six critics'. At the interval, the question was not so much 'Do they like the show?' as 'Are they talking about it?' Some directors had the sense to check out the audience: some audiences applauded before the interval, not because it was a good show, but because now they knew they could creep out to the bar for the second half.

FoH wasn't always uneventful. Facilities were, to say the least, limited. One time filling the urn in the sink in the Gents (the sink was actually for the cleaner and designed to take a mop bucket, but, hey, what people didn't know didn't hurt them), water pressure suddenly increased and there was a fountain. My trousers were soaked. Somebody was despatched to get a fresh pair from Cranbrook Avenue and, I can now admit, I sat behind the desk, selling tickets trouserless, as the audience started to arrive before the replacement trousers. The other FoH staff had to make sure that I didn't stand up; there was a near-miss when the phone (which was behind me rang). 'I'll get that', I said about to stand up; 'NO' came the chorus from the rest of the FoH staff.

Now, about the jelly fight: I feel that I owe an apology to the cast of *Toad of Toad Hall.* As Props-Master with a limited budget I could not use brand name jellies: I had red colouring and gelatine. At first, the jellies were fairly jelly-like in consistency; however, at the end of the night we collected 'usable' bits and these were recycled into the next night's jellies. As one of the throwers (I was in the show too), I soon got the hang of this and realised that the softer the jelly, the more likely to disintegrate and to be unusable. So, as the week wore on, they got tougher and tougher; seriously, they just bounced and stayed intact. I didn't have to recycle them, just collect them and wipe them down. By the end of the week you could have used them to cut diamonds. Barbara Mackie made me promise to throw the jelly *round* her rather than *at* her as it was likely to cause bruises. Other people were not so careful, so apologies for any permanent damage.

If it all sounds like youngsters playing around, that's not what it was. The Department had a work ethic that would make the average Protestant look like a slacker. Late nights, weekends, whatever was required.

It wasn't unusual for students to work on two or more shows at the same time, as well as doing their course work. Whatever we say, we did do our coursework. At weekends, the Gulbenkian was full of people working on various shows – and, yes, I do remember climbing out of the window because we had got locked in and Adrian Lukis telling me I had about a foot further to go. I launched myself out of the window to find that he had severely underestimated the distance and I landed in an undignified heap. It wasn't the first time and it won't be the last. If I take just one message from my three years in the Department it would be this: 'Take your work very seriously, but don't take yourself seriously at all'.

A Sandwich Changed my Life

Liz Parker. Single Honours Drama, 1979
English Lecturer

In 1976 I was attending interviews at pretty much the only five universities that did Single Honours Drama. I had visited Manchester, Bristol, Birmingham and Exeter, but could not make up my mind. Something was missing. My father was driving north on business and I said I would travel with him as I wanted to attend an 'all-day interview' that I had been invited to at Hull University. My father commented facetiously 'Is there a University at Hull?' but reluctantly agreed to an easterly detour.

I had been sent a long list of what I had to prepare and half-heartedly set about reading Max Frisch's, *The Fire Raisers* (as requested) and rehearsing an audition speech from Tennessee Williams' *Suddenly Last Summer* (my long term memory is still good: my short term memory non-existent; I lose my car every day in the multi-storey).

I arrived. It was raining. It was grey. My father had been right: I should not have come. I was taken to the Green Room and was greeted by three cheery students clad in their clogs and denim – Mike Scoblow, Sue Lovett and Anthony Minghella. Now this is when a sandwich changed my life. Aware that most interviewees had travelled a long way, the Drama Department laid on a friendly feast of corned beef [*probably from Jack Kaye's, left over from the war. Ed.*] sandwiches (see what I mean about good long term memory?). These sandwiches symbolized the spirit of the Drama Department (note all the language devices from the new English lecturer), fun, friendly and feisty.

On the way home I broke the news to my father that I was going to go to Hull if I was offered a place. I had the most wonderful three years there and met friends that are still best friends today. To name my four alumni 'bestest buddies'; Heather Williams, Sarah Greene, Jeremy Myerson (who lives in the next road) and Chris Jury. I see many others and we always gloat about the secret that was Hull University Drama Department, much to the irritation of long suffering partners who have had tee-shirts made up with the words 'I didn't go to Hull f….ing University'.

Postscript:

I passed on my audition speech to Sarah Greene. She used it for her audition at Manchester Library Theatre and it was entirely responsible for her subsequent success.

I never ate another corned beef sandwich.

I instilled in my children from week 1 the idea that they should go to a northern university, but on showing them around Hull they renamed it 'Hell' and my daughter opted for Durham instead. I am still hopeful my son will go to Hull.

I used the skills I learnt at Hull in a 30-year career in theatre and television. I am now a lecturer at Kingston College and hope that I can pass on some of what I learnt at Hull to my own students.

Cricket – a Dramatic Game

Gary Rees. Joint Drama and English, 1979
Primary School Headteacher

Some years ago I was attending a Headteacher Conference, at which one of the guest speakers was the erstwhile Poet Laureate, Andrew Motion. At lunchtime, as luck would have it, Andrew was brought by the organisers to sit at the same table as myself. Upon being introduced, I remarked that I already knew Andrew as one of his former students, whereupon his face fell – evidently thinking, 'Oh God, that's all I need, someone wanting to reminisce about past lectures and seminars at Hull'. To his undoubted relief and curiosity I produced a photograph, which I had brought with me on the off-chance of having a brief word with the luminary. Much to the vexation of the others on the lunch table, we then spent the next 40 minutes talking about cricket.

The photograph I had brought with me was of the Drama Department cricket team that had played against the English Department. Andrew clearly recalled having played against us, not least because it was the last time he had actually played a game of cricket. Neither of us could remember the result [*We won, of course. Ed.*], but as we pored over the faces we agreed that there can rarely have been a cricket match that featured both two future Arvon Poetry Award winners, one to become Poet Laureate, and a future Oscar winner.

I have many photographs of past productions at HUDD, but the photograph of the departmental cricket team is perhaps my favourite for many reasons. As well as having the privilege of captaining the team, I have many happy memories of net sessions on the sports field the other side of Inglemire Lane, plus actually winning some games against other departments, in particular against the Psychology Department. For some reason Psychology students thought that Drama students were too effete to play sport and were often heard voicing their prejudices before a game. The majority of our team turned up in a variety of clothing, which was not usually white, which only served to reinforce their views. So giving them a good spanking (not literally), as we invariably did, was particularly gratifying.

This photograph, though, is of the team after a match against the other old rivals, the English Department. There is one face in the photograph I can't put a name to, who may have been a ringer, but what a team. It features Tony Pearson (scorer), Mark Morley (all-rounder), Ross Brittleton (vicious fast bowler), Tony Minghella (dramatist and director-to-be, generally useless, but enthusiastic and owner of a trendy cardigan which would later feature in *Old Times*), Adrian Lukis (batsman, often seen playing British aristos on TV), Olly Reynolds (published poet and useful bat), Don Roy (Head of Department and spin bowler), Mike Walton (batsman, always correctly dressed), Gary Rees (captain, with a split in his trousers), Steve Pugh and Andy Crook (both all-rounders).

Andrew Motion, playing for the English Department, hit a four at one point, only for Alan Bower (later Dean of Arts), the batsman at the other end, to call out 'Oh dear, Andrew, you've knocked the head off a daisy. Now you'll have to stop and write a poem about it'.

I refrained from reminding him of this, but after lunch the Poet Laureate addressed the conference, reading some of his poetry and talking, as he always does, about Philip Larkin. Andrew spoke of the great love that he and Larkin had for football, but on a personal note he added that he had been reminded that day of an equal love he once had – for the game of cricket.

Après Hull le Déluge

Andy Crook. Single Honours Drama, 1980
Freelance Teacher, Director and Performer

What has Hull University Drama Department ever done for me? I knew one thing when I left Hull in 1980 and that was that I needed to study more; in fact I needed training. This is in no way an indictment of my time spent in the Drama Department nor of the teaching, far from it. I was in fact 'lit up' by my whole time there, so enthused I wanted more. The things that had driven my passion were mask and chorus work with Mike Walton, a summer production of a *Commedia* piece with John Harris, Brecht with Tony Meech, Beckett with Anthony Minghella and, above all, dance and movement with Viv Bridson. I realised that I was not cut out for naturalism.

I now needed to get away and do something else. I needed foreignness (although Hull in the late '70s had seemed quite a foreign place to me) and so I went to Paris and to L'École Internationale de Théâtre Jacques Lecoq, as it is now called. I had had a year between Hull and Lecoq working as the world's worse assistant stage manager for a small touring theatre company based in Loughborough. I had got that job because Andrew Manley, the Artistic Director of EMMA (East Midlands Mobile Arts), liked Hull graduates. My crimes against theatre during that year included turning up to a venue with lights, but no cables, turning up with the wrong set and playing the house music all the way through the first half of a show (the box was sound-proof and I was working off visual cues though I did think the actors seemed a bit uncomfortable).

That year was also a time I was supposed to be saving up for Lecoq and learning French, neither of which, of course, I did. Luckily, I managed to get a scholarship from the French government via The British Council and that paid for my fees plus a small stipend. I still had no French. Finally I got to Paris and was terrified, but thrilled. My lack of French was in some ways a boon. I would get up for an improvisation, fall flat on my face and be told by the teachers that I was a disgrace to acting and to theatre. Luckily I did not understand anything of what they had said and thinking I had not done too badly would get up again next time. The teachers thought I was incredibly brave to take such flak. Had I understood what they were saying I would have

147

fled back to England in the first couple of weeks. I know this because by my second year my French had improved and I was shocked by what I heard. I was bad, but I loved what we were doing and so I stayed, though there were times of great mortification and introspection. I was also lucky in that I was surrounded by some great and very talented students; Simon McBurney was in the year above me and I remember telling him that a theatre company called Theatre de Complicite would get nowhere.

Commedia was my saving grace at Lecoq. I can still see the surprise on people's faces as they realised that I was not absolutely terrible, in fact I was quite good. I rediscovered the joy that I had found playing around in John Harris's summer production of a *Commedia* piece the name of which now escapes me but was huge fun.

I have worked in several Lecoq companies, one a *Commedia* company named I Gelati. We did mask work and proper plays including Brecht's *Good Person of Setzuan* and I discovered a talent for movement work.

I now teach and direct, as well as perform, and my work is rooted in what I learnt at Lecoq, but in areas that I first met and played with at Hull. I didn't really get away to do something else. I built on my experiences in class and productions in the Gulbenkian. Recently I have been performing with the American director and teacher Phillip Zarrilli developing a repertoire of Beckett pieces. I think often of Anthony Minghella whose passion for Beckett was a big reason for me wanting to go to Paris. I have that passion for Beckett still and I know that it will always be there.

I was not a great student at Hull, but I learnt a lot. The more I look back now at what we did then, the more I see that it is still influencing my work and my teaching. I also made friends with people whom I still see today and who are my closest friends.

Hull University Drama Department did quite a lot really.

Happy Times!

Gillian A. Choa (Carolyn's younger sister). Single Honours Drama.
1980
Head of Academic Studies and MFA Programme Coordinator, School of
Theatre & Entertainment Arts, Hong Kong Academy for Performing Arts.

Cold, snowy, windy evenings on my bike. Smell of fresh bread down
Newland Ave.

Reading on the bench in the foyer. Switching off lights outside the theatre at
midnight.

Waiting for tutorials in the corridors. Smelly fish days.

Snow drifts and burnt toast in De Grey Street. Cheap wine and bopping.

Horrible sweet curry in the cafeteria. Long distance calls in the W.

HUDDLEs. Tulips in the spring.

Tranquility in the theatre. Cricket in the summer.

Lunchtime dance classes.

Bacon sandwiches in the middle of the night. TV Snooker in black and white.

Summer Vac Course.

Ordering last drinks in the pub. Making props all night.

Tea at Anthony's.

Eccentric friends. Sweet Barbara [*Carmichael*].

Directing, acting, miming, dancing, 'teaching'.

Happy times!

Z Theatre Company: Year One

Matthew Diamond. Single Honours Drama, 1980
I T Consultant

Sometimes the best ideas are hatched after the third pint.

In June 1980 Mark Morley and I decided to take our third year Director's Option double-bill to the Edinburgh Fringe. Flushed with acclaim by our peers, we lamented the fact that it was all over after three performances during April. In fact this idea didn't come completely out of the blue; we'd both independently found out that another hugely entrepreneurial student, David Hurst, was managing The Heriott Watt Theatre near Princes Street that year and still had the graveyard lunchtime slot to fill. So, fuelled by a mixture of ego, delusion and Sam Smith's Bitter we hatched our plan in the Union Bar the night before one of our Finals.

This was of course an act of insanity. What the hell were we doing forming a theatre company when we should have been in the library re-reading ancient Chinese plays about civil service exam candidates? If I'd asked myself this at the time, the answer may have gone something along the lines of 'If I haven't got to grips with Yuan dynasty literature now I never will', but is more likely to have been 'Sod it. This could be fun'. So it was decided: Genet's *Deathwatch* and Ionesco's *The Lesson* were going to The Fringe.

We had to think of a name for our company and fortunately this was decided by circumstance. As I remember, Mark phoned the Fringe Office asking to be included in their annual programme [*David Hurst, in person, he says. Ed.*].

'You're too late', he said. 'It's already being typeset'.

'What if we called ourselves Z Theatre Company? Could you slip us in on the last page?' A short pause. 'Put a cheque in the post and we'll do it'.

And that, my children, is how ZTC got its name.

Now, anyone who has been to the Fringe knows one thing – it's expensive. Venues cost a fortune, Edinburgh landlords greet the month of August with '£' signs in their eyes and even the pubs add a few pence onto the price of a pint. Set against this challenge, Mark and I had bank balances typical of a finalist reaching the end of their third term. Having persuaded the cast and crew of our respective shows to come with us, we had to get some money.

By a combination of extended overdrafts, a book sale, a clothes sale, a benefit concert and parental indulgence we just about managed to eke out the venue deposit, accommodation deposit and printing costs for leaflets and posters. We asked the Drama Department for some money and got a firm but friendly 'No', although they did let us use the original costumes and to rehearse in The Gulb. Yorkshire TV gave us £50 at a time when they seemed to give £50 to anyone who wrote a convincing enough begging-letter. A van rental company agreed to lend us a Ford Transit for half price in exchange for a publicity photo at Hadrian's Wall. We managed.

It was during this desperate flurry of fund-raising that a member of another Department Fringe-bound company approached me, booked to play the same venue? She cornered me in the refectory and, without saying hello, snapped:

'What do you think you're doing?'

'Taking *The Lesson* and *Deathwatch* to Edinburgh'.

'You're making fools of yourselves'.

And then she uttered the sentence (here quoted verbatim) which finally made me realise why taking ZTC to Edinburgh was the right thing to do:

'You don't stand a chance compared to us. We're the Cool Ones'.

I wish I could remember my witty rejoinder to this, but in reality I probably shuffled in my seat and mumbled something non-committal because in a sense she was right. The Acolytes Theatre Company had money behind them; they had a primetime slot at the same theatre; they were staging the British premières of three acclaimed feminist plays from the US. To add to this their membership included some of the most beautiful, popular, talented and – yes

– cool students in the Department. In my self-appointed adversary's eyes we were two mediocre finalists at the anorak end of the style spectrum who'd somehow corralled a naive bunch of first-years into our self-indulgent ego trip. We were upstarts, wannabes, *arrivistes*.

What better reason could there be to go to Edinburgh?

We rehearsed for a fortnight in Hull, then crammed into a white van stopping at the Wall as contractually obliged. The cramped travel arrangements were the perfect preparation for Edinburgh. 13 of us shared two and a half rooms off Leith Walk, the 'boys' room consisting solely of mattresses and ashtrays.

The Fringe itself hit us like a hurricane. It seemed like every performer in the World was leafleting The Royal Mile and there was only one way we could rise above them: we'd have to be *deeply* uncool. I quickly scribbled down a re-written parody of the old Ran-Dells hit *The Martian Hop* and we worked up an *a cappella* arrangement to perform on the streets. We proceeded to murder the back catalogues of Buddy Holly and Phil Spector. The real hero in this part of our story was Pat Tulip, our administrator, who ensured that the company was a well-oiled marketing machine despite hangovers, fatigue or the occasional hissy fit. That ZTC existed beyond its first year is down to Pat.

By the end of the festival we had made our money back, got a decent press and even a full house. So ZTC's first Fringe was an unqualified success. Blessed are The Uncool for they shall get rave reviews in *The Scotsman*.

So what did the experience teach us? From a theatrical perspective it taught us how to travel light, how to create theatre out of a cast, a room and very little else. Whatever else, friendships were forged during that August which survive to this day. Of the original company some became actors, some teachers, some writers, a few went into arts admin and sadly two, Dennis Baker and Warren Bowling, are no longer with us. I ended up on the comedy circuit for a decade and a half before a middle-age career change took me into IT.

How uncool is that?

Oh, What a Lovely Course

Jane Prowse. Single Honours Drama, 1980 Writer/director TV/theatre; novelist

What to say about HUDD?

Friends forged for life, time and space to try everything.

Freedom, creativity, timing rehearsals to the 10-minute drinking-up time across the way.

Boobs popping out during *And So To Bed.*

Pasting patches over Oliver Reynold's eyes for Bond's *Lear.*

Chris Keenan stabbing himself in *The Pearl.*

Having the dogs set on us while playing *Turandot* to the children in the parks.

So many triumphs and disasters.

Designing costumes for *Oh What a Lovely War* with Veronica Smart – Pierrot outfits made of cheap white nylon, decorated with hand-wound black wool baubles. Production over and I washed and tumble-dried everything for the costume store. They fried.

Came back to find a molten mass of sticky nylon – pinned to the walls by Ruth Stuckey as an example of gross stupidity and neglect. Whatever else I learnt at Hull, I can honestly say I've never misused a tumble-dryer since.

My time at Hull defined me, inspired me. I loved every minute.

Thank you all.

'What Flavour of Winegum Would Shakespeare Be?'

Jane Dale. Joint Drama and English, 1981
Freelance Project Facilitator, devising and running creative projects with
older people and people with memory difficulties

My first memory of Hull was when I came to the Drama Department for an interview in 1977. I was interviewed by – sorry, completely forgotten his name as he never taught me. He had retired by the time I started – Harry somebody? [*Thompson, of course. Ed.*]. He was wearing carpet slippers and a sort of a smoking-jacket and asked me 'What flavour of winegum would Shakespeare be?'

I remember answering his question really seriously and earnestly, concluding that Shakespeare would be the port wine flavour because of the richness of his language and the complexity of his characters. I don't think he was paying much attention to my reply. I had just been interviewed at Exeter University where I had to smell walls and demonstrate waiting for a train without moving so this seemed positively tame by comparison. I was surprised when I was offered a place.

Some of my strongest memories of Hull are connected with Anthony Minghella. I remember being in one of his Modern British Drama seminars and a fellow student, Andy Wood, was talking about seeing *Romans in Britain* by Howard Brenton at the National. The play had caused an absolute furore at the time (1980) due to the simulated male rape scene. Andy persuaded me to get on all fours so he could demonstrate to the rest of the tutorial group how 'the scene' had been choreographed. At that moment, Don Roy, Head of Department, entered the room. Andy and I froze, Don looked bemused and Anthony just said 'We're discussing Howard Brenton, Don'.

Towards the end of my second year Anthony asked me if I would be interested in developing a play with song, about a group of women. The cast spent many hours playing games, getting to know one another, improvising, going on a trip to the seaside and having a lot of laughs together. Gradually bits of the script would appear and the play started to come together. It was called *Whale Music*.

The play was shown in two parts over two nights and my character appeared in the second part. The night before opening I was seriously ill with a stomach bug, spending all night on the bathroom floor and all next day in bed. Somehow I managed to make it to the Gulbenkian and get through the play, even coping with the scene where I was force-fed doughnuts.

At the very start of the play, I remember standing on the stage area as the audience came in and they were running to get a good seat. I don't think I fully understood until that moment the anticipation and expectation surrounding a new Anthony Minghella play. It was exhilarating being a part of it and I will always be grateful to him for such a fantastic opportunity.

In the year I graduated (1981), Anthony decided to leave Hull and move to London to try and make it as a writer. When I told my mother she said 'What's he thinking of, giving up a steady teaching job like that?'. The rest, as they say, is history.

The fact that such a creative force and uniquely special person is no longer with us is still too painful to comprehend.

'You'll Never Get Away With It': or How Hull University Drama Department First Got to Perform on the Edinburgh Fringe

David Hurst. Single Honours Drama, 1979-1981; withdrew after Year Two
Marketing Director

I only ever wanted to produce and not to act. This was the answer I have always given when asked why I studied Drama at university in 1979. And I also wanted to take a show to the Edinburgh Fringe. You see, I knew just how to do it. At least I thought I knew.

Oh, my, the ambition of youth. The summer before starting at Hull had been spent working in Edinburgh, first as the grandly titled Fringe Publicity Officer, which meant loading my beaten up green Renault 5 with Fringe programmes and delivering them to all the Tourist Information offices within 50 miles of Edinburgh. 'Great,' they proclaimed, 'It's Fringe time again'. This was followed by selling tickets for the hundreds of performances on sale in the Fringe Box Office. What a baptism of fire that was. You quickly learnt what sells and what doesn't and why some shows were popular and others were not. You went to see the shows that were selling well and checked out those that weren't, where cast often outnumbered the optimistic audience.

Armed with this first-hand experience, I arrived at Hull waiting to see a production that would make it in Edinburgh. And in the spring term of 1980 it happened: the play was *River Journal*, a moving and symbolic morality play by American playwright Martha Boesing. All we needed was a catchy company name to appear on page one of the huge Fringe programme. As Aardvark and AA Productions had already been taken, together with the play's director, Carrie Hitchcock, we agreed on Acolytes.

Then I had to find a venue, certainly the hardest and most important task of any would-be Fringe producer. My old boss and Fringe administrator, Al Moffat, persuaded me to take not just a 'slot' in someone else's theatre, but a five-week lease on the fine Heriott Watt Students' Union building in the very central Grindlay Street, the most popular multi-space venue in Edinburgh before Bill Burdett-Coutts had even thought of using the Assembly Rooms for his 'Festival within a Festival'.

But empty spaces need equipping. My brainwave was to approach the then Head of Department, Don Roy, and ask to use all the theatre equipment from the Gulbenkian Centre to equip three performing spaces of very different audience capacities. 'He'll never agree', they all said but, to my total astonishment, after I presented my case in full, Don did agree, just as long as everything was fully insured. So, with lorry and van fully loaded, off to Edinburgh we went: Hull University Drama Department making its first foray into public territory, using the creative name of Acolytes in case the venture failed. We were quickly followed by late entrants Z Theatre Company [*see Matthew Diamond above*], the breakaway troupe bringing two riveting Fringe-worthy classics in Jean Genet's *Deathwatch* and Eugene Ionesco's *The Lesson*. They were late in applying, but my relationship with Al Moffat meant that he accepted them into the programme he was typing when they applied, just as long as their company name began with a letter after 'M' – hence 'Z Theatre Company'.

The five-day build was slowed when we realised the 15 amp plugs on our 100 lanterns would not fit into the ancient 13 amp sockets. The next major problem came on opening night when the council Health and Safety officer would not grant the licence as there were no kickers (don't ask) on the scaffold-built seating rostra. Panic, then compromise. We opened on time.

At the end of the 27 days, the three theatres and 27 companies performing at the Heriott Watt Theatres proved a big, if stressful success, with Alexei Sayle, Roger McGough, Angus Deayton and Radio Active, Arthur Smith and the National Revue Company, pulling in the crowds from 9.00am to well past midnight for all three weeks of the Fringe Festival. And Acolytes made it through too. Although performing in the 7.30pm evening 'star slot', houses for *River Journal* fell disappointingly below target. However, HUDD and ZTC had made it to Edinburgh, the company enjoyed the adventure and performed to family and friends, the producer broke even (!), and all the equipment was returned intact to the Department.

At a recent visit to the Fringe, I let on to a ZTC member that I was involved at the start of the 'HUDD Adventure' to Edinburgh. After effusive thanks, she admitted that THE reason she chose Hull was precisely because she knew of the tradition and opportunity of going each summer vacation with Z Theatre Company to be a real part of the Fringe Festival. Some legacy.

Somebody Else's Something

Kate James. Joint Drama and English, 1981
Journalist, Actress and Creative Director (advertising)

10 years older than everybody else, newly emerged from a couple of years of 'locked-in syndrome' and almost six-foot tall, I left my home in Singapore, determined to blend in unobtrusively.

It was quite a wrench. I was also married, with two little boys. The childrens' setup at home, however, had been organised around my paralysis, so it also worked for my absence. Servants, chauffeur, housekeeper were all in place. Of course it was painful, coming and going for three years. But I'd had time for a good, long think during my two years of silence and a good, long look at my life. I'd been a catwalk and photographic model, published a few short stories and also done time as an actress.

Actress? You needed a sense of humour. An Asian cast, one white actor, and it *was* usually just the one. The temptation to put me in a blonde wig, whatever the role, was rarely resisted. Rarely successful, either. I shall not forget the reviewer's comment, when I gave my Helena in the *Dream* (I really thought I was particularly affecting wandering in the forest, sad scene: wistful, fragile, alone and vulnerable, yet speaking with caressing resonance in a luscious, velvet voice). 'Kate James was like Dolly Parton doing Eeyore'.

Time to get sorted.

I applied to Hull, and only to Hull, and was interviewed by John Harris. He took a punt. He said he hoped I might bring some 'exotic fizz' to the Department and that he would look forward to seeing how I might emerge from my education as a person in my own right. He suggested a persona beyond wife, mother, clothes-horse. My objective was to 'Stop being somebody else's something', as he put it. An intoxicating idea.

So, in October 1978, I arrived.

It was wonderful. We had such freedom. Kids today, you have no idea how free we were. Free to shine, academically and dramatically, of course. But also free to stay in the Gulb all night long, rigging or dismantling lanterns, as one small example, on the old 'lean over and grab' method, without Health and Safety insisting you had to come down the ladder and move the platform and then climb up again between times.

We were free to experiment, which led to some dazzling drama and to some complete cringeables: actually, the all-important freedom to fail was entrenched among us, just as it should be. We worked within a generally supportive framework of gentle good-humour and hilarity. And, when something took off, even a little lunchtime show, the enthusiasm was always wild. I think we were all a little in love with each other.

It was cold. Most of us were poor. Student accommodation was largely unheated and incredibly shabby. A pack of wolves had been let loose for a fortnight without food in the house I rented in Victoria Avenue. How else to explain the state of the curtains and the half-eaten armchairs, the scratch and claw-marks on the varnish?

Goodness, it was fun.

My housemates, David Williams (Drama and English), Nigel Odell (European Studies) and Steph Chambers (English) were probably the best friends I ever had. Outstanding minders, all. Gentle, giggly Anna Douglas (Drama and English), always big-eyed with some kindly cause or another, and the amazing Nikki Minton (Law) were our frequent visitors.

The blokes in the Drama Department were all top talent, which nobody can deny.

In the end, as I always knew I would, I did the right thing and went home to Singapore. Never again the skin-tight drainpipes, never more the 1940s fur coat, cut from hundreds of little black animals. No career moves in the UK. And no contact with anyone, lest my heart should break.

Singapore now presented amazing opportunities. Lee Kuan Yew appointed a Minister for the Arts, who was tasked to create instant Cultural Vibrance. He went on a fact-finding mission, and came back saying foreign newspapers had Lifestyle sections all about Music, Drama, Film etc. on Sundays, only it would be better if they were daily so *The Straits Times* should crack on with that. Four weeks to launch.

I became part of that, covering theatre, for nearly four years. All forms of theatre, in all four of the national languages.

English and Malay I could speak, so I had to wing it with the Indian and Chinese. Handily, Indian and Malay theatre is often dance-drama (Artaudian), and the first Spoken Drama in Chinese turns out to have been a show called *No Rah* in 1938 Shanghai, aka *A Doll's House*. It provoked riots and the poets and practitioners fled south, to Singapore.

Oh, and then I had some adventures, got social, did advertising, made money. That took me all over Asia-Pacific and, yes, once to Hollywood. I specialised in financial products, airlines and cars.

Watching *Top Girls* recently, 20 years after first seeing it, I did recognise myself once again. Not the head of the agency. All the houses I bought, all the potatoes I ate. Still the Geisha. Still somebody else's something?

50 years of HUDD. 50 brilliant years and how many grateful students. Can I, without conjuring Forrest Gump, describe our courses of study as a box of chocolates? A box I imagine we all still dip into and always will. My time there certainly shaped my life and my thinking. That was the real enrichment. Thank you, HUDD. I owe you so much.

And, it's fair to say, as a proud graduate of that thing called Hull, I did eventually become Something else's Somebody. I hope John Harris would have approved.

I Know I'll Go to Heaven 'cos I've Spent My Time in Hull

Kieran Balfe. Joint Drama and English, 1982
Teacher

I went to Hull after dropping out of my journalism course at Preston Poly and subsequently failing to enjoy living in a bedsit in Stamford Hill. I was so bored by the wonderful world of work (temping for Reed Int.) that I dreamt of writing essays again. This seemed to go down well at my interview in the Gulb where, as the snow slowly melted out of the gaps in my brothel-creepers, I obviously came across as suitable despite mistaking masks on a Greek urn for decapitated heads. I did worry about the leotard requirement but it never became an issue.

I actually wanted to do 'straight' English but lacking a French O' Level I was given a list of possible 'Joints' and thus chose Drama 'cos it looked the nearest to English. Ho-ho. I knew little about Drama when I arrived and knew a bit more when I left. I soon lost interest in English to the point in Year 2 when they lost interest in me and tried to chuck me out, but I got back on appeal.

What it all was on Planet Gulb was experience. Experiencing all the usual student stuff plus sharing a Cranbrook room, avoiding Morris dancing, not avoiding *The Beggar's Opera*, doing a Mummers' play for York tourists, helping form ZTC and doing Edinburgh, going to the NSDF twice, being in a film kissing my best mate, going to Greece to perform *The Odyssey* on a beach, leaving Greece early with sunburn and heartache. I spent a large part of my second year doing a HUDDLE and repeated it as a NSDF entry in my third (didn't get in). Despite the fact that everyone knew far more than I did about Drama I had a good time and got the key role of Treasurer of the GRC (unopposed). I tried to direct a main-slot but luckily didn't. Concentrating on the social side as my contemporaries settled down to work and steady relationships, I achieved a certain notoriety for remembering pointless stuff, like the names of everyone in the Department, plus acquiring a yellow Cortina, running trips to the Humber Bridge Viewing Point and spending six months doing another HUDDLE in my final year.

Wangling a job teaching in Peru gave me five months to hang around Hull before leaving. My finest hour was my leaving-party which was so much fun I left Peru after a year and came straight back to Hull to have a home-coming bash. Shortly after I returned to London and have been in the South-East ever since.

Somehow, I became a proper teacher, possibly by doing a Drama PGCE three years after leaving Hull, rather than going straight onto one. I've now been a Drama teacher for 25 years. I go to the NSDF practically every year. I still use my lecture notes, particularly the ones on the meaning of drama, Brecht and Stan, and 'mental'.

I've had at least three ex-students go to Hull to read Drama. I run the *Hull University Drama Department Reunions 2011* Facebook page. I have a large group of Hull friends whose achievements I rarely fail to admire and envy.

I love the fact that so many of my lecturers at Hull stayed there (except for Antony Minghella and Viv Bridson). I'd like to apologise to them (and the English ones, and my parents) for not working hard enough and gaining a 'poet's Third'. If I'd paid £9000 a year perhaps I would have worked harder, but then perhaps I wouldn't have come. We used to talk about being Thatcher's Children and I remember the Department under threat in '81, but it was a lot easier being a Drama student when all you had to moan about was imminent nuclear destruction and the difficulty of getting an Equity card. I got this essay in to Mike on the last day of August (the final deadline). I'd like to think it's better than my first Drama homework which was to think of a set design for *The Merchant of Venice*.

My answer: Blue.

First and Lasting Impressions

Kath Burlinson. Single Honours Drama, 1982
Theatre maker

My first impression of HUDD had a lasting impact. I was attending my interview and in the office, sprawled on a low chair with his feet on a table, was David Phillips (now theatre critic David Benedict), chatting away to Barbara, the departmental Secretary. I loved the fact that a student could behave in this way. The atmosphere felt great. Then I really enjoyed my interview with Tony Meech, who asked me what kind of theatre I would make with an unlimited budget. I remember my answer and realise now that this is still the kind of theatre I love to make (poetic, devised, ensemble-type stuff). After my interview, I put Hull at the top of my list.

I had an incredible three years and met many friends to whom I am still close, 30+ years on. We felt in the early '80s that we were in the vanguard of a revolution in sexual politics. Discussions in Anthony Minghella's 'Political Theatre' course were hot and heated. We had amazing 'Crazy Colour' haircuts to go with our feminist polemic, specially when Alison Stewart (now Goldie), Bea O'Sullivan, Heidi Griffiths and I headed to Edinburgh Fringe 1982 with our feminist sketch show, *Heavy Periods* (yup, that was the catchy title).

I returned to Hull on a couple of occasions to perform in the Gulbenkian and at Hull Truck theatre. On my most recent visit (10 years ago or so?), Robert showed Alison and me the trendy cafés now lining Newland Ave and I remembered the thrill we felt in 1980 when the first pizza place in Hull opened near Pearson Park. This was where Cathy Wigglesworth, David Allman and I went to pretend we were Americans (we were rehearsing *Kennedy's Children*). All was going swimmingly until the dessert, when David (Olly to all his mates) ordered an ice-cream sundae 'without the noots' – his Stockport vowels giving him away and making Cathy and me hoot.

There are so many powerful memories (many too intimate or illegal to share, I am proud to say). I think my final year was my favourite: 1981-1982. We were such a 'gang' and we felt so incredibly *alive*. I was living in Suffolk St, off Beverley Rd, with Toby Follett and Nigel Hollidge, Mary Bullen and Phil

Harmer, not a Drama student but an honorary 'piece of furniture' who features in our Class of '82 photo being sat on by Toby. We would have endless parties and heady discussions about Grotowski while referring to the television as 'the fascist'. It didn't matter that we had no central heating, everything was always covered in a fine film of soot, the house was infested with cockroaches, slugs frequented the kitchen and we had to use the departmental shower or the Hull baths to keep clean (bet they've gone now – those enormous taps turned on by women with equally enormous biceps). 'Bliss was it in that dawn to be alive'.

Of course there was also deep, deep angst, *Sturm und Drang* (thanks Tony) and lots of existential despair. But there was always a HUDDLE or a fadge (gone too, I gather) if you needed cheering up.

There was also something very special about Hull's unique blend of industrial decay and Victorian grandeur. Its geographical isolation was significant, as was its relatively small size, giving us the sense that Hull was, in some way, 'ours' (which of course it was not). The Humber Bridge was built during our time – we were never quite sure what it was supposed to connect.

In the 30 years since I left the Department, I have frequently met HUDD graduates working in every aspect and at every level of the profession, from theatre admin to LX, directing to stage-management, in film, TV, dance, radio. This is testimony to the extraordinary way we were allowed to develop our interests and passions, as well as to the resources at our disposal. We were remarkably free, we were trusted to make our art and we created vast numbers of shows. Few of us worked hard academically, though I did experience a flurry of intellectual thrill during my final year courses, especially 20thC Russian and American theatre. But it was the *whole* experience that was so extraordinary. What a privileged generation we were, with 12 Single Honours students per year, no fees and grants on which to live. The continuity of the staff also meant that *generations* of us were taught by Tony and Robert and Mike and Keith. It is still extraordinary to meet HUDD graduates who are so much younger than I am, and be able to discuss the staff as well as the streets and clubs – oh, Spring Bank, the Silhouette, fringed jackets.

HUDD, I do trust that your spirit remains. May you forever thrive.

A Respectable, Scholarly Student

Alison Stewart (Goldie). Joint Drama and English, 1982
Theatre-maker

I was going to apply for straight English at university but in the nick of time a school-friend pointed out that it was possible to read Drama, surely a natural for the class show-off. Delighted, but cautious, I applied for Joint Drama and English, prioritising Hull as I wanted to feel a long way from home.

My all-girl school was antediluvian and hadn't bothered to prepare me for The World. I'd done my own tentative teenage research into sex 'n' drugs 'n' rock 'n' roll, but academia was a mystery. As was the North of England. When the train first trundled into Hull, I gawped at the brown brick two-up, two-down terraces, so different from the mimsy *cul de sacs* of Southern suburbia. I subsequently lived in a Hull-special for two years, a dear little house which only let us down when one of us fell through the wormy kitchen floor. It was easy to burgle too, but on student incomes there were slim pickings – the thieves took half a loaf of bread and Kieran's aged Doc Martens.

I'm not sure if I'd heard of Philip Larkin before I arrived, but it was hard to escape his looming, Lurch-like presence in the library. Ah, the Library. I never learnt my way around it. The difficulty of finding a book in a depository 20 times the size of my school's sent me into a massive crisis of confidence; in-depth study never became my forte. I was not alone. Mrs Meech once memorably commented that she'd seen Drama students sitting blankly at the library desks as if hoping to absorb knowledge 'by a process of osmosis', a word with much greater musicality in Liz's Manchester accent.

The practical side of my degree was definitely the jollier. The sturdy 'Gulb' gave all us drama-kids an enviable hub, where we hung out, chewed the fat, and were allowed, nay encouraged, to mount productions, from lunchtime HUDDLEs in the Green Room to full-blown three-acters in the Main House. There we posed on the steps in gaudy second-hand garb from Pauline's overstuffed shop (patron, the mother of handsome Roland Gift, of the Fine Young Cannibals – I would ogle him shamelessly on Beverley Road to no effect whatever). I suspect that all Hull students NOT doing Drama, barring a few souls who crossed over to our dark side, thought us loathsome.

At the end of my first year, I decided to have most of my (long, blonde) hair chopped off: it was half shaved and half spiked and my Mum cried. It was one of the more outlandish coiffures of the Drama Dept, along with Kath Burlinson's and Heidi Griffiths', and it cut down my casting possibilities drastically. For a while I was only allowed into Absurdist plays, grotesque sketch comedies or crude *a cappella* choirs. It expanded my comedy repertoire though – for much of my career, I've earned a buck purveying comedy in one form or another. Without that haircut, would I have become a great Shakespearian tragedian?

At Hull, my worst role ever was Helen of Troy in *Dr Faustus*. After a momentary flush of pleasure that I should be chosen to play this ravishing creature, I realised she had no words, and I must merely stand, simpering interminably. My second worst role was as a nun in *The Marat-Sade*, also non-speaking, but at least I got to hit lunatics with a stick. My third worst role was as a bride covered in blood, carried around in a coffin by four limber gents. Can't remember the play, but it was completely nuts; again, no lines. I have been writing myself a lot of words to say in plays ever since these mute times.

In spite of my inner Judi Dench remaining nascent, I had an absolutely brilliant time at HUDD. I made some great friends, particularly Kath B, with whom I've had a ball in two different performing incarnations, *The Wild Girls* and *The Weird Sisters* – we plan on doing *The Old Crones* for a late outing. I love my Hull mates like siblings, no matter how seldom we meet. Recently Mick Cahill celebrated his 50th birthday and a good selection of HUDD-types were there: balder, greyer, wrinklier, but still vital, in mind and body.

HUDD gave me tools for life and work it would have taken ages to acquire otherwise. I learnt my way around a theatre; how to treat a theatre building and the stage as my home. Our teachers were mellow, wise and forgiving. Hull was utterly welcoming (apart from the time that local bloke punched me in the face in the street for having blue hair and a leopard skin coat, but then, I did look … challenging). We lived the Life of Riley and I am a better person for it. I'm not fond of 'Best of…' Lists but if my life depended on it, I'd say that my three years at HUDD were right up there as some of the best I've had.

Exit ALISON, *weeping sentimentally.*

Comme il Faut

Nigel Hollidge. Joint Drama and French, 1982
Actor

I have often thought about the uncanny rightness of my choice of university course. I studied Drama and French and, 30 years later, am now an actor working in French.

You can't get better value for money than that, dear taxpayer.

I had wanted to go to drama school, but after several refusals, had settled on the university route. When I finally did go to a drama school for a year after leaving Hull, I was shocked by the conformism and lack of search in these actor factories, such a contrast to the feeling I had in Hull that theatre was full of numerous possibilities and that it was up to me to find my way.

Being with people interested in writing, designing, film-making, or just doing bugger all, expanded my suburban acting horizons.

30 years on, and 20 of those as an ex-pat, many of those characters are still part of my life, a fact that fills me with much joy.

Thank you Gulb.

Still a Student

Malcolm Newton. Joint Drama and English, 1982
Theatre Musical Director

It was either Hull or Exeter for me – Drama and English at both. I had spent a couple of days at a workshop interview in the pretty city of Exeter and one day at Hull … not quite so pretty.

I did like Exeter, but, although Hull seemed a million miles from my home in the Surrey gin-and-tonic belt, the warm, welcoming and down-to-earth staff and the exciting potential of the gorgeous Gulbenkian (a 'proper' theatre) won me over.

A good job really, because I didn't get the A level grades for Exeter. Well, I didn't quite get the grades for Hull either, but thankfully they let me in. Extra-curricular theatre activities at Godalming Sixth Form College had meant that I hadn't put enough time into my A Level studies. Perhaps the tutors at Hull had recognised the value of such extra-curricular activities. They certainly encouraged the continuation of such activities in addition to my course work.

When I arrived the one thing I did know was…that I didn't know much.

I was occasionally intimidated by the apparent maturity and confidence of some students. 30 years later, although I have now learned a lot more about theatrecraft and, in my particular case, about the many different uses of music in theatre, I continue to be reminded daily that I still have plenty to learn … such is life.

At the time of writing I am Musical Director on a production of *The Tempest*, working closely with theatre director Adrian Noble who used to run the Royal Shakespeare Company … and I still feel like a student.

Anyway, as an 18-year-old I must have seemed particularly young to my tutors, and yet I never felt patronised, only ever encouraged. I did my best to soak up their learning and wisdom. Some subjects sort of went 'over my head'; for others I struggled to summon up enthusiasm. But for the majority, it was the enthusiasm of the tutors which fed my enthusiasm.

And re those 'extra-curricular' activities, it was as though we could 'have a go' at anything and everything we wanted to do. Some of our projects must have seemed absurd, naïve even, but (and I don't think this is rose-tinted spectacles) I have no memory of ever having been dissuaded. Guided and nudged in helpful directions maybe, but never discouraged.

I also learned from other students and their variety of theatrical passions. Lots of lovely, clever, funny young people. One frequent collaborator, playwright and lyricist Ashley Bramwell, remains one of my best friends. And I value his opinions today as much as I did 30 years ago, perhaps even more.

As for The Gulbenkian Theatre – what a well-run gift. Many projects and productions overseen by residential staff, guest staff and students. In my case this included much time spent developing music theatre projects with Ashley – we had some successes and we made some mistakes. We learned a lot.

The time spent experimenting, performing and learning in the building set me up for life. In fact it was to be two or three years after my graduation before I 'graduated' further in my career to work professionally in similarly 'proper' theatres. There is no question that my three years in Hull University Drama Department provided vital foundations not only for my career, but also for my life. And, importantly, it was a happy place.

In no particular order, thank you Don, Mike, John, Anthony, Tony, Robert, Jim…and many other inspiring, influential and helpful faces which roll through my memory.

Bridge-Building

Eileen Ryan. Joint Drama and English, 1982
Wife and mother

I arrived at Hull in 1979. It was a strange city. A place that seemed never to have recovered from the Second World War. Walking down a street, you would be brought up short by the fact that the houses had suddenly stopped where the bombs had fallen 30 years before. Terraces looked out over empty spaces where their neighbours opposite used to be. Entire streets had never been re-built. I lived off Sculcoates Lane and would walk to a friend's house near Stepney Lane. My route lay across a wasteland of missing houses, grassed over, like an unplanned green space amidst the dense housing. I remember Sunday walks along disused railway lines, green canals, derelict industrial areas. It was a place out of time. Even the children who played in the streets outside our house looked like kids from a Bill Brandt photo.

We took one of the last ferry boats across the Humber and cycled for miles through the quiet countryside we found on the south bank, stopping to picnic in the ruins of a lonely abbey where the man in the gatehouse was singing loudly to keep himself company. I think it must have been Thornton Abbey.

As the Humber Bridge was being built, we would sometimes drive out at night to see how it was coming along. I have a terrifying memory of walking out onto the unfinished bridge with a friend and sitting on the edge with our feet dangling, high above the Humber, as if we were fishing off the end of the pier. There was no fencing to stop us. Such a Health and Safety lapse would be unthinkable today.

Later, the bridge complete, we drove over it and visited the newly-redundant railway station on the south bank where we had disembarked from the ferry with our bikes a few months previously. I still have the photos – railway tracks going nowhere, buddleia sprouting on the platforms.

I found all this urban decay fascinating and beautiful. I could afford to. I was leaving. It was just a three-year adventure.

A part of the adventure was the houses where we set up camp, houses with outside lavatories and baths in the kitchen.

Houses which had no central heating, no washing machines, often not even hot water or a television.

I imagine that very few of us came from homes where this sort of pre-war existence was the norm. Yet we accepted it as part of student life. It was part of not living at home with mum and dad.

In keeping with the pre-war tenor of our existence, few of us had cars; most of us walked or biked. For miles, backwards and forwards across the city. God, we must have been fit. And when we partied, we dressed in original 1940s frocks that we found in Pauline's extraordinary jumble sale of a shop.

The adventure came to an end and we left, many of us migrating to London to seek our fortune. I only went back once, a couple of years later. Never since.

I hear it has changed. As I write this, I'm planning to go a symposium at the Hull Truck Theatre on Anthony Minghella's *Whale Music*, the première of which I was in as a student in the Department. And I am nervous about seeing the city in its new clothes. How will they compare with a '40s lace dress from Pauline's?

Hull Days

Anna Douglas (Thompson). Joint Drama and English, 1982
Charity Project Manager

Coming from a single sex, catholic school where everyone's aim was to do Medicine or Law, I had always felt 'different'. Entering the Drama Department was like being given a new lease of life. Anything was possible and it was a virtue being 'different'– highlighted by the number of people who wore dungarees and berets and evidenced by the fact that as a Drama student I could live in Cranbrook Avenue, not Halls, because Drama students kept irregular hours.

Highlights included the summer vac course musical we did based on Posy Simmonds' *Mrs Weber's Diary* with Gary Yershon as MD; I can still remember most of the words to 'God, I hate Dick Pearce'.

Being a founder member of Z Theatre Company and taking Ionesco's *The Lesson* up to the Heriott Watt Theatre for the Edinburgh Festival. Busking around Edinburgh with attention-grabbing songs, such as the unforgettable ditty extolling the virtues of incest written to the melody of 'Puppy Love' by Donny Osmond, rejigged by the comedy genius that is Matthew Diamond.

Performing *The View From Our Attic* on a precariously high platform in Mal Newton and Ashley Bramwell's series of musical images, based on Bill Brandt's photographs, *Through the Iris*. David Allman's rendition of 'I'm not Rene Magritte' was a highlight.

I also have vivid recall of the time spent filming *Nicky* – a short film about an old lady and a dead dog, penned by the multi-talented, illustrious writer and wearer of all manner of suede and leather wear with fringing, Mr Robert Cheesmond. I played the part of the old woman, despite being no more than 20 at the time, who, until the intervention of two students was blissfully unaware that her unresponsive dog, had shuffled off this mortal coil. Despite still having a copy of the script somewhere I never did get the promised video copy of it and would love to see it. Robert!

And So to Z

Patricia Tulip (Munn). Single Honours Drama, 1982
Arts Marketing; then living abroad in Indonesia and Germany

Having been 'encouraged' at school to apply for English or History courses, I discovered by pure chance through a neighbour of ours that it was possible to study Drama at university.

This line of further education was not encouraged by my school.

Once I had applied and been accepted for interview, a raw, wintry weekend in Hull followed where I met a number of my soon-to-be fellow undergraduates and life-long friends.

It is not with nostalgia or romantic hindsight that I knew as soon as I walked into the Gulbenkian Centre it was where I wanted to be. It felt new, different, interesting and exciting, but most of all, just right. I can't explain why it did – it just did.

There followed three amazing years and so many memories – not all of which have anything to do with the Drama Department.

So many opportunities and experiences and, for me, the direction of my career established – starting with the very first year of Z Theatre Company in Edinburgh in 1980.

If only everyone had the opportunity we did.

Whale Music

Alison Watt. Joint Drama and English, 1982
Writer-director

In the second term of my first year I was approached by my then course Tutor, Anthony Minghella, and asked to get involved in a project he was planning. The project was to be an original play with an all-female cast, which he was going to write and direct. I was to be one of the performers, if I was 'interested'. Extremely flattered to be asked this by one of the Lecturers, I was also very excited by the proposed working methods. It seemed Anthony hadn't actually written the script, yet, as such, but was intending to work through improvisations and other assorted acting exercises to generate ideas. He said he had selected certain women from the Department whom he thought would create stimulating work together. I didn't spend too long thinking about it before I said yes.

During the script development process, I particularly enjoyed one activity, which meant taking photographs. The purpose of this exercise was for each of the cast to explore, through images, what we understood by the term 'being a woman'. There were some entertaining and wildly differing results. I opted for 'arty', indeed probably pretentious images of the mermaid fountains in the Avenues. Jane chose a chemist's shop on Newland Avenue. Tina chose cows. Eileen, the sea (possibly near Spurn Point). And Alison, a tree without its leaves. My character, Stella, ended up as a beach photographer in the final version of the play, so maybe this exercise had script impact, for my character, at any rate.

Some of our improvised character activities worked really well. Others maybe, a little less so. One activity involving an imagined wolf hunt had to be abandoned mid-flow because none of us were really sure of what we meant to be doing or feeling. But then Anthony, still learning his craft, was finding his way too, I'm guessing. Certainly, nothing was ever wasted.

One of my overall, favourite memories of the process (and something which helped immensely with company-bonding) was a cast and crew trip to the seaside at Bridlington. This was an action-packed, fun-day involving fish and chips, paddling, the discovery of a used condom on the beach (which, as an idea, found its way into the play as the 'silly fish' gag) and a journey later up the coast to Flamborough Head, where the cliff top footie game resulted in a lost ball in the crashing waves below. Somewhere there is a great photograph of that day out, with us gathered around the cannon on Bridlington sea front.

Finally, over the Easter holidays, the script was committed to paper (well, the first half, anyway). During that period, Anthony had decided to call the finished play *Miss*, which went down like a lead balloon with the rest of us. Generously, he provided a list of alternative names and eventually we all agreed on *Whale Music* instead. Anthony was very good at listening with patience to our suggestions and, if it made sense, he'd take it on board. I remember once in the Rehearsal Room, he and Jane seated on the cushions, working together to develop one of her speeches to add more character depth. Another memory from that time in the Rehearsal Room was of Joe Jackson songs booming up through the floor from the theatre below – scene change music for another production (Pam Gems' *Dusa, Fish, Stas and Vi*). Anthony was to use this music in the first professional production of *Whale Music*, which he directed for Leicester Haymarket.

On the actual performance nights in the Gulb, we had to split Act One and Act Two over two nights because of it being a 'late night' show. The performances themselves are a bit of a blur, but I do recall smoking an awful lot of cigarettes on stage (it felt like I lit a cigarette in nearly every scene I was in), eating avocadoes (which Anthony put in the play because he really liked them), singing songs especially written (which never saw the light of day again after our production) and riding a bicycle around the 'in the round' staging, hoping not to land in the lap of the front row. The whole project, from start to finish, was an amazing experience, achieving almost cult status at the time. Looking back I realise now how much I learnt as a performer, writer and director from that show. I'll always be grateful to Anthony for giving me those opportunities. Trying out new techniques and methods? Being open to new influences. It was the stuff of life, then. It still is.

The Source of the Sound

Paul Arditti. Joint Drama and English, 1983
Sound designer

I typed this with one finger on my iPhone last night in the back row of the Upper Circle at the Duke of York's. I should have been paying attention to the preview of *Jumpy*, but I was able to use my bullshit skills (finely-honed during Drama Department tutorials) to get through the director's notes session at the end without revealing my ignorance of what had been going on all evening.

I first entered the Gulbenkian Centre, much like any other neophyte Drama student. I was unsure of my politics, sexuality, faith and especially my vocation. My dress sense was pretty dodgy too. By the time I left it in 1983, I had added a few more big, unanswered questions to the list. Why the fuck was I losing my hair at 21, for example? After three years, I was sure of one thing though. Jim Lambert, the Drama Department's doughty lighting and sound technician, knew what he was on about.

For me, reading Joint Honours Drama and English at Hull was all about the things not on the syllabus. I was more traumatised than enthused by the English Lit seminars, but Jim Lambert, for whom I never wrote an essay, taught me more about the practicalities of the theatre than all the books in the Brynmor Jones. Thing is, I don't remember talking much to Jim. We freshers were given a few hours no-nonsense instruction in how to use the exciting-looking lighting and sound kit: not much else. However, I do remember being given unlimited access to the tape recorders, microphones and speakers of the inner sound sanctum – The Control Room – whenever I was attempting to design sound for a student show. This accounted for most of my waking hours, so was a big plus. Extra-curricular access to Jim's precious stuff was a perk not accorded to many Single Honours students, who were mostly actors and therefore not to be trusted. Either Jim spotted some artistic promise in me, or I was deemed the least likely person to trash the place. Nearly 30 hugely enjoyable years later, I'm still trading on the confidence of that trust, and a few unshakeable basic principles of sound design.

It's not just the dons that make a difference. Cheers, Jim.

The Language Barrier

Mick Cahill. Single Honours Drama, 1983
Actor

The names of the other actants in this recollection have been omitted to protect their dignity.

It was my 2nd year and I had the privilege to be cast as the lead in Brecht's *Baal*. At the audition the director, a mature exchange student from Belgium, explained that some nudity would be involved. I had no problem with that.

When I turned up in the Rehearsal Room it was still a surprise when the Director announced that this would be the first nude rehearsal. It was far more of a surprise to the two actresses in the room when he announced that he felt we would all be far more comfortable if we were all nude. Before any of us could protest he had stripped and had adopted his preferred directorial position, the crouch. He was a pale, skinny, but quite hirsute man and, it must be said, the sight proffered was not the most attractive.

It was only then that the pricklier subject could be addressed. One of the actresses (averting her eyes, I'm sure), pointed out that, far from agreeing to nudity, she had been assured that she could keep her 'slip' on during these scenes. Quickly it became apparent that a linguistic hurdle had intervened. In greater Europe 'slip' means 'panties', not the longer British garment.

After a good half-hour of negotiation it was resolved that, for the good of the piece, she should appear topless and the rehearsal commenced.

The rehearsal went well. The scenes gained shape, and after a couple of hours the actresses were, once again, fully dressed. I was sitting behind a desk, my modesty covered. The Director was crouched naked, all a'dangle.

At that moment another student entered looking for a friend. Confronted by a seemingly clothed cast and a naked director she made her excuses and left.

Nude or not, the director did a fantastic job. But the memory of that rehearsal, even after more than 30 years, still makes me laugh.

Unconditional

Nick Perry. Single Honours, Drama, 1983
Writer

I've nodded off during Eisenstein's cinematic masterpiece *Battleship Potemkin* several times over the past 30 years, but the first time was in the Gulb on a sultry autumn afternoon in 1980. I was lucky to be there. I'd failed to get into university on two previous attempts, but for some unknown reason Hull University Drama Department made me an offer anyway.

I didn't have to think twice about it, but I did. Hull had been bottom of my UCCA preference list. It was miles from anywhere. It didn't sound all that cool. But then, hang on ... wasn't that me too? Weren't me and Hull the perfect fit? Of course I accepted the absurdly generous unconditional offer with barely another thought.

It would be fair to say that my son owes his existence to that offer, since I met his mother at Hull [*see below, Maureen Glackin*]. My closest friends, with whom I exchange inane emails every day, I made there. People speak laughingly of the Hull Mafia, but Ant [*Minghella*] introduced me to my agent of 25 years, Alan Plater got me my first theatre commission, Simon Moore encouraged me to go to film school and Brian Thompson gave me a leg up into radio. My whole life was seeded in those few short, golden years. Nothing since has quite matched them.

I remember *Baal*, the production directed by Philip Demeester, with Mick Cahill magnificent – and intermittently bollock-naked – in the title role. What really stuck in my mind (settle down) was the programme. Everyone involved was listed in alphabetical order – cast, crew, director, writer, front-of-house – instead of according to the conventional pecking order. It probably wasn't the first time anyone had done it, but it was the first time I'd seen it done and it seemed perfectly to capture the Hull spirit. We lived and worked and passed our leisure time together. We were all part of a single lecture-fed, play-mounting, idiot-dancing organism and in between times we lounged in the foyer of the Gulb like jewels in a display case, stirring campus-wide resentment – or so we were told (we would have been far too self-involved to have noticed, or cared, quite frankly).

I thought that this was how it was always going to be, a life full of co-operative artistic ventures ... but it isn't. It's a life full of people who didn't go to Hull. Some us wanted it to go on forever, I recall: we could have left in the summer of 1983 right after graduation, but hung around until Christmas, at which point we began to feel like a bunch of Alan Rickmans at Juliet Stevenson and Michael Maloney's engagement party, and finally shuffled off.

Last year I went back to visit the grave in the Ella Street cemetery of Moshe Tsvi, the very first of my ancestors to set foot on British soil. He arrived in Hull exactly 100 years before I did – except he came by land and by sea, making the long and arduous journey from Russia with his 12-year-old son Isaac whom he hoped to save from conscription in the Tsar's army, the fate of most Jewish boys at the time – while I got a lift up the M1 from my Dad. Neither of us then had much idea about Moshe and Isaac, or that so many of our dead lay buried nearby, but looking back it seems to me that the actions of my father and his great-grandfather resonate, as they brought their sons to Hull in the hope of meeting some nice people who might help them get on in life. Isaac wound up a tailor in Wardour Street, a few doors from where my first movie was edited. We've a lot to thank Hull for.

Memories

Brian Thompson. Joint Drama and English, 1983
Writer

During a tutorial in my first term at Hull, we were posed a tricky, but fairly general question. Not wanting to risk saying the wrong thing we all kept quiet and waited to be told 'the answer'. But instead, our Tutor just looked mildly miffed and then moved on to the next thing. This puzzled me at the time, but after a bit of reflection I got the message: if we weren't prepared to think for ourselves, Hull wasn't going to do it for us. (The Tutor's name was Anthony Minghella).

One of the things I learnt at Hull was to do it yourself. I'd come straight from a northern grammar school where you just did what you were told. At Hull, direct a show? start a magazine? write a play? The doors were open and you could just get on with it. Whether you ended up working in the drama world or not, I suspect it was an equally valuable lesson to learn.

Pete [*Leafe*], a fellow Drama student, was sharing the flat on Pearson Park where Philip Larkin used to live. His room overlooking the park was the one where Larkin had written some of his most famous and miserable poems. Having undergone a 'Drama Department' makeover the walls were now covered in brightly-coloured balloons and the room housed a massive collection of teddy bears. Somehow that sums up the Hull experience.

Back in the bad old days, Oxbridge types used to make snide comments when you said you'd been to Hull University. I quickly learnt to name-drop that my Drama tutor was Anthony Minghella, my English lecturer was Andrew Motion and the bloke running the library was Philip Larkin. It worked.

Okay, I probably also ought to mention that I met my wife in Hull University Drama Department. Well, obviously, she wasn't my wife at the time; she was a beautiful young woman called Anna Douglas. I know this is very uncool, but we are still married, she's still beautiful and our children are now looking at which University to go to...

Admissions – Not As You Know Them

Peter Aughton. Joint Drama and English, 1984
Retired Theatre Manager

My admission interviews were not at all what I expected. I was anticipating in-depth questioning, not least to establish why I wanted to go to university at the age of 40. That was not what happened. Just before Easter 1981 I was invited for interviews at Hull. My first was with John Harris, the Admissions Tutor for the Department of Drama, at 11.30, after which I would go to meet Rowley Wymer, Admissions Tutor for the Department of English. I was living in York so I gave myself plenty of time. I got to the university about 10.30. That gave me time to have a look around the campus and find the Gulbenkian Centre. Reporting to the office I was taken along to John's room that clearly indicated many of his manifold interests – lots of masks, I seem to recall. He talked a bit about the course, asked me if I was doing any theatre at present, which I was (I had just played Fred Castle in *The Bed Before Yesterday* by Ben Travers). I asked some questions about the Department then John said I would probably be offered a place, assuming the English Department were agreeable.

I think John then rang Rowley and he could see me straightaway. John told me to come back after I had seen Rowley. I think he must have given me a room number because I don't remember going to the office in the Department of English. Anyway, I got there, knocked on the door and heard a voice say: 'Come in'. In I went. There was no sign of Rowley and for a moment I thought I had misheard until this figure uncurled itself from the corner of the room behind a stack of books. This meeting too, was fairly brief, again with a brief description of what I could expect and the only question I remember Rowley asking me was what I was reading. When I told him I was reading *Titus Alone*, the third part of Mervyn Peake's *Gormenghast* trilogy, he said 'Oh good. Send me about a thousand words with your thoughts'. I got the distinct impression that this was just a formality, but I spent four days over Easter penning my thoughts. Rowley never did respond, so it couldn't have been a disaster.

There then followed a slightly surreal experience. I went back to the Gulbenkian and John said 'Do you fancy a beer?', or words to that effect.

Though I was driving, one beer was acceptable, so off we went to Staff House. Here, I got a shock. I was anticipating starting in October 1982, if I was offered a place, but John intimated that I might be offered a place that year, 1981. My interview was just before the Easter vacation and I got the formal offer of a place, and, yes, it was for that October. The letter came soon after Easter. My wife and I had to go into planning overdrive. Those were the days when a student got a full grant from the local authority and support for children. Application forms were a matter of urgency.

Thinking back over the events that day and the subsequent offer, I have often thought the Drama Department liked to have a bit of maturity in each year. There were three mature students in my year. Whether we were of value is not for me to say.

There is an interesting codicil to events. I was working for a construction industry supply company at the time. I kept quiet about my plans, proposing to hand in my notice after return from holiday in August. On my first day back, because there had been some re-structuring, I was offered an alternative post to the one I had, or redundancy. The reader will not be surprised – I took the latter. The settlement was a very welcome buffer and enabled me to buy a car to replace the company one. Travelling to and from Hull became a pleasure not a trial.

Gulb

Maureen Glackin (Perry). Joint Drama and English, 1984
Head of the School of Education, St Mary's UC

Hull was the last place to interview me, but from the moment I arrived at the Gulb I knew that this was where I wanted to spend the next three years of my life. Being accepted by the Drama Department meant that I was allowed to join an elite crew permitted to use the Gulb as a playground. And boy, did I have fun. After a slow first year, I flourished and 'grew into myself', developing a confidence and self-belief through the friendships that I made.

The Gulb became the centre of my universe, socially and academically. I recall spending large amounts of time sitting in the windows of the foyer watching the world go by, revelling in my fey status as a 'Drama student'. I also remember spending hours upon end in the Gulb rehearsing, developing a physical and emotional understanding of the dramatic genres I was at the same time exploring academically. And then there were the parties, the sandwiches (the '19 Ryde Street' consisted of peanut butter, jam, strawberries and cream) and Z Theatre Company. They were wonderful years in the course of which I was inspired by the enormously talented people that I had the pleasure of being an undergraduate with, and by what I would now, as a professional educationalist describe in professional educationalist terms as the relational, pedagogical practice of the staff who facilitated an environment in which mind, body and spirit were allowed to flourish. And I really mean that.

I am aware that these musings may seem pure nostalgia, and indeed to some extent they are … but then, why not? Surely that's the joy of reflecting on life when you were on the cusp of it and everything seemed possible. So now, after more years than I care to take note of, what do I know? I know that the discipline, the professional attitude and the performance skills I learned at Hull have stood me in good stead in a career that has taken many unexpected turns. For me, Hull was a life-forming adventure: I had my heart broken, more than once, to the soundtrack of OMD and Sondheim and had it mended and made whole to The Jam, to which Nick and I are still listening.

How Hull Made Me a Theatre Critic

Chris Jones. Joint Drama and English, 1984
Chief drama critic for the Chicago Tribune

I have three short stories. The first week I arrived at the Department, this short boy from Rochdale was a tad intimidated by all the posh accents, handsome looks and the natty attire. I remember my dad coming to visit and my explaining my sense of being a scruff. I persuaded him to take me to Beverley to buy a cravat. It looked ridiculous on me. God knows why I thought I needed it. But it was one of my happiest memories of time with my dad.

Some time in my second year, I think, I was appearing in a production of *The Comedians* by Trevor Griffiths. I was the cheap pub piano player. My main prop was a pint. I was hanging out upstairs at the Gulbenkian, pint in hand, when Robert Cheesmond took one look at me and my pint, wrongly deduced that I'd come from the union with booze in hand to watch the show, and angrily kicked me out. Missed my cue and all.

And then there was my appearance as Stingo, the landlord in *She Stoops to Conquer*. This fine performance was reviewed in that little Department magazine: 'Chris Jones' performance sent me off to lots of Hull pubs to see if this Smike-like publican was anywhere to be found in them', said the writer, 'Alas, I didn't find any'.

Bastard!

I've written hundreds, if not thousands, of reviews in my 20-year career as a critic, but the fact that I can write that down, precisely, without looking up anything is a useful reminder that we rarely forget bad reviews, even years and years later. This is why so many Chicago and New York actors can't look me in the eye.

And lastly: I did do something I remain proud of at Hull – a TV production of *Another Country*. I still have the tape.

Making a Crisis Out of a Drama

Oliver Jones. Joint Drama and English, 1984
Ex-actor, Arts Journalist

It's funny to think that they used to riot at theatre first nights. I'm talking Jarry, Synge et al (in case you failed to arise for those lectures). Speaking as someone who crossed over to the Dark Side after Hull – reviewing plays for *What's On* in London through the Noughties before marrying a newspaper theatre critic – I've sat through a lot of bad plays, but I have only once seen a press-night fracas. And that was a ruckus after a really good show, involving a critic who had forgotten to take his medication (I'm on a reduced dose now).

But tempers frequently boiled over during my '81-84' stint at Hull's Drama Department – and usually it had nothing to do with the emotional fallout of those recklessly experimental, pre-Aids days. It was, after all, inexcusably bourgeois to care in matters of the heart – unless the proletariat was involved. But we did care about our Art. I remember my own fury after a HUDDLE performance of a new 'work' entitled *Open Door*. Coming into the space, we were presented with a number of chairs arranged around a half-open door. We sat down and eagerly awaited the show. After some 10 minutes of non-action, it became clear that nothing was ever going to happen, although the 'director', lurking in the back row in a mask did start chortling to himself.

OK, there wasn't a riot as such. But I and the current Chief Press Officer of a major northern producing house, were both quite vocal about our feelings. Happily, the show's creator went on to acquit himself admirably, casting me in a number of ambitious main-house productions before abandoning it all for a successful career in pop music. He's still a friend and I remain indebted to him – though I've now got it down to under a grand.

Far more incendiary was the hullabaloo surrounding our end-of-first-year vacation project, for which we were given 'Rape' as our theme. As I write in 2012, Republican senate nominees and Assange supporters are demonstrating just how much the general male mind-set has 'progressed' on this score. I have little doubt that the combined forces of the first-year Joint and Single Honours streams could have come up with a thoroughly trite and unenlightening dance-drama on the subject, but three individuals insisted that the topic should not even be broached, let alone theatricalised. We argued all day, for what seemed like weeks. The majority eventually bowed to the intransigent Gang of Three and we cobbled together an anodyne piece about the 'Iniquities of Advertising' at the last minute. I dimly recall that at least two of the Gang left the Department soon after, immersing themselves in activism. They clearly picked up a few showbiz skills before they left – watching television one night, I witnessed the two girls hogging the News at Ten cameras at Greenham Common, dancing together in pink dungarees (I may be confusing their '80s dress sense for that of the aforementioned Press Officer). Still, we now know that the Greenham Common women put the Americans off the idea of using the UK as their launch-pad. So, again, I'm grateful to former sparring partners.

I am also glad to report that the bad behaviour continued well after my time in Hull. I returned in the mid-'90s for the festivities surrounding Don Roy's retirement. On learning that we were to be entertained by current Drama students, a really rather well-oiled mob of Drama graduates piled into the auditorium, ready to snark at some bright young things' attempts at a Brecht *Lehrstücke* or Beckett short. And what did we get? *Grease* – the abridged version.

We were, without doubt, the rudest audience of which it has ever been my privilege to be a part. I apologise in retrospect for any hurt feelings – the performers looked pretty aghast at the time. I suppose it was good practice for any of them planning a career in inner-city TIE. As it happened, the worst heckler among us is currently a Senior Lecturer in Education in the Arts at a major Welsh university. Needless to say, 'Grease' – an end-of-first-year summer project to rival our own for rabble-rousing, was not the students' but the tutor's choice.

A World Service

Wanda Petrusewicz. Joint Drama and French 1984
Assistant Editor, BBC World Service News

I'd had my heart set on studying Drama in the bright lights of London – but as soon as I walked into the Gulb, I knew where I wanted to be.

My time in the Drama Department is full of wonderful memories, from the inspiring lectures (where I took no notes as I just wanted to listen) by Anthony Minghella, before he moved on to the dizzy heights of directing films, via HUDDLEs (do they still exist?), to full-scale productions.

There are many which stick in my mind – I can't listen to anything by the band 'Chicago' without remembering David Mamet's *Sexual Perversity in Chicago* one of the first productions I was involved in, helping Paul Arditti with the sound.

Another memory is my role as Gratiana in the black, white and red splendour of *The Revenger's Tragedy* in my second year. I'm still periodically reminded of the scene where a few couples cavorted at the back of the stage to demonstrate a debauched society.

Our Vac course production of *Peer Gynt*, with three students playing the main character as he ages. My chief memory of that is cycling around Hull's antique shops trying to pick up various nautical artefacts as well as going to Marine House to beg for a real boatswain's whistle.

Those intense few weeks made it hard to leave the Department behind and spend my required year abroad in eastern France – that year I saw a lot of Jane Mercer (Drama and German) who happened to end up in Freiburg just over the border in Germany. In those pre email and Facebook days we survived through the odd letter postmarked North Humberside to tell us what was going on. We did at least manage to get to the end-of-year party in June 1983 as the rest of our year graduated.

My final year highlight was stage-managing Pinter's *Homecoming*, directed by Keith Peacock. A personal triumph was finding three china flying ducks to adorn the set in the days before they became a kitsch collectors' item.

I then had a sunny summer at the Fringe as Stage Manager with the Z Theatre Company, performing at the Celtic Lodge, living 10 to a room and spending several evenings with the Hull Truck company soon after John Godber had taken over.

On graduating, I applied to the BBC as a Studio Manager and, although I didn't get in the first time, I tried again and was successful. My creative theatre experience proved invaluable, especially when working on radio drama, walking in trays of gravel and opening and shutting doors.

I've been with the BBC ever since – graduating from Studio-Managing to production and am now an Editor. I suppose I'd imagined working for some nice Arts programmes, but have ended up in the harsh reality of BBC News. But with plenty of Hull graduates around in London, there's always an opportunity to reminisce. I'm grateful for the organisational skills of Kieran Balfe who somehow manages to get us all together regularly.

The A to Z of HUDD (and its aftermath)

Richard Shaw. Single Hours Drama, 1984
Executive Producer, Television

A is for Anouilh, the writer of a very slight and irredeemably camp one-act play called *The Orchestra,* a 1983 production in which J. Michael Walton made a memorable appearance. His dedication to the role even drove him to shave off his beard.

B is for Miranda Ballin, an irrepressible committed Welsh firebrand, a dedicated SWSO member and someone I always wished I'd kept in touch with.

C is for Robert Cheesmond, the unfathomable, uncontrollable, heroic force of nature who was a lecturer when I was there and is still there today, looking even more like a wild man that he did in the '80s.

D is for Don Roy, that gnomic, unfathomable, totally impenetrable Head of Department who talked about peeling away the layers of the onion and cranes bowing at Churchill's funeral, and who lived in a parallel universe to the rest of us. But he did get a theatre named after him.

E is for Everything But The Girl, the shop, not the band. The shop was actually called Turners Furniture and EBTG was its slogan. Ben [*Joint Drama and English*] and Tracey were way too cool to be my friends, although *Idlewild* is still on my playlist. I bought a bed there.

F is for Fame, a consummation that eluded every single one of our year group, a dismally low-achieving bunch of flakes.

G is for *Götz von Berlichingen*, the ill-advised *Sturm und Drang* epic staged by Tony Meech and Robert Cheesmond. In a vain attempt to butch us up they made us make our own swords and dress us up in leather jerkins and shout '*aghhhhhh*' a lot: we were hopeless. The play contains the most irritating line in all of theatre '*Swim on brave swimmer while I lie dying here*'. Just try saying it convincingly: it's impossible.

H is for Hull University Student Radio, an expensive folly that kept me happily occupied for many hours presenting nonsense to nobody.

I is for Iran, where the extraordinary film *Be Like Others,* the story of the Iranian transsexual community was filmed, I was lucky enough to be the co-producer on it. The film went on to compete at Sundance and in Berlin. Iran's revolutionary politics also figure in our most recent feature-length documentary *How To Start A Revolution*, a film about the politics of non-violent revolutionary change.

J is for Jonathon Cowap, who I always wish I'd got to know better, he seemed so balanced and centred, as opposed to so many others in the Department. I occasionally stalk him online in a slightly creepy way listening to his podcasts from BBC Radio York.

K is for the Krankies, whom I booked to appear in panto when I went back to work at Hull's New Theatre after graduating. Who knew that a degree course in Drama would lead to such sophisticated taste in casting?

L is for Lion Television, where I've worked for the last decade. The job has taken me to the far ends of the earth in search of obscure commodities, sent me out in the footsteps of Charles Dickens and Mark Twain, following their globetrotting adventures, and given me the chance to explore the world with chefs, explorers and scientists, bringing more thrills and excitement than anyone could reasonably expect from a job.

M is for Mask-Making, my number one all-time favourite course with that amazing Renaissance man John Harris who also taught us Tai Chi. John also opened our eyes to *Commedia dell'arte* and Japanese *Noh* Theatre and *Kathakali* and talked about faraway places in South East-Asia where he caught malaria and studied shadow puppets.

N is for the New Theatre, in Hull, a venue that I returned to professionally two years after graduating, to refurbish and run with William MacDonald, the inspired theatrical entrepreneur who would go on to be my mentor for over a decade.

O is for *The Oresteia*, the awesome production that came out of the National Theatre when I worked there briefly in the '80's. It was a strange and testing time professionally, after which I headed back to the challenges of classical ballet and opera which I always thought had bigger sets and better tunes.

P is for the irrepressible, awesome, adorable and impossible Philip Pellew, who much preferred a good game of tennis to attending lectures.

Q is for Quepos, on the Pacific coast of Costa Rica, one of the first filming locations for the Rough Guide travel series that we resurrected for British TV a few years ago.

R is for the Royal Opera House, where I spent a very odd few years helping out with the refurbishment and re-opening, struggling with the impossible contradictions of running an international opera house in the shadow of a New Labour administration. Enormous egos, vested interests, billionaire donors, political interference, ugly newspaper headlines, spiralling costs and delays, resignations and walkouts; plus, somehow in the middle of it all, some great art from the Royal Opera and Royal Ballet making for a heady few years of high drama.

S is for the Silhouette Club, on Spring Bank in Hull, a seedy smoke-filled den of iniquity full of drugs, goths and gays, very popular with HUDD students, long since closed.

T is for Patricia Tulip, who bequeathed me (somewhat reluctantly I felt at the time) the awesome responsibility for running Z Theatre Company for it's 1983 and 1984 Edinburgh Fringe Festival seasons. We triumphed.

U is for *Ubu Roi*, a magical, terrifying, grotesque, circus of a show we staged in the round with enormous puppets, psychedelic lighting and a terrifying score. Perhaps the only time that the entire year-group came together in our only near pitch-perfect presentation.

V is for Villa Vajra, a breathtaking private estate in central Bali where, inspired by the course on South East Asian puppetry at HUDD, I once hired an entire *Wayang Kulit* puppet troupe and full Gamelan orchestra to perform a truncated version of the *Ramayana* for the assembled guests and staff.

W is for Walton, J. Michael, unpredictable, inspiring and occasionally infuriating. You hear people talking about 'that important teacher...'; well, he's mine.

X is for Xiangkhouang, in North-East Laos. After losing contact with Guy Levesley for over two decades we met up again in our early 40s and started travelling the world together to random far-flung places including Burma, Vietnam and Indonesia. Xiangkhouang in North-East Laos was one of the least successful journeys we did as I made him camp out in the Laotian jungle for a night. He (almost) never forgave me.

Y is for Yemen, a spectacularly desolate, dramatic and challenging country where I went searching for the source of frankincense and myrrh for a BBC series about the origin of spices with Kate Humble.

And **Z is for Z Theatre Company**, the HUDD-based student theatre ensemble that flourished in the early '80's and finally set me off on my producing career.

Inspired by the Greatest

Neil Ruckman. Drama and English 1985
Teacher, examiner, storyteller, writer

I remember the day of my last Finals exam. Sitting in the huge sports hall with only a few other students scattered around, I was faced with the last question on my Drama paper. It read something like this: 'The greatest dramatists have learnt from their failures. Discuss in relation to a drama practitioner of your choice'. I chose to write about Erwin Piscator and his controversial adaptation of Schiller's *The Robbers*. From awkward beginnings, Piscator developed his vision of epic and political theatre, elements of which could still be seen in the Olympic and Paralympic opening ceremonies.

In my grandest dreams I saw myself as a mini-Piscator. Had I not built a wall between the audience and the actors during an experimental HUDDLE performance? Had I not managed to spurt fake blood all over myself and fellow actors during a 'political' piece of theatre, turning intended tragedy into absolute farce?

Hull University Drama Department was a safe place in which to try out one's maddest dreams. I loved the peace of Wednesday mornings, mask-making to classical music in John Harris's room. I loved the intense discussions of Thursday morning seminars in Robert Cheesmond's tiny office. And I loved to immerse myself in late-night rehearsals after a session in the Union bar.

I benefited from being part of a very able group of students supported by talented tutors and lecturers. There were some great productions. There was *The Mystery Cycle*, with the whole Department. I can still feel the trepidation with which I carried the speakers for God's voice to the grid at the top of the theatre. There was *The Misanthrope* with its great set and stylised performances and *Piaf* stuffed full with passionate performances and fantastic singing.

We were taken on some great adventures beyond the bounds of the University campus. I remember during our two-week study of Grotowski's techniques we were all required to befriend a stick. I took my new 'friend' out on to the streets of Hull and drew some unwelcome attention from local youths. Fortunately I could run quite fast. We also staged *Hamlet* at the newly refurbished Spring Street Theatre, an experience which rekindled my love of Shakespeare's plays.

One of the most extraordinary and wonderful experiences was the two-week summer vac course at the end of our second year in which we put on a gothic melodrama by 'Monk' Lewis at the old Grammar-school hall in the centre of Hull. We had such fun with this, learning to play the melodrama completely straight and so extract maximum laughs. The 'hands on' experience of putting on a production from scratch has informed much of my work since leaving Hull.

Hull University was truly life-changing for me. My time in the Drama Department gave me the confidence and belief to take risks and to continue to learn. I can still pursue my maddest dreams – some of which have yielded their own successes.

Bookends

Rick Russell. Single Honours Drama, 1985
Film Editor

The idea of contributing to this 50th Anniversary record of HUDD immediately sparked two very different thoughts. One from my very first experience at the department nearly 30 years ago and one from the immediacy of today.

In 1982 I was eagerly applying for Drama courses at all the leading Universities, excitedly thumbing through glossy brochures before filling in my UCCA form. It turned out that the daughter of some family friends was in her final year at HUDD, her name was Rebecca Harbord. She had won a best actress award at the NSDF for performance in a one-woman play about the actress Sarah Siddons, a monologue which develops as her portrait is painted by Gainsborough.

Becky invited me to come for a weekend during term-time to see what undergraduate life was like. I departed from King's Cross to the wilds of Humberside with a mixture of excitement and trepidation. No sooner had I arrived at her flat in Pearson Park than she whisked me off to the 'the Gulb'. It was already late in the evening. The campus was imposing in the dark, but light still shone out of the tall glass windows of the foyer. She took me straight into the theatre. The working lights were on and we were welcomed by students in overalls and with punk haircuts. Becky had come to work.

I was handed a roller and a bucket of black matt emulsion and instructed to paint everything in sight black. It was a strike and we were returning the theatre back to the neutral space after a production. I loved every minute of it. We stayed late into the night and then returned to the student digs where we talked until the wee hours and drank cheap red wine. Quite a thrill for 17-year-old.

I was completely smitten with the theatre, the atmosphere, the people. It felt like I had found my home. Nothing else would do. This is where I had to study.

My three years at Hull, from 1982-85, were so full of experiences and happy memories that I couldn't do any of them justice in this brief essay. Suffice it to say that I carry the sense of belonging to this *Alma Mater* with me even now.

This brings me to my second thought. Anthony Minghella had already left the Department to pursue his writing career professionally by the time I was a student, but he had left an indelible mark even then. He became even more of an inspiration to me as I eventually found my vocation in life, to be a film editor.

After a long career working principally on TV commercials and music videos and founding a company which has expanded from London to include New York and Los Angeles, I had been keen to return to my first love – drama.

I am currently editing a major feature film about the life of Nelson Mandela based on his autobiography, *Long Walk To Freedom*. The coincidence is that Anthony was working on the project with the producers for several years and was due to direct the film, to be denied by his tragic and untimely death.

Anthony was the best of ambassadors for the Department and would never miss an opportunity of expressing his eternal gratitude to the incredible start to his creative career at Hull.

I can honestly say that not a day goes by in my professional life when I don't draw on the bank of knowledge and experience of acting, directing, writing, design, music and film which I attained at HUDD.

Finally, the Department was threatened with imminent closure in 1981 as Thatcher was hell-bent on cutting arts courses at Universities, and here we are celebrating 50 years of HUDD. Pretty damn impressive. Roll on 50 more years.

Amazing People.

Ruth Curtis. Single Honours Drama, 1986
Actor and worker for MS organisations

One of the reasons I chose Hull University Drama Department was because I knew a couple of people who had been there (and were working actors). I was lucky the Department also chose me. I did things at Hull I probably wouldn't have been able to do elsewhere. It was not officially 'training' as you might get at a drama school but it was an amazing practical experience. I learnt loads. Where else could I have been involved in so many productions in so many ways – acting, directing, lighting, sound, flying, stage-management? The Gulb was a great theatre space and we believed that we ran it ourselves. The lessons I learnt there have stood me in good stead in my subsequent life and career as an actor and director.

The other day, I was on a job with a fellow actor who, coincidentally, had been at HUDD a few years before me. We realised we know lots of people in common. Many of them are Hull graduates. Memories flowed about productions and people. I recalled going to Denmark in a play by the famous Danish playwright, Ludvig Holberg. No, as first year drama students we'd never heard of him before either, but in 1984 Denmark hosted a festival to commemorate the 300th anniversary of Holberg's birth. A group of us from Hull travelled with students from the Royal Scottish Academy of Music and Drama (including now well-known actors John Hannah and James Macpherson). I think our production was called *Hans Molehill*. I don't remember many details from that amazing week except we arrived in Copenhagen on my 21st. I know when John Hannah suffered appendicitis because he spent that day being as sick as a dog and it wasn't from drinks to celebrate my birthday. A few weeks later, back in Hull, I was sick. A lot. We all said 'well at least it can't be appendicitis. That would be too much of a coincidence'.

I had my appendix out at Hull Royal Infirmary in an emergency operation before it ruptured. When I subsequently suffered a stitch abscess I was put in the University Health Centre for daily dressings. One time, Philip Larkin wandered into the clinic whilst I lay there with my stomach exposed. He was completely unfazed and just wanted to retrieve his forgotten coat or umbrella.

Somehow, Hull just seemed to be one of those places where that sort of thing could happen.

I started working with (the now disbanded) Remould Theatre Company whilst still a student because my (then) boyfriend and ex-HUDDite, Andy Crook, got a job with them. After graduation, Remould created a job for me which allowed me to stay living and working in Hull for a few more years. I lived in a flat in a house on Marlborough Avenue, not far from Pearson Park. It had previously been occupied by Drama student Phil Pellew. In fact most of the flats in the house were occupied by present or former HUDDites. Deborah Clarke was in the flat above. She is still my friend now, as are many of the people I knew in those fabulous Hull days.

I am grateful to HUDD for leading to me going to Denmark, to NSDF, to Edinburgh. Whilst with Z Theatre Company, our street routines to get audiences for shows at the Edinburgh Fringe, led to a feature article in the *Los Angeles Times* (with photo, those distinctive black and white ZTC tee-shirts had a lot of impact). It was just one of those HUDD things.

I'm never really surprised to hear someone in the business is a former HUDDite. We get everywhere and we carry our experience with us. For some of us, it informs who we are and what we do. Nowadays, I occasionally work with Kepow Theatre Company, doing impro shows and workshops. Kepow was founded by Kevin Tomlinson and Paul Jenkins. They both studied Drama at Hull.

One of the Coldest Places on Earth

Alison Boam (Duffy). Joint Honours Drama and English, 1987
Director at Per Diem innovation consultancy. Studying part-time for a
Masters in Innovation, Creativity and Leadership at City University

I look back fondly on my time at Hull. I often wonder where everyone is, as I
have incriminating photographs to share.

Oh, how we laughed. Robert Noble and Daniel Wain trying to out-ham each
other. Jeremy Ward in that Action Man costume in *Troilus and Cressida*. The
lycra outfits we wore for Viv's dance spectacular (my husband still doesn't
believe it was me). The beautiful *Trip to Scarborough* costumes, complete with
white fluffy wigs that made us look like sheep. The wonderful *Women Pirates*
for which I was required to have a thick Irish accent. I can still remember my
lines.

And the lecturers. John with his beard full of cigar ash; Robert squeezed into
his leather trousers.

I think of Hull as one of the coldest places on earth. I remember sitting on my
bike one snowy night at the traffic lights on Cottingham Road. Mike Walton
drew up beside me on his, unrecognisable, covered in several inches of snow.

The Union café was always nice and warm. Remember the red plastic teapots
and those enormous Chelsea buns?

It had some interesting rental properties too. I remember moving into a house
with four young men – very brave. Poor David Connor got the last room to
be allocated. The one with the silver thread in the carpet (slugs).

I didn't go into acting when I left. I knew I was more interested in publicity
and sponsorship. Working at the Design Museum and Shakespeare's Globe, I
did have my share of luvvy excitement though, brushing shoulders with
Terence Conran and a whole host of designers; Robert de Niro, Helena
Bonham Carter; lunch with Mel Gibson and Sam Wanamaker; royal charity
film premieres. Aah, those were the days. However, drama has been very
useful to me, and particularly now, in my work as a facilitator and trainer.

Drama at the Olympics

Gordon Farquhar. Joint Drama and English, 1987
Olympics and Sports News correspondent, BBC Radio

Like many students my first taste of Hull was the interview. Some time in 1984, I walked out of the railway station and hopped on the blue and white bus with Orchard Park on the front of it. As you do, I tuned into the conversation going on in the seat in front of me between two women, '...and ahd urnly ad uh draigh waight waighn and uh frowt jowse'. I thought me and my Lancashire vowels are going to get on fine here. If they'll have me. I'm pleased to say they did.

I've lost the Lanky twang, flattened out of me by years of talking proper on the radio. And, truthfully, not being a native of East Lancs, I was only borrowing the accent anyway. What I've never lost is an appreciation of how those three years at Hull set me up for the rest of my life.

They disabused me of the notion that I was any good as an actor. They gave me a confidence in using my voice and standing up in front of a crowd; an outlet for creativity, ways to communicate and how to listen. They introduced me to radio and television production, and the Union bar introduced me to my wife.

I remember the Drama Department fondly: it was disciplined, but benign: it allowed us to make mistakes and experiment and somehow managed to galvanise a crowd of complex individuals into something greater than the sum of their parts (very BBC in fact). Some of the skills I learned I use every day, others, like the correct way to bow like a Regency prince and how to keep a sheep's heart looking fresh after a five-day run, have in truth yet to find themselves in demand. That said, I muck about with my kids, stage-fighting all the time, thanks to the production of *Women Pirates*, where I also learned how hard it is to remember lines after you've been accidentally kicked in the testicles by fellow cast member.

Yes, thanks Hull.

'not anymore and not yet'

Matthias Frense. Single Honours Drama, 1987
Head Dramaturg, Ringlokschuppen Mülheim, Germany

Clov: … It's finished. We're finished. *Pause*
Hamm: … We're getting on…

Samuel Beckett, Endgame

One of my most lasting memories of being a student in Hull is based on a technical aspect. Whenever a production in the Donald Roy Theatre had been put on for the last time, part of the closing ritual involved the entire cast and crew dismantling all the equipment and distributing it between the workshop, props room and rubbish bins. The flying equipment was lowered and all the drapes, spots, loudspeakers, cables and so on were removed and taken back to storage. The stage floor was swept clean and the workshop was tidied up. In no time at all we were left standing in the bare black box where there was not a single object to remind us of all the work that had been put in over the previous few weeks. The 'strike' had been completed successfully. The only thing that was left was the memory of the complex social happening that makes up a theatre production.

And then we partied.

To my mind, this seemingly insignificant procedure actually represents one of the most fascinating phenomena in the theatre: its concrete tangibility in the here and now on the one hand – and its absolute transience on the other. The fact that art is always concerned with interpreting memories as well as the remembering process itself may go without saying.

But in these times when data can be stored and retrieved at any time, this quality of temporariness which is inherent in theatre holds special potential: it asks each member of the audience to concentrate on that particular moment, it offers us the chance to take up our own individual standpoint within a group and, at its best, it can change our view of reality by the time we leave the performance. This point of 'not anymore and not yet', where one performance is put on hold or finishes and the new one has not yet begun, is one of those 'great moments' which rarely – but repeatedly – happen for me in theatre. It is that moment where feelings of joy and sorrow almost coincide.

Over the last 20 years the different forms within the performing arts have changed radically. There have been many interesting developments at the interfaces to the visual arts which traditionally focus on people's perceptions. Theatre-makers seem to be becoming more and more distrustful of narrative; it obviously arouses suspicions of being manipulative or ideological.

After all, apart from cinema, today's 'great productions' are put on for political or business reasons. Which is why it is even more important today, where all aspects of life seem to be valued according to their cost-effectiveness, for the performing arts to interrupt what is considered normal.

It's all about the opportunities which changed perspectives can create with exceptional situations to enable us to envisage something new.

HUDDLE: A Drama in Three Years

Rosie Millard. Joint Drama and English, 1987
Journalist

1984. A windowless room, in a large octagonal building, decorated with pin boards, cast-lists and a poster of Arthur Scargill. Pattering on the roof indicates that it's raining.

Enter three Drama students, namely:

ROSIE MILLARD, *young, enthusiastic, in a pearl necklace and shorts.*
ADAM JOHNSON, *slightly older wearing a miner's jacket.*
ROBERT NOBLE, *lanky boy in cricket whites.*

ROSIE *(in Received Pronunciation)*: God, it's grim up North. I'm freezing. Is it always like this, Adam?

ADAM *(in Lancashire drawl)*: You Southerners have no idea. That's why coming to somewhere like Hull is so good for you. Thank God for the Gulbenkian. Drama is about the only course at the University which welcomes people south of the Watford Gap.

ROBERT *(musing)*: If only I'd been born here. Could have played for Yorkshire. Or are we in Humberside? What IS this room anyway? I say. *(heralding ageing academic with a rolled-up copy of* The Hull Daily Mail*)* Good man! Can you tell me where we are?

(MIKE WALTON, for it is he, bearded, in a tweed jacket, clutching a copy of Stanislavsky's My Life In Art, *peers myopically around the door.)*

MIKE: This is the HUDDLE room. This is where you will put on 40-minute plays, at lunchtime, with a budget of 5p. *(A faraway look crosses his face.)* Here you will learn that drama, like an onion, can be peeled any number of ways and still bring tears to the eyes. You will all use this room in ways predictable and unpredictable. It will be your honing-ground, your laboratory, your testing-zone. Here you will have the Right To Fail. Some of you, Adam, will stage agit-prop. Some of you, Rosie, might put on worthy and earnest pieces of drama. Others – and, Robert, I am thinking of you – might stage entertaining talks with theatrical giants such as Donald Sinden.

ROBERT (*sighing with delight*): Really?

ADAM: Sinden? That old ham? You must be joking. I didn't come to Hull for that sort of tripe. I came to Hull to understand the urgent political need behind all great drama.

(*The three look at one another, trying to fathom their motivation.*)

ROSIE: Well I came to find out that what I didn't want to do was end up in the theatre.

ROBERT: I came here because I wanted to put the show on – as they say– right here.

ADAM: I want to do the Film Option. As well as explore the pages of *Towards a Poor Theatre*.

(*Outside, there is a sound of tap-dancing in the corridor.*)

ROBERT (*joyously*): Oh, good, a musical!

ADAM (*with loathing*) : Oh, God. A musical!

(*In bursts* TOBY PARK, *a ludicrously good-looking youth with a brilliant smile. He is wearing tap-shoes and a laboratory coat.*)

TOBY: Hull will be the perfect place for me to hone my absurdist skills in dramatic comedy. In adulthood I have a feeling I will form a theatre company and wow the world with madcap versions of *Moby Dick*, *Oedipus* and *The Hound of the Baskervilles*. Often, I shall be naked. But that must all wait. First, I must astonish the Gulbenkian with my jokes, looks and my charm and, of course, along the way I must lose a packet of money with Z Theatre Company at the Edinburgh Festival.

ROSIE: That sounds like fun. Can we hitch-hike up there, stay in a basement, and live on nothing but cling peaches for a fortnight?

(*There is a loud banging on the door.* MIKE *turns round in alarm.*)

MIKE: I don't want to seem hasty, but this is my next Tutor Group. I'm packing them in. Greek tragedy, the niceties of French farce, Russian kitchen sink, we are by far the most popular Department in the University, you know. Don't know how we manage, frankly. Bye, all. I've got only an hour to spend on *Battleship Potemkin*.

(*He hurries off, but not before handing a sheet of paper to* ROSIE.)

ROSIE: Oh, God. Mike's requested me to make 50 costumes for a Sheridan drama cycle.Tonight. Out of hessian, buttons and old J-cloths. It's to be performed on location this Sunday at Fountain's Abbey. Of course, I'll do it. for him…

(ADAM *and* TOBY *groan.*)

ROBERT: Teacher's Pet. You wait until I get Cameron Mackintosh on my Christmas card list.

ROSIE (*ignoring them*): …of course. But why is this place so ludicrously ambitious?

ROBERT: Because we have to aim high here, old thing. I think one should always liken playing The Gulb to playing at Lord's. It's the highest. It's the top.

TOBY (*singing, on a unicycle.*): It's the Coliseum! It's the top! It's the Louvre Museum!

(*The door opens.* JOHN BERNASCONI, *Curator of the Hull University Art Collection, bearing a glass of Claret, peers in.*)

JOHN: Er, not quite, but I like the analogy.

(*Enter a range of fresh-faced students, one playing an accordion, all singing 'Mack The Knife' from* The Threepenny Opera.)

ROSIE: Isn't that the show that made Gay rich, and Rich gay?

ADAM (*rolling his eyes*): At last. Brecht. And Weill. Dramatic names I really can honour and admire.

MIKE (*reappearing, leading a posse of Second-Year students dressed in Russian peasant garb.*): That is, of course, the point of the Department. Here you will grapple with the pinnacles of world theatre. You will have the chance to extemporise. To range from showbiz to Shakespeare, with a good slug of Brechtian anti-theatre in between. To applaud. Or to leave the auditorium silently. To have the opportunity to lose it all, make it all, and feel loved and supported throughout. Pity, fear and a dash of Feydeau. That's the formula. The rest of the University will envy you the confidence, daring and *brio* that is the hallmark of a Hull Drama student. Then you will graduate. You will go out into the world. You will use all you have learned at Hull to be creative. And you will succeed. You all will.

(*He looks around. To his embarrassment the entire student body is openly weeping.*)

Exeunt students to The Polar Bear.

[*I shall leave it to the lawyers of others to seek redress for the gross distortions perpetrated here. I never liked Stanislavsky (nor tweed jackets) and she had at least four days notice to design and make the 45 costumes for* A Trip to Scarborough, *performed not at Fountain's Abbey, but Beningbrough Hall which is much nearer Hull and easier to get to. Any more of this nonsense and I will be forced to reveal the truth about her performance as Cressida. Remember, I was there. Ed.*]

Hull Hath No Fury

Robert Noble. Joint Drama and English, 1987
Deputy Managing Director, Cameron Mackintosh Ltd and Producer

The extraordinary aspect of Hull University Drama Department is that it seems to inspire such great feelings of loyalty.

Meet anyone and say that you have been to Hull and studied Drama and find that they have done the same, even if you don't know them at all and they come from a different generation, there is a common kinship of values, a certain understanding. It prompts a certain smile, a certain skip in the step and a certain knowing look that says we have both travelled the same path. There is normally an immediate rapport. I have not found this with any other organisation that I have either attended or belonged to.

The Hull Department was never a clique, even if the rest of the University looked somewhat warily at the very trendily dressed Drama Students on the left hand side of the Union Bar compared to the rest of the students on the other side. I failed the trendy dress set with my cords and yellow jumper, so I think the rest of the University must have thought, had they been interested, that I had gate-crashed the Drama Students from the Theology Department.

What the Drama Department seemed to inspire was a great eclectic mix of people from different backgrounds and attitudes whom the lecturers had selected to do this course. Somehow, being thrown together, the mix seemed to work. We were allowed incredible freedom to do what we wanted to do, which was work in a theatre for as long as possible.

My visits to lectures were intermittent, particularly within the English Department; Rosie Millard's notes were an inspirational help although even with them (considering her future acclaim as an author and newspaper columnist), I could only get to a 2.2: I hardly deserved to get anything higher.

That was because the Gulbenkian was central to my world, other than the Drama Department's annual victory over the English Department Cricket Team each year, a triumph Mike Walton seemed to care more about than his academic teaching, although I think a certain Adam Johnson may have run out

Mike for 0 one year and was immediately down-graded to a 2:1, rather than a cast-iron First. I am not sure why my cricketing skills did not deserve a higher classification – perhaps I really got a Third.

The Gulbenkian seemed to be a treasure-trove, where you could act, direct, design and produce to your heart's content. You could be involved, seemingly, in a different production every week of the year; here you felt you could fail or succeed without hindrance. It was a place to try everything and hopefully find your niche, so that the chrysalis at Hull could become a butterfly when we finally faced the outside world.

I am now the Deputy Managing Director of Cameron Mackintosh Ltd, entrusted as part of Cameron's team to looking after his canon of blockbuster musical productions all over the world, as well as handling Matthew Bourne and producing his stunning dance-works internationally. I feel I have been very lucky to have travelled the world producing quality theatre.

But I have to admit that if someone asked for my main thrill in theatre, I would have to say it was producing in Hull a James Bond Extravaganza called *Hull Hath No Fury*, with dancing girls, cars actually driving onto the Gulbenkian Stage through the scene-dock doors, a roller-skate chase, and the Don Roy Theatre becoming, in the final scene, the Centre of Mission Control, for Blofeld to enact his evil plan to destroy the world. With the legendary John Barry film music playing through the theatre and sterling performances from Farmer, Millard, Crawley and others, *Hull Hath No Fury* was perhaps a slightly different experience from the normal on the Campus in the aftermath of the 1984 Miners' Strike. Popular Entertainment was not necessarily top of the agenda within the Gulbenkian's repertoire, yet the queue at the box office stretched from the theatre foyer right into the Union Bar. A true blockbuster had come to the Gulbenkian at last.

The GAFTA Awards have become a major part of the Drama students' celebrations at the end of every year since 1985. It's maybe arrogant, but perhaps we all want to have some kind of legacy, however trivial that legacy may be, that allows our memory to live on in a special place. It was Rick Russell (now a highly successful film editor) and I who dreamed up the inaugural GAFTAs in 1985 as a 'Celebration of the Year Past'.

We decided on creating a Morecambe and Wise show, with the lecturers and Jim Lambert and their PAs (Barbara and Audrey [*secretaries*] and Ruth from Wardrobe) coming down a glamorous staircase on Stage dressed in top hat and tails. It was a complete surprise to the whole student fraternity as we managed to rehearse in secret. Alongside G (for Gulbenkian) AFTA Awards there were sketches in which we ruthlessly parodied the entire Department, especially the great actors/dancers/writers of the previous session. Again it was highly unusual at that time for the Department to dress up and be glamorous, even if only once a year, but I remember we had a ball, albeit I'm glad it was never filmed. The memory is often preferable to the reality. None the less, it seems to have created 27 further Ceremonies after this one, so we must have done something right; I only hope all the people who finessed those Events/Ceremonies enjoyed it as much as I did, with Rick and then Nick Crawley (sadly deceased) who took it over on my departure. Long may the GAFTAs continue.

That is quite enough of Memory Lane. Much to remember and much to be grateful for. I hope Hull still inspires its current group of Drama students.

Mike's notes say, if we get over-enthusiastic we will be cut or edited. Hopefully, I won't be edited if I recall Mike's graceful off drive [*one in my life and it was caught by Rowley Wymer. Ed.*] on the cricket field. That normally did the trick as far as improving his mood on a Monday morning.

'Ah Yes, I Remember it Well'

Em Whitfield Brooks. Single Honours Drama, 1987
Director, singer, songwriter, choral leader, facilitator; Artistic Director of
Helmsley Arts Centre

First thoughts looking round the Department at interview: 'Why did I put this place fifth choice? They'll never have me'.

First question from Mike Walton in interview: 'Why did you put us fifth choice?' 'Er, well…I put Bristol first – leading smoothly into a gentle discourse from Mike about Drama at Hull being more practical, more focused, more fun, more fulfilling. Convinced I'd blown it I stopped trying to impress and enthused about Gordon Craig and wanting to be a director. I got in.

First proper conversation with anyone: Toby Park, a week after arriving, in the student union bar, already cast in a lead role in the first big production (Buchner's *Leonce and Lena*), already in girl trouble – still a dear friend.

First HUDDLE: *A Seaside Postcard* involving stripping naked beneath small beach towel in small rehearsal room with big audience, alongside Jo Walker. A lifelong friendship was born.

First play: the main part in Paul Zindel's *The Effect of Gamma Rays on Man-in-the-Moon Marigolds*, as the mad mother. Jenny Brent, Ganyat Kasumu, Helen Brown in the cast. The piece opened with a four-page monologue on the telephone. One night as the lights went down, I froze: turning to Jo, 'I can't go on'. She disagreed, pushed me hard onto the stage – and I did it.

First friend not in my year: Richard Kennaugh, in his third year when I was in my first. We met in an upstairs Gulbenkian corridor, noticing each other as we were both wearing identical coats. We lived in flats in the same Pearson Park house and spent a lot of time together. Anyone who knew Rich will recall his broad smile, his dry turn of phrase and his exceptional talent as a lighting designer. Lost to cancer at the tender age of 33. His work on *Murder in the Cathedral,* which we all thought heralded the start of a long and glittering career, was the piece of work he was proudest of at his death. After leaving Hull he designed lighting for The Yorvik Centre in York and then 'got

210

distracted' and remained in the corporate sector. His deep regret that he didn't stay working in theatre, his true love, is something I've never forgotten. I think of him often, especially when I need tips on lighting – although Geoff Farmer is great on this – and I'm still in touch with his mum.

First show I directed – aargh! Can't remember. As part of the Directing Option Mike gave me an Arthur Miller one-act play called *I Can't Remember Anything*, which I do recall. Other acting moments: playing another mad mother in Franz Xaver Kroetz's *Stallerhof*; a music-hall star alongside Clare Denham in Peter Morgan and Mark Ludlow's *Pax Britannica*, which we took to the Edinburgh Festival; acting alongside Simon Hudson in a Russian comedy, unable to keep a straight face and convinced he would become a huge star; and who can forget the original musical version of Sheridan's *A Trip to Scarborough* for the National Trust at Beningbrough Hall? With music by the great Nick Phillips. I can still remember the songs after all these years. It took a while to get my Brechtian head into the fluffy silly country bumpkin that was Hoyden, but I loved her in the end. Lots of clear memories: Julian Howarth's song 'Hoyden hath charms', Geoff's honest servant character, Gordon Farquhar as the dashing hero, Rosie Millard's costumes with Jo Walker in a giant purple frock kicking the whole thing off in that marble hall singing *Take a Trip to Scarborough, the finest of resorts...* and all those huge wigs – it was fun.

It was all fun. It was fulfilling. It was practical. It set us all up for varied, distinctive and versatile careers. Many of us still work together. Recently I've met and worked with two great practitioners who were Drama students after me, Kate Bramley (Badapple Theatre) and Ruth Paton (currently designing the touring show I'm directing). Both have an open, skillful, multi-talented approach that is perhaps the mark of what we were all encouraged to find. I'm also in touch with Middle Child Theatre, some of whom have only recently graduated, and again, their work is confident, creative, impressive, vivid, exciting.

We were lucky. We are lucky. It's all still going on.

A Degree of Possibility

Henry Little. Single Honours Drama, 1988
Opera Director; Chief Executive, Orchestras Live

'Don't be surprised if you don't get a place, it's the most competitive course in the country'. These were the words of my tutor the day before I boarded the train in 1985 to Hull for my interview. Hardly the most encouraging advice, but I was determined to study in a place as far from my native London as possible. And for me, Hull was the number one choice, a city not too large, as culturally and socially different from London as it gets, and with a sense of confidence and ambition about the Drama Department that was inspiring.

The Gulbenkian Centre felt like a place where anything was possible. As one of only 11 Single Honours undergraduates, the course and the Department with its first class theatre facilities (probably then the best anywhere in the country), available exclusively for Drama Department students, offered a fantastic opportunity to be involved in every aspect of practical theatre-making. And that's more or less exactly what I spent my time doing. In contrast to several of my peers who arrived with Theatre Studies 'A' level, my engagement with drama had been primarily through a local youth theatre. In contrast to several of my peers, with relatively little knowledge either of theatre history or of contemporary theatre theory, I needed to hit the ground running.

Three incredibly intense years at the Drama Department gave me the chance to do everything from lighting design (badly) to performing (averagely) to conducting and playing the piano for numerous productions (occasionally quite well). We were encouraged to engage in every aspect of theatre (technical, stage-management, publicity, design and performing), and I think that's what drove me to directing several productions in my final year and my ambition to follow a professional directing career. What I also remember is a fantastic sense of community support across all three year-groups and a (certainly false) sense that we, the undergraduates, were running the building and making it the success that it was. Such intensive creative working is a powerful catalyst for lasting friendships and Mark Jones and Martin Lowe, who graduated respectively in 1988 and 1989, remain among my closest friends today.

On the academic side, I remember some inspirational afternoons in a group as small as four, being given what felt like a 5 star teaching experience on why theatrical genres from the past could be directly relevant to theatre practice in the present.

And having come to the Department from a musical background, it made total sense to focus my work on Music Theatre and Opera. Working with Nick Phillips on a production of Sondheim's *Sweeney Todd* in 1988, encouraged me to explore the opera and music-theatre field. From Hull, I spent a year in Banff, Canada, as a Resident Assistant Director on their Music Theatre Faculty before returning to the UK to work as a Resident Director at The Royal Opera, Glyndebourne and English National Opera. It was at Hull that I realised that for me opera combines the very best of theatre and music and it remains my professional passion today.

Taking an undergraduate degree aged 20 to 23 is less about the class of degree that's awarded at the end. All 11 of us got 2:1's as it turned out, prompting some cynical remarks from our Joint Honours colleagues who felt that they'd had to work considerably harder for the same outcome), but it's much more about the degree of personal change over three years. I entered the Department as a quiet, shy and a little unsure individual and emerged with a sense of confidence and ambition that I could sustain a professional career in theatre.

My three years in the Department were certainly eclectic and that career pattern has continued today where, after moving into Arts Administration, I worked for the Arts Council for 10 years before joining *Orchestras Live* as Chief Executive in 2008. The point is that none of this would have been possible without three really formative years in the Department, getting a thoroughly rounded experience in all aspects of theatre. For me the change over three years was tangible, unequivocally positive and inspiring; and for that I look back over my time at the Department with pride, gratitude and affection.

**The Untold Stories of Narnia or Life Inside the Wardrobe
(to the memory of Nick Crawley, beloved friend, natural comic,
sensitive soul and fellow-student who was taken from us far too
early, but who left his mark on all who knew him)**

Lloyd Llewellyn-Jones. Single Honours Drama, 1988
Senior Lecturer in Classics, University of Edinburgh

During my time in the Drama Department between 1985 and 1988 (happy, happy years), hardly a day passed by when I didn't spend much of it on the top floor of the Gulbenkian, tucked away at the end of the 'service' corridor, in the Wardrobe department. I had no need of a Narnia; it was the Wardrobe itself that was my dreamland, my Nirvana, my Shangri-La, my Elysian Field … I could go on.

I had secured my place at Hull thanks to the strength of my costume design portfolio, I think. I remember lugging it – too big and too full – from Wales to Humberside and thudding it down on Mike Walton's desk. And I recall that he looked through it and made sympathetic noises at the end. And five months later, or so, I was studying at Hull with my mind set on a future career as a costume designer. So it began.

For three years, and after a few nice (and welcome) forays into acting (such as Moritz in *Spring Awakening* and some effete Parisian count in *Total Eclipse*), a bit of sound design and contemporary dance (!), I became known for my work with costume more than anything else. I costumed modern dramas, period dramas, dance pieces, HUDDLEs, operas, and musicals. I worked with good healthy budgets, I worked with laughably poor budgets, and I worked with no budgets at all – they were often my favourite productions in fact (anyone remember *Cupid and Death*?). For *The Great American Backstage Musical* I had the challenge of creating an American musical in miniature, which traced the careers and lives of six characters between 1930 and 1950; there were over 40 costumes on a budget of £150. I mainly used lining fabric and a lot of glitter and glue.

Harlequinade, two *Commedia dell'arte* plays directed by the much-loved John Harris, was my favourite production. Two scenarios were chosen for performance, one from 1620, the other from 1760. I had a wonderful time costuming the same cast in two period designs and the final result was very beautiful. John thanked me with the gift of an inscribed book on costume history. I still have it. And I use it often.

My final production at Hull, *Sweeney Todd*, directed by Nick Phillips, was a fun job – but problematic because of the sheer number of cast involved. Solved by vast quantities of bleached calico, a lot of machine dyeing and spray paint. By my third year I was known as 'Jones the Frock', a title worn with pride.

Wardrobe was the best place to meet people. I met Sir Anthony Quayle in the Wardrobe. I met and learned so much about the art of costume from Betty Bourne and the Bloolips gang when they visited Hull. Sitting and sewing, Wardrobe was the place for conversation. I first made friends with Nick Phillips there. That's where Claire Rosier and I bonded first and where Scott Smith and I laughed the most. At some point everyone passed through Wardrobe. It was a social epicentre.

And at the heart of it was Ruth Stuckey, the Wardrobe Mistress. Always patient with me (even though I knew that at times I drove her to distraction). Ruth was an excellent teacher who led by example. I count myself fortunate to have studied under her and I will always be grateful to Ruth for allowing me free expression and for facilitating my hunger to work with costume.

After graduation I did work as a costume designer – first at Covent Garden, then at the BBC. In 1991 I co-founded Mappa Mundi Theatre Company in Cardiff, and I am glad to say we are still going strong. In 1995 I began post-graduate study at Cardiff University and by 2000 I'd received a Ph D and started a new career as a university lecturer. That is what I do now, but I still utilize my Hull training in costume: I've published extensively on dress history and on costume design. And I still work as a costume designer and director.

I recently came across a piece I wrote for the Department magazine shortly before my Finals. It purports to be a complete inventory of the Wardrobe department's stock and was meant to be a legacy for my successor as Student Wardrobe Supervisor.

Inventory of the WARDROBE Department, March 1988

10 pairs black leotards (slightly soiled/stained/strained) – Shakespeare, modern dance, avant-garde Chekhov.

Ruff (no starch) – Shakespeare comedy, *Commedia dell'arte*, pantomime, *Oh What a Lovely War!*.

17 shoes (various periods; none a matching pair).

Apron (gingham; pink/white) – *Oklahoma*, *The Crucible* or any other post-War American drama.

Lady's bodice with pasta shell trim and spray paint – any period play c. 1500-1915.

Shirt (white; size 14 collar; buttons missing) – contemporary drama post 1980/with collar turned up: any drama pre-1915.

Boots (thigh-high) – Shakespearean hero, pantomime principal boy, Nazi high command.

Hooped skirt (all hoops missing) – *The King and I*, *Desire Under the Elms*, *East Lynne*.

Corset (laces missing) – any Restoration comedy, *Commedia dell'arte*, burlesque.

Glove (white; single) – mime, burlesque or Germanic cabaret.

Handbag – Wilde, Shaw, Ibsen, Pinter.

Pantomime cow (front end missing; back end stained) – pantomime, Shakespeare comedies, avant-garde Chekhov.

9 pairs American tan tights (gifted by anonymous donor, labelled 1967) – Any post-War British drama, pantomime.

Bra (off-white, missing hook) – Any post-War British drama, any Tennessee Williams play.

1 pair roller skates (size 13) – *Starlight Express*, avant-garde Chekhov.

73 sequins (various colours) – Broadway style musicals, Shakespeare comedies, *Oh What a Lovely War!*.

Hotpants (mustard and blue) – Post-War British drama or Broadway-style musical.

White vest (torn) – any Tennessee Williams play.

Glove (black; single); see above – Glove (white; single).

Feather-boa (plucked) – Coward, burlesque, burlesque Coward.

Satin dressing-gown (burgundy; no belt) – Wilde, Shaw, Ibsen.

1 pair lederhosen – *The Sound of Music*, *Spring Awakening*, any post-War German drama.

3 ladies' dressing-gowns (pink nylon) – any Tennessee Williams play, Japanese Noh drama, *The Mikado*.

Kilt (waist: 50 inches) – *Macbeth*, *Brigadoon*, *The Prime of Miss Jean Brodie*.

23 Laura Ashley wedding dresses (various styles; shop-bought; still in shrink wrap) – pantomime, *Seven Brides For Seven Brothers*.

1 pair silver tap shoes – Shakespeare, modern dance, avant-garde Chekhov, Broadway musical, *Oh What a Lovely War!*.

Bed sheet (white; heavily soiled) – Greek tragedy, Shakespearean tragedy, Orton.

1 'Sesame Street' T-shirt (Ernie and Bert with 'thumbs up' gesture and the motto 'Where's My Rubber Duckie?' – avant-garde Chekhov.

Shattered Dreams

Martin Lowe. Joint Honours Drama and Music, 1989
Musical Supervisor and Orchestrator, Stage and Film

Hull was the making of me. It really was. And the Drama Department was somewhere a Joint Honours student could run away to when Harmony and Counterpoint got too difficult. And yet, this Department that I loved shattered my dreams; and every day I am thankful that it did. I'm serious.

I had rocked up at Hull thinking I'd change the world by writing musicals. I hadn't actually seen the world at this point, but you had to admire my ambition. I quickly learnt that The Gulbenkian Theatre could be a cruel place. For a start, it seemed to take forever to get noticed. I think if I hadn't surprised my peers by playing 'Day by Day' from memory during the First Year Vacation course I'd still be hiding away in the Music Department pretending I enjoyed Early Music.

Marianne Elliott, Stewart Harcourt and I had been inspired by Ntozake Shange's piece *For Colored Girls…*, and wondered whether we could create a similar show dealing with, and I hesitate even to write this, paedophilia. I know, I know – we should have opted for something a bit easier, but we were young and ambitious and had grand ideas for the future of Musical Theatre.

It turned out to be traumatic from start to finish. I hated every minute of writing it and couldn't quite reconcile the idea that this was the profession I had allegedly elected to pursue. I was anxious, miserable and constantly watching the clock worrying if I would get it finished in time. I had also stupidly decided to orchestrate it for 14 musicians; naively thinking that if I used the same instrumentation as Sondheim's *Into the Woods* it might actually sound the same. It didn't.

I would add at this point I had elected not to take the Orchestration course or the Composition course as part of my Music degree, so as to give myself maximum time to write musicals in the Drama Department. A logical decision?

218

Having given myself three weeks to write about 75 minutes of music, I then had about six weeks left to orchestrate it. I had to persuade a few friends to hand-copy the entire score for the band. We rehearsed for eight long weeks for one performance on December 2, 1988. I had that date engrained in my head from the day I started work on it – and not because I was excited at the prospect of the world finally hearing my great masterpiece, but because I just wanted the whole thing to be over and to have my life back.

Our show was to be performed at a Studio Night. Studio Nights weren't open to the public and had been created to shield the world from seeing potentially disastrous student productions. We were on a double-bill with Athol Fugard's *A Place with the Pigs* and whilst Studio Night shows were never supposed to be a competition, I figured it was a slam-dunk for the child-abuse musical.

Hmmmm … the reaction? Deeply underwhelming. How did I know? Well, sometimes you just know that your show is not a hit. No one needs to say anything – you can just tell. But that was not the end of it.

Oh no! You then had to endure the dreaded post-production discussion. It took place, for those of you not familiar with this departmental imposition of the mid-'80s, a few days after a show was performed. The days and hours leading up to the dreaded event were probably more nerve-racking than waiting for Michael Billington's review to appear in *The Guardian*: unless it wasn't your show that was in the firing-line when they could be quite good *shadenfreude* events.

The real skill was how you handled these discussions and the insurance policies you put in place to minimize the damage. You could either try and find someone really nice to moderate it for you (which worked wonders after a particularly disastrous student-directed *Total Eclipse*), or, as was the case with Nick Phillips' mega departmental hit *Sweeney Todd*, you could open the discussion with a blanket apology to anyone you might have offended during the process and then get on with explaining your vision to the room.

Where was I? Oh yes – shattered dreams. If writing the show had been torturous then the thought of the discussion afterwards was like awaiting execution. The meeting began diplomatically enough in that British way, with some mild admiration for the scale of ambition at not only writing and producing an original musical, but persuading 14 members of the Music Department to come over and play in the band. The debate about our show climaxed with a ghastly outpouring by a so-called friend, who completely dismissed the production – accusing us of undermining a serious subject with schmaltzy music and a boring text. And then, to make it worse, almost without taking a breath he proceeded to lavish praise on *A Place with the Pigs*, saying it was the coolest thing ever.

And that was it. Our allotted discussion time was over. The show was history and we were on to Athol Fugard and his beautiful prose. It was clear that our show wasn't very good. That's not fair. My contribution wasn't very good; and I knew it. I just didn't have enough good ideas as a composer; what's more I'd hated the process. And yet I was clinging to this idea that I had come to Hull wanting to become a Musical Theatre composer. It seemed time to put that ambition in the drawer along with being a taxi driver, monk, fireman and every other silly childhood fantasy.

However, all was not lost. As one dream was shattered a new plan was starting to hatch. I might be a rotten composer, but I was turning into a rather good Musical Director, and whilst writing made me miserable, the process of teaching and pulling a musical together was thrilling to me. I didn't know a single person who worked in musicals, let alone the West End, but this became my new ambition.

It's funny how things turn out. I think what happened in Hull saved me an awful lot of heartache later in life. Sometimes, when I'm feeling insecure about work, I find myself dwelling on my student dreams of being a composer and the Paedophile Musical, and wonder whether I should have hung in there, but most days I know I made the right decision.

Occasionally, if someone asks me nicely, I will write music for a show. And to date the royalty cheques I receive are for the following :
    A deliberately terrible song that is sung by a has-been actor.
    A deliberately terrible song that is sung by a bank manager.
    A deliberately terrible song that is performed by a deliberately terrible amateur theatre company.

I leave you to draw your own conclusions.

A Heart Still in Hull

Mark Batty (Taylor-Batty). Joint Honours Drama and French, 1989;
Ph D, 1995
Senior Lecturer in Theatre Studies

I could have gone to Goldsmiths. I wanted to do Drama and French somewhere and they were willing to take me on my lower A-level results in 1984. But I had liked the look of the Gulbenkian so much during my interview day that I took a year out to re-take my French A-level and get the grade Hull needed. My dad dropped me and my guitar at my student digs on Cottingham Road in September 1985 and I eagerly set out on Monday morning to begin work in that lovely building. I would not finally say farewell to it until all of eight years later, having returned (after a year in Sweden) to do a Ph D under the meticulous supervision of Donald Roy (or 'Roi', as he was affectionately known).

So I got two bites at the Gulbenkian cherry, as both undergraduate and postgraduate, and I remember those happy Hullish years fondly. Including the smells of fish and cocoa carried on the wind which blew directly at you, no matter in which direction you cycled. I never learned to play the guitar, though.

I don't think I made a great deal of impact on the Department over all that time: I was mostly silent in seminars and failed nearly every audition I took, but I embraced the culture that was on offer, absorbing an education from all the extra-curricular activity in the cavernous studio that was, in reality, the spine of the Hull Drama experience. The Rehearsal (Green) Room, the wardrobe, the workshop, the stone-floored foyer – as well as functional areas – all of these were community spaces that we were encouraged to own, to populate, to keep breathing.

My first experiences of productions were as a vaguely incompetent ASM (sent to get powdered tomato soup to concoct stage blood, I could only find minestrone and was committed to filter out the dried pasta), or as a breathless and tuneless supernumerary thought-policeman in a musical version of Orwell's *1984*. By the time I was a Ph D student, I was confident (and competent?) enough to direct my own shows and enjoyed making a low-budget production of *Royal Hunt of the Sun* look vaguely epic using stacks of 50p broomsticks from the market and bags of dry leaves harvested from the campus grounds. I remember my own well-meaning ASMs rubbing hand cream into the leaves in a desperate bid to keep them supple. What goes around...

Now that I'm a Theatre Studies lecturer myself, I'm aware that a lot of my own pedagogical and pastoral practices have their roots in those seminar, lecture and rehearsals rooms back in Hull. Robert's energy and warmth, Tony's witty precision, Mike's barely disguised enthusiasm for his subjects, Keith's calm, casual professionalism, John's eccentric tangential anecdotes, Jim's open-door helpfulness: I like to think all of these reside somewhere in my own attitudes to current cohorts. When my own students are staring at their shoes in tutorials, I remember how my own silence was managed and my contributions negotiated. When I'm lecturing in front of 100 faces, most of whom are checking Facebook these days, I still remember the specific lecture strategies that kept us interested and even inspired. I think I still borrow some of the same jokes, for my sins.

When I left Hull in 1993, to go straight into my first lecturing job in Bolton, I had spent a total of a quarter of my life to date in Hull. It was more than a place of education, it had become a home town, a place where I'd discovered friends, myself and a profession. It will always be home, not just an *Alma Mater*.

A Legacy of Curiosity

David Bridel. Joint Drama and English, 1990
Director, Writer, Choreographer, Performer, Educator and Clown

I still marvel at the breadth and depth of the education I received in the Drama Department and its impact on my subsequent work and career. In my case, the connections between the various academic classes, seminars and lectures and the output that followed is almost embarrassingly obvious.

My lifelong love of the *Commedia dell'arte* was, naturally, inspired by John Harris and has led me to write, direct and publish the play *I Gelosi*, telling the story of one of Italy's best known *Commedia* companies, adapt Gozzi's fabulous *Green Bird* for the stage and even start my own school devoted to the study of clowning.

Mike Walton's course in Russian theatre infected me with a bug that won't leave, leading to hallucinations masquerading as original plays *The Death of Mayakovsky* and *The Party*.

Tony Meech's infamous passion for Brecht descended, like the gods, to aid a twice-produced *Caucasian Chalk Circle* and a clown show based on that truculent Teuton's *Legend of the Dead Soldier*.

Keith Peacock's TinTin-esque pursuit of several elusive absurdists has repeatedly led me into the delectable labyrinths of Ionesco, Pirandello and Beckett.

In the meantime, multiple productions of Shakespeare, Chekhov, Ibsen, Orton, Priestley, Dumas, Marivaux, Corneille and many others have all been lashed by the same classical whip that once drove me onwards in those formative years. Even when I work in entirely contemporary media, the structural underpinning of a classical education retains its powerful influence. Much as I succumb to the clichés of my university years in conversation – the beer, the pranks, the bad haircuts – the real legacy of my time at Hull is apparent in the work that has thrilled, challenged, confounded and inspired me ever since.

As an educator myself, I know too well the likelihood that a student will leave my charge and never appear to look back: I find myself guilty of this exact folly. Graduating from Hull, I was about as foolhardy and eager as they come, and I wasn't inclined to spend time on gratitude when it could have been spent on throwing myself at new opportunities, like a puppy let loose in a playpen.

But perhaps these words can, in some small way, express the thanks that I feel for the experiences I had in the Department. Thanks to the wisdom, knowledge, patience and bloody-minded perspicacity of all those who created and developed it, the Hull University Drama Department is the place where I – like hundreds of others – wrote, directed, performed, produced, designed and stage-managed for the first time.

It is the place where I met the tradition that I continue to try to expand and preserve. It is the place where a whimsical teenage dream gradually transformed into a permanent search for new ways to express and interpret the various joys and terrors of being alive. And it is the place where the curiosity of others – staff and peers alike – awakened a faith in the sometime magical, frequently maddening, utterly earnest and endlessly ironic practice of making theatre, which will sustain us as long as we dare fool with it.

Always Something Going On

Chris Megson. Joint Drama and English, 1991
Senior Lecturer in Drama and Theatre, Royal Holloway, University of
London

During the middle term of my second year (Spring 1990), exactly half-way through my degree at Hull, I decided to keep a diary. Each evening, or more accurately in the very early hours, I'd settle down in my room on Duesbery Street and write up the day's events. I can't remember what prompted this turn to introspection but, during the three intense months of that term, I wrote on a daily basis about life in the Department, the ups and downs of rehearsals and studying, and the general whirl of university life. After graduation, the diary was stored in a box in my parents' attic and I've only recently – nearly 20 years later – retrieved it. Reading it through after all this time triggers inevitable feelings of nostalgia (mixed with spasms of toe-curling embarrassment), but the experience has refreshed my sense of what is was like then to be a Drama student at Hull.

I was involved in a number of theatre projects in that the time which were gathering pace or reaching fruition. I was cast in a minor role in *The Power of Darkness*, directed by Robert Cheesmond. I often got the comic parts, in this case a drunken peasant.

After that, I appeared as the Hotel Manager in a student-directed version of August Stramm's manic expressionist play, *The Awakening*.

At the same time, I was preparing to perform the role of – wait for it – Ma Ubu in a puppet version of Alfred Jarry's *Ubu Roi*. This was staged in a huge canvas-covered booth: the three actors, one of them me, wore black clothing to make all but our heads invisible to the audience, while the bodies of outrageously-costumed latex puppets (which had somehow been corralled from the satirical TV show *Spitting Image*) were strapped to our necks and operated by puppeteers from below using wooden rods. It was crazily ambitious, but we took the show to the Edinburgh Fringe that summer and played to good reviews in the courtyard outside the Pleasance Theatre.

It strikes me now – although it didn't then – that the three plays are all rarely-performed classics of the European repertoire, each inflecting different kinds of modernist innovation, Naturalism, Surrealism, Expressionism. This was consistent with the experimental thrust of much of the theatre practice in the Department. It's worth noting, too, that two of the three projects were entirely student-run. All of these shows held out particular challenges for me, not least being required to grow a beard for *The Power of Darkness*. 'I'm going to shave the sides and leave the chin as it is' was my final exasperated comment, dated 23 January.

There were, of course, student HUDDLEs, of varying length (and quality). During a staging of Edward Bond's *Black Mass*, I managed to forget the opening lines of the play and it was downhill from there. Aside from such inglorious failures, there were some extraordinary achievements, numbers of occasions when student-directed or student-written pieces were performed over several nights in Main House slots to a public and paying audience, offering a remarkable opportunity for creative development and feedback.

Aside from the friendships and the discussions on theatre and the increasingly energised student politics at the time (by November 1990, Thatcher had been forced out of Downing Street), my principal recollection is that there was always *something* going on. And if the rounds of activity felt occasionally claustrophobic, then the skies and avenues of Hull – wide and expansive – provided a good counterbalance. In short, it was a wonderful environment to learn and grow.

Given that I now work as an academic in a University Drama Department, my debt of gratitude for those formative years is unambiguous. Thank you and a very happy 50th to all.

Freaks and Geeks

Joanna Nadin. Single Honours Drama, 1991
Speechwriter and novelist

There are too many moments.

Some of them, say-cheese Kodak ones, I'll keep forever. Jani in a beard and someone else's dress. Four of us on the rooftops of the Royal Mile.

Me at graduation with last night's dark circles. And Peppino's puppy fat.

Some I've torn and trashed: the arguments, the casting disappointments, the mistakes and misdemeanors.

And, while both I and Keith Peacock knew from my first improvisation as a toaster that I was never going to tread any boards beyond the Gulbenkian, I have still taken from HUDD more than a scrapbook of memories; I've taken a career.

HUDD was where I learned that loving words could be an end in itself. It was where my obsession with books wasn't just tolerated, but nurtured, in offices lined with titles I had never read, by playwrights I had never heard of at my North Essex comp; where I was encouraged to be too clever by half and know it all; where I realised the power of the perfect soundbite; where I learned to love politics and hate Thatcher – my teachers, not talk show hosts, or campus campaigners, but Brenton, Brecht and Bond.

It was where I learned that there was gain in being the geek after all. That I could quietly shine without making a song and a dance or taking the stage. That being behind the scenes, writing words to put into other people's mouths, wasn't just enough, it was everything.

I would never go back. The binned memories outnumber the ones I've kept in glorious Technicolor. And I never felt 'special', despite our title. But I wouldn't have come so far without those three years, without my tutors, and without my peers. It taught me what I wasn't, and helped make me who I am.

Have Doc Martens: Will Travel

Daniel Smith. Drama and English 1991
Music Publisher

I suppose the strongest recollection is being free of parental ties and having a grant.

After getting my record player sorted out, I headed straight down to the Army and Navy supplies and bought a pair of eight eye-hole Doc Marten boots – which I knew would annoy my mother greatly.

My second purchase annoyed my student neighbours greatly; namely a Peavey Pro Audition amplifier and an electric guitar. Yes, I was the irritating student with the biggest hi-fi and the dominating parents.

Inevitably, the Doc Martens and amplifier had a higher-profile social life than I did: they appeared in *Oi For England* (Edinburgh Fringe 1989) and *She Walks Alone* (Edinburgh Fringe 1990).

The role of Props-Master was unusual in undergraduate drama and was often twinned with that of Stage-Manager. Happy amateur days when roles blurred into who had the biggest chutzpah; now it's Production Managers and IT consultants.

The Docs came back from Scotland as an unequal pair and the amplifier came back covered in black paint.

20 years on, I still wear Doc Martens; not the eight-eye-hole boots of old, but comfortable flat heeled shoes, though at 67 quid a pair they can hardly be rated as the students' favourite in 2012.

I also still play guitar and have had several, which have been traded up, down, to the left, to the right and even given away to the ubiquitous charity shops which clog up the High Street like mushrooms in a student spag bol.

My student neighbours might be pleased to learn that I now play acoustic. Anything from The Stranglers to The Doors and back again.

The Start of a Good Journey

Nat Taplin. Single Honours Drama 1992
Sustainable Transport Marketing

Sometime during my first term, Mike Walton gave me back an essay saying 'You know, if you work *really* hard, you could get a First'. I thought: I'll work *quite* hard and get a 2.1.

What I most value about my time at Hull was the freedom: freedom to stare out over the Yorkshire Wolds from the top of the library; freedom to come and go from an exciting black building at all hours of the day and night; freedom to direct my own production in a 'real' theatre; freedom from fashion (black polo neck every day); freedom from debt (no tuition fees and a room to rent for £10 a week); freedom to grow a beard; freedom to shave it off again; most of all, freedom to work out what I might want out of life, or the next installment of it anyway.

It was – perhaps almost by accident – a fantastically vocational course. You left the Department able to turn to your hand to almost anything: writing, criticism, design, electrics, first aid, marketing, group work, management, public speaking, PR, counseling, procurement, improvisation and problem-solving of any kind… (and even performing arts).

20 years on, I am running my own small company, 'Good Journey', promoting sustainable travel and tourism. Many of the impulses that carried me here have their roots in Hull. 1992 was the year of the Rio Earth Summit. I was already buying eco cleaners from Hull's then tiny Bio-D Company and campaigning to get recycled paper into the Union photocopiers. I was struggling to stay awake in a seminar after returning on an overnight ferry from an earnest environmental conference in Strasbourg. I was exploring the Yorkshire coast by train, bus and foot. And I was mortified that my dissertation of environmental themes in drama was seen as rambling rather than fascinating.

I feel that my year group (1989-92) were lucky to come through before the cuts and competition really took hold. I was lucky to grow up with little TV, lots of fresh air, no internet, no mobiles, British Rail, YHA, 'Young Playhouse'

(£1 theatre tickets) and freedom to roam the countryside. We were the last generation to be given the keys to the school hall and allowed to rehearse plays and build sets unsupervised. We were the last year group small enough to be able to direct our own personal productions. We were the last students to leave university largely free from debt. Perhaps too, we were at the tail end of a great tradition of education for its own sake.

But perhaps every generation comes to view the past as a golden era?

A Technical Rehearsal

Kristine McIntyre. MA in Theatre Production, 1993
Opera Director

As I write this, I am currently directing a new production of Tchaikovsky's operatic masterpiece *Eugene Onegin* and thinking about how doing my MA in Theatre Production at Hull has played a huge part in my career.

Growing up in an American arts landscape of stand-and-sing opera and well-made kitchen-sink theatrical dramas, I was eager to explore new ways of thinking about these art forms. I didn't even know what was really possible until I came to England for my third year of university and discovered an entirely new theatrical language. I knew from the first moment I saw a conceptual opera production at the English National Opera that I had found an artistic home and that I needed to come back to the U.K. to pursue my postgraduate study.

In America I would have been relegated to a Music faculty, but at Hull it was not strange to anyone that I should want to pursue an MA in Theatre by directing and writing about opera.

Mike Walton and Robert Cheesmond were willing partners in this endeavour and encouraged me to look at opera through a theatrical lens and created opportunities for me to do so. Under their tutelage I wrote about concept opera for my dissertation and worked on the biennial opera production as the major directing project for my degree.

When the budget for the opera was slashed, the directing and design team knew that we needed to totally rethink the production concept. I learned not only how to update a piece quickly and completely, but also to do good work with extremely limited resources – perhaps the best real-life lesson for working in the arts. The result was England's first foray into grunge opera, an updated, Camden Town production of Delius' *A Village Romeo and Juliet*. It's a credit to the Drama Department and to Robert that the production was such a success.

231

At Hull, the theatre itself was our laboratory and the success of any idea was determined by how it played out in practice in the theatre and the effect it had on the audience. I learned not only how to stage things, but how to think about theatre and how to assess what works and why.

As a director who has made a career focused on new, updated and often conceptual productions, I can think of no skill more important or critical to my life's work. My time in the Drama Department at Hull set me purposefully on a path that I still follow with joy and conviction.

Broadening Horizons

Dean Turner (Conrad). Single Honours Drama, 1993; Ph D, 1999
Writer

Back in 1990, when I was applying for undergraduate courses, there were fewer than 80 universities in England. What's more, there were only five to which this 19-year-old theatre-enthusiast would even consider applying to study drama: Bristol, Birmingham, Manchester, Exeter and Hull (not necessarily in that order). But then options got tighter. Bristol and Birmingham didn't interview me; Manchester's facilities were limited to the small 'Stephen Joseph' black-box space; and Exeter's campus theatre, the Northcott, was available to students only as an end-of-year exhibition space. Only Hull University Drama Department had a credible, fully-functional laboratory theatre space, Gulbenkian (now the Donald Roy) Theatre.

It's difficult to overestimate the value of a facility like the 'Gulb' to a serious Drama student: a fly-tower over the stage, a working space beneath it, good lighting and sound, rehearsal spaces, wardrobe, a TV studio, a workshop – albeit too small [*then*] – and one of the UK's last remaining paint-bridges. I had worked for three years as an assistant theatre technician at Essex University Theatre, on regular professional and amateur productions, MA projects and weekly touring shows. Essex had been my laboratory space and so three years studying Drama at a university that didn't have a working theatre seemed pointless. I had to go to Hull.

The problem was, I didn't have the grades.

Hull attracted students with three 'A's at A Level and could afford to demand at least AAB. I had left school and home shortly before my 17th birthday with no A Levels and so little hope of stretching my formal education any further. I did eventually sit my A Levels at a local college, writing my first ever English Literature essay in the examination itself. I know now that I should have been proud of the C and two Ds that I earned, but at that point these were a long, long way from the grades I required. It may be why Bristol and Birmingham stayed silent; it's certainly why Exeter and Manchester said 'No'.

I'm still not sure why Hull offered one of its premium Drama places to a naïve 19-year-old who had barely heard of Stanislavsky, let alone Brecht and Artaud. The intake for my year was 15 Single Honours students, up from a mere 8 the previous year, but still fantasy numbers in the era of mass education that has followed. The risk that HUDD took with me was, and remains, somewhat of a mystery. It was, perhaps, a reflection of an ethos natural to departments whose right to exist is initially questioned by the university community at large. It is likely to be a tribute to individuals, like Mike and Don, who nevertheless recognised and championed the value of practical experience in a university drama setting. All know is that I am grateful that somebody was brave enough to take a gamble on me.

I duly attended every lecture on the course, saw every show in the Gulbenkian, tried to get to every HUDDLE and represented my year group on the Staff/Student Committee. I wasn't a brilliant student, but I did learn a lot. And although I never really did catch up and fit in with those AAB students, the graduate me of 1993 was a more complete person than the student me who had arrived in 1990.

After a year away in America, I returned to Hull for my Ph D, under the supervision of John Harris, whose wit and kindness were brought to an end by his untimely death in 2008. A much-loved friend, John is sorely missed.

I can't say that my experience at Hull was entirely free of downsides and disappointments; in fact on occasions it was bloody frustrating. But time moves on and perhaps only the churlish would allow those shadows to eclipse what has generally been a positive outcome. The gamble paid off for me: I got my doctorate and I have done my best to encourage other students to take risks in their turn. Back in 1990, Hull University Drama Department took a largely un-schooled boy out of Essex – the first in his family to get A Levels, and the first to leave the shire – and it gave him what all good universities should: education and opportunity.

Happy Birthday HUDD.

Biology to Drama

Zinnie Harris. MA in Theatre Production, 1994
Playwright

I came to Hull to the take the MA in Theatre Production straight from studying Biology at Oxford. It wasn't what you might call an obvious progression and, when I arrived, I knew next to nothing. I had been directing student plays, but not much more. Don Roy later told me that they let me in on sheer enthusiasm alone. I am so glad they did. What I encountered blew my mind. I spent my year not only taking the MA course – terrific in itself – but I persuaded various tutors to let me sit in on undergraduate lectures to try and make up for my lack of Drama degree. I guess Don's comment on enthusiasm was right. I even remember writing and submitting undergraduate essays for some reason that escapes me now.

I loved the open access of the place. If you had the energy and an idea, it seemed to me that the tutors and technicians would support whatever enterprise you engaged with, whether letting you into the radio studio at the weekend to write and produce a short radio play, or staging an open-air *Tempest* with life-size puppets on the Gulbenkian steps, or giving you the studio to stage a play of my own, with zero budget and zero set, just because I wanted to see a particular scene on its feet. My highlights were Gary Yershon's vague, anecdotal and largely hilarious sessions on musical theatre (God, did he really get us all to sing?); assisting Don on what can only really be described as the 'dubious success' of *Breasts of Tiresias*; performing in Stephen Artus's production of *Gum and Goo*; and trying to get a whole cast of first years to speak with a convincing Scots accent for Liz Lochhead's *Mary Queen of Scots got her Head Chopped Off*.

The Department for me was a vibrant place where anything was possible, but above all full of people, students and tutors, who were as serious about theatre as I was and who had the will to see each and every one of us succeed. The confidence in a girl who had come straight from the science labs, fuelled me for many years after leaving, and is something for which I will always be grateful.

Can I Call You a Name I Will Remember?

Christopher Simpson. Joint Drama and English, 1996
Actor

I remember my mum deftly negotiated a last-minute place on the course (unknown to me as I was rehearsing a play that summer), arguing eloquently and persuasively that I was deserving. I had been looking after her and she, who had always prized a good education, talked me into my place at Hull.

I remember Guy Bass disbelieving I had travelled up to Hull from London on my own without my mum.

I remember, after two weeks in Hull, receiving a self-addressed envelope with a letter from her inviting news of her now deeply-ensconced son's as yet unreported adventures.

I remember there was a student who kept coming into the Department in the first week and insisting on calling me an arbitrary name of his choosing.

I remember being in Hull afforded me inspirations, ideas and memories.

I remember Mike Walton quietly releasing me for a few days so I could go and see Peter Brook's *The Man Who* at the Lyttleton Theatre in London; and John Harris generously writing me a glowing letter of recommendation to accompany my hopeful letter to Peter Brook. Later I was to visit the Bouffes du Nord and do a cartwheel on the carpet in the theatre I had dreams of working in.

I remember reading Adrian Kiernander's book about Ariane Mnouchkine and *The Theatre du Soleil* which inspired my spending two and a half intensive months learning with the company.

I remember hearing for the first time that theatre is fire and that actors are athletes of the heart. I remember reading all the extant ancient Greek texts in an episode of academic zeal [*That is a one and only. Ed.*].

I remember licking the back of someone's ear during a falsely-daring improvised HUDDLE created with Guy Bass and enjoying the ensuing not-so-worthy outrage.

I remember I asked Nike [*Imoru*] if she had any suggestions as to how I could improve as an actor and she told me to learn how to close my face.

I remember answering my essay questions before I read the books and constructing essays through the night.

I remember the first time I met Hilary Otto in the library.

I remember Liz Besbrode asking me to find the game in improvisation.

I remember dancing to funk at the Welly almost every Friday.

I remember not knowing what else to do after my mum had died in my final year, but to come back up to Hull early to rehearse *Man Equals Man* directed by Matt Readman.

I remember being so sad on my graduation day that my mum wasn't there, misplacing the hired mortar board in a haze and having to borrow Jay Lusser's to walk across the stage.

I remember being touched by Mike Walton's sensitivity as I realised the folly of not having told him my mum had died until graduation day. When I think of my time at Hull, I remember endings and beginnings.

I remember being delighted that I was offered the role of Dromio of Ephesus in the first production of my first term, directed by Paul Jenkins, and feeling included in the possibility of creating shows immediately.

I remember knowing I could try anything, even if I didn't have the wisdom to.

My mum didn't see me graduate, but I am so thankful she spoke her magic. Going to Hull gave me friends for life and vital frames for engaging with all manner of creative endeavours.

Seeing Through Their Eyes

Debbie Standage (Brace). Single Honours Drama, 1997
Every Child a Talker (ECaT) Early Language Consultant

In a hugely important three years of my life, Hull University's Drama Department set me on my life's course.

Seeing Matthew Brace, a fellow Single Hons. Drama student and knowing from the first moment that we would spend our lives together, is the single most important meeting of my life. 14 years later we are continuing to build our future together and with two little Brace boys to accompany us on our journey, we couldn't be more grateful to the fact that I flunked my A levels the first time around and had to beg a deferred entry from JMW. Mike was able to see things through my eyes and know that Hull was where I needed to be.

I always knew I would be a teacher and work with children, but didn't want to embark on a formal teaching degree. Drama enabled me to take an alternative path into primary teaching. Creating performances with young children, using many of the techniques and skills I learned, experimented with or was inspired by in the Gulbenkian, was a learning experience for me as well as a great pleasure.

The 14 years since graduation have been varied, but I can honestly say that my degree has proved invaluable both for my career in the classroom and also in the work that I now do in 'Early Years'. Being able to see and imagine things through someone else's eyes is highly skilled work and a key feature of successful performance. This skill is fundamental when working with very young children and central to the work I now do with families as I support, encourage and inspire the crucial role that adult plays in developing children's communication skills.

I am proud to have completed my Drama degree at Hull University.

Take The Plunge

Peter Bramhill. Single Honours Drama, 1997
Actor

It's not without a pang of nostalgia that for the very last time, I politely interrupt Don Roy's tutorial on French Renaissance Theatre, to draw his attention to the rapidly cooling cafetière standing on the shelf behind him.

Don, as always, jokingly berates us for not reminding him sooner and turns to address the neglected coffee-pot.

And during this brief decaffeinated hiatus from Beaumarchais' *The Marriage of Figaro*, I debate whether I had time to get to the Zoo café and back, or would I have to face yet another sandwich from the Union shop before catching today's HUDDLE of Jean Anouilh's *Antigone*, in which, unbeknown to me, I would witness my future wife being born out of a black bin-liner.

Leaving this conundrum unresolved, other than adding 24-hour Jacksons [*Sainsbury's these days*] into the mix, I turn my thoughts towards a few more of the unanswered questions I had from my time in the Gulbenkian.

Such as, was it right to use the Emperor from Star Wars as my inspiration for the Old Man in Keith Peacock's production of Strindberg's *Ghost Sonata*?

Was the gimp-masked serial killer in *Pulp Fiction*-themed contemporary dance piece *To Comfort Ghosts* my last taste of Edinburgh and the National Student Drama Festival?

Should I have attempted that Jamaican accent for the Rastafarian tea-boy in office radio drama *Kiroshi*?

Did I successfully walk like Death? And would Mike Walton's translation of *Alkestis* be my only ever stab at playing him?

Was the recording of various objects being dropped into the first floor toilet a convincing sound-scape for prison boat drama *Female Transport*?

Was it wrong to have turned my housemate's sleeping-bag into a pair of toasty trousers for absurdist Studio Night, *Transient Blues*?

What are the chances of the newly-adopted foyer bar, which I'd hastily constructed as a prop for original musical *One More Kiss*, not collapsing before graduation?

How many Marlboro Lights did we all get through in order to save up enough empty packets to make the set for Sean Buckley's *Gravegardening*?

Would the minor fencing in a fat-suit injury I'd sustained during last night's *Weird Sisters, the Musical* affect the choreography of tonight's sword fight?

If I really thought about it, did I actually fully understand my own dissertation title?

And finally, with these halcyon Gulbenkian days almost over, was I properly ready to enter this profession for real?

Then, just as I'm beginning to get the fear, Don turns and with hand hovering over the cafetière, provides the perfect answer 'Right, I think we're ready to take the plunge'.

From Dancing at Lughnasa to Dancing in Siberia

Joseph Long. Single Honours Drama, 1997
Research Fellow, Max Planck Institute for Social Anthropology

In the spring of 2006 I found myself on the shore of Lake Baikal with a group of Buriat-Mongol friends performing the *yokhor*, their traditional circle dance. By this time I was half way through two years of anthropological fieldwork in Siberia researching local ritual and performance traditions. As I surveyed a lake still thawing after the long winter freeze, I remember reflecting on the course of events that had led me there. Both Siberia and the discipline of anthropology seem a long way from the Gulbenkian Centre sometimes, but much of my later interests was formed in my three years in the Hull Drama Department and learning, dancing and writing about the *yokhor* has often led me to reflect on that journey.

At Hull, Mike Walton's final year course on Russian theatre and his accounts of early Soviet social and artistic transformations nurtured my growing interest in all things Russian. I decided to study contemporary developments in Russian theatre at postgraduate level and took time out to learn Russian and travel extensively in a country emerging from 70 years of communism. After pilgrimages to the Moscow Art Theatre and Chekhov's house, the journey took me gradually east, away from the artists of the metropole and towards the indigenous peoples of Siberia. The steppe landscapes drew me in and in the Buriats I found a people with their own performance traditions, rooted in shamanist ritual, but shaped by the conventions of Russian and Soviet theatre.

While the experience led to a change of direction for me, the foundation of this interest lies squarely in my experience in Hull. Drama at Hull was always about studying theatre in its political and historical context, whether that was Ancient Athens, Medieval England or post-war Germany. It was at Hull that I had first read about social and cultural impacts of the Russian revolution and read theorists of performance, bridging the divide between Drama and Anthropology. Whatever the label, the study of performance processes in a wider cultural and social milieu forms the basis of my ongoing research.

Looking back it's a wonder to think anyone at Hull got anything read at all, given the dynamism of the Department in its production work. Switching from stage-management one week to directing the next, taking on lunchtime, evening and touring productions, playing Ceilidh, folk and rock gigs in aid of Z theatre company and a group of us running a drama project in a local special school: all seem to be something of a blur now, but I think they were pretty much a blur at the time. Often academic work didn't begin until the evening, when rehearsal or performance ended and I remember getting through my final semester thanks to a coffee machine purchased at a car boot sale. The year's were a creative blur in which production experience and writing about performance informed and fed off one another.

In my final year at Hull I was cast in *Dancing at Lughnasa*, Brian Friel's beautiful piece that exposes some of the pagan elements underlying Irish Catholic culture. In the play dance is both a communal experience and a space for transgression of the formal strictures of everyday behaviour; I think that Friel expresses this more effectively than any anthropological analyses that I know of. And therein lies the paradox of writing about performance – words on a page can rarely communicate as directly as, nor evoke the vitality of, live performance, the power of which makes it such an attractive object of study. This was a paradox well understood in the Hull Drama Department with its ethos of combining academic study and production experience, blurring any distinction between theory and practice. It is an approach not so different from the methodology of participant observation that underpins anthropological fieldwork, the kind that finds one dancing with friends on the shores of Lake Baikal.

The power of performances as social acts remains an important thread in my academic work, a thread that has run from Hull through graduate studies at Cambridge, Indiana and Aberdeen to fieldwork on the Southern Siberian steppe. In *Dancing at Lughnasa* I played the batty Uncle Jack, recently returned from missionary service in Africa, having immersed himself a little too deeply in the traditions and dance of the local people. Having worked my way through the literature of a new discipline I now recognise the ethnographic sources that Friel drew on to form Jack's stories. I also recognise the feeling of constantly having a part of myself somewhere distant, among people with whom I have lived, worked, made offerings to their ancestors; and with whom I have danced. It has been, and continues to be, an incredible journey, one that started in Hull in a flurry of rehearsals, library fines and black coffee.

You Never Leave Hull University Drama Department

Hannah Miller. Single Honours Drama, 1997
Head of Casting, Royal Shakespeare Company

Some of us call graduates of HUDD the 'Hull Mafia'. We might as well have a special handshake. There is something that unites those that have experienced time in Hull, in the Gulbenkian Centre, creating, learning, debating, hammering, cutting, stitching, arguing, struggling, achieving. I bump into people working in the theatre who may have graduated before or after me, but there is a connection, an understanding of something intangible that we have experienced in Hull that is just a little bit different for a Drama Department. A little bit less pretentious (OK, it's still a Drama Department and there may have been a certain hour-long improvisation inspired by Strindberg's diaries), but a little bit more rooted, possibly because it is in Hull.

It started for me at my interview day with the feeling that all the sessions were genuinely as much a chance for me to find out about the tutors, the course, the resources, as it was for them to check me out. I was sold, despite a night spent in a dodgy B and B on the Beverley Road.

The opportunities I had, and took with both hands, gave me the foundation for everything I do, certainly professionally and in many ways personally too. Simply, I wouldn't be doing what I am doing now without HUDD – not that I'd have ever guessed I'd be doing this job either. The breadth of everything you can get involved with in the Department allows you to explore and enjoy so many different disciplines and subjects; I felt the world was my oyster when I graduated. What an amazing gift. The course allowed me to try everything and discount nothing, so I found out on my own where my strengths and passions lay and where that could lead me.

Most importantly, I still count about half of my year as good friends, 15 years after we graduated and have gathered other alumni along the way. The most important thing to me was whom I spent those three years with and whom I shared these experiences with. The tutors at Hull seemed to know how to put a good team together.

Sensations

Ruth Paton. Single Honours Drama, 1997
Theatre and Opera Designer

Of the many reasons to be grateful for my education in the Drama Dept at Hull, these stick out:

Hull provided me with a historical, cultural and social backbone that gave me the confidence to tackle any project with any director.

I never felt compartmentalised into being a certain type, or having to perform a certain role.

The atmosphere of creativity that surrounded our practical work fostered a work ethic of collaboration and investigation that I still rely on today.

I remember the smell of the recording studios;

the pleasure of knowing the Donald Roy Theatre inside out;

sitting in a small room having meaty discussions with my tutorial group;

the excitable atmosphere in the upstairs studio we used for HUDDLEs;

feeling empowered by a Sarah-Jane Dickenson lecture;

marvelling at studying foreign plays in published translations by members of our staff;

the feeling of hemp rope, and meeting some brilliant, quirky people.

The Right Direction

Kate Bramley. Single Honours Drama, 1998
Theatre Director and Playwright

I still remember vividly my interview at the Drama Department where strangely, perhaps due to my decision to take a gap year, I was the only student interviewed that day.

I had an extremely relaxed walk around the building with the gentlemanly John Harris, who gently quizzed me on my interests and any ambitions for my time at Hull University, should I attend. I cautiously offered the idea that I would really quite like to be a theatre director. His response was along the lines of 'Well, you'd best take a look in here then'.

'Here' was, of course, the theatre and I fell in love instantly with the space, with its many flexibilities and staging potential as enthusiastically described. And the thought that mere students were allowed to direct shows for that wonderful space. I am afraid that it was that simple, positive conversation, and the feeling that I could somehow fit in with the world John was describing, that pushed Hull to the top of my university list.

I have never regretted that decision for a second and, since graduating, have met so many other Hull Drama graduates working professionally in the arts who have the same fondness both for the theatre space and the spirit of the Drama Department that shapes our collective memory.

My interest in directing did not wane through my three years at Hull University. If anything it intensified with the guidance and support of so many of the lecturers. I was encouraged to consider academic and practical approaches and diverse styles of performances: all of which nudged me towards a fledgling interest in writing, about which I had little instinctive confidence. I had felt stubbornly, certain at 15 years old, that I wanted to be a theatre director, but three years at Hull University gave me an intellectual scene-dock stocked with a plethora of ideas.

It was the kindness of Administrator Joy Ward who, mid-way through my third year, launched me off into the next phase of my theatre apprenticeship, recommending me as an Assistant Director for Hull Truck Theatre. That blossomed into a 10-year involvement with the company as a regular director for John Godber.

This again dramatically shaped my thinking about the theatre process and opened a new debate in my head as to why, as well as how, theatre should be made – something I had naively never considered prior to that.

And who for.

Nowadays, I write and direct for my own touring company [*Badapple Theatre Company*], specialising in new comedy, with audiences at the heart of the process. Our own 'Theatre On Your Doorstep' scheme takes high quality theatre to the smallest of venues nationwide. My work is laughter-filled, original, hands-on, bitterly hard and utterly rewarding.

I remember my time at the Gulbenkian Centre as being exactly the same way, and will always be grateful to those who guided me through.

A Very Interesting Journey

Fiona Czeschel. Single Honours Drama, 1998
Senior Program Assistant, Faculty of Education, University of British
Columbia

I was a late applicant to HUDD. *'Almost* a mature student'. J. Michael Walton sat behind his desk and I tried not to take it personally. Having had very little notice of the interview, I had been running on adrenalin for days. I can't quite recall the drive from Scotland and certainly don't remember driving back.

I do recall feeling a sense of belonging and a terrific excitement when I arrived at HUDD. I wondered about the wonderful masks and photos on the walls in Mike's office. I can still see a photograph of a woman dressed in a yellow cheongsam detailed with beautiful embroidery. She looked like a performer from the Beijing Opera. The background of the photo was dark, but had a rectangle of light in the distance. Something about the image was captivating. I could see from the costume that she was probably from a noble family, but what struck me more was the look on her face. Travelling somewhere and a little apprehensive about going. Behind the makeup, the look in her eyes was sad, but the energy in her face said she was ready for whatever lay ahead. Of course, being young and enthusiastic, I explained all of this to Mike, who sat patiently and didn't confirm or deny the story I generated about this photo.

At the end of the interview, convinced I hadn't done enough to gain admission to the Department and that I'd never see Mike or Hull again, I asked about the woman and her story. He had taken the photo in the wings during a street production of Chinese Opera in Singapore. The woman was, indeed an actress.

It was then that I realised that this was a course I very much wanted to take. Unknowingly, I had uncovered my love of costume and costume design, which I got to realise in the Wardrobe department throughout my three years. I also discovered my uncanny knack for making up stories with an element of truth, which I got to exercise as Co-Editor of The GRC Grapevine (1995-6).

My HUDD experience was a very interesting journey, full of wonderful and not-so-wonderful moments that have shaped who I am. I loved (almost) every minute and am grateful to have been part of such a great Department.

Full Circle

Hannah Chissick. Single Honours Drama, 1998
Theatre Director

In August of this year I did something I have not done since I was a student at the University of Hull. I spent the entire month at The Edinburgh Festival. Although it had crossed my mind that this might provide somewhat of a trip down memory lane, I was totally unprepared for the nostalgic overload that the month would be.

In the summer of 1997, I, along with many of my year, packed up and headed bright-eyed and full of optimism to the world's largest arts festival. Guided by the 18-year-old, but already brilliant Emma Gersch, who was our Company Manager, we packed ourselves, our luggage and also the sets for four shows onto the coach.

That summer was in many ways a coming-of-age for me and one I will certainly never forget. It was the first show I had directed that was on sale to the general public, it was my first three-week run and the first time my work was reviewed by the press. It is absolutely true that I was sick with nerves before every single performance for the entire run.

It was certainly an eventful month, I was woken at 4 am to be told that my technical rehearsal had been moved from the following afternoon to 5 am, one of the other shows' sets was removed by overzealous bin men and never seen again, and I spent most of my days hanging jelly babies by tiny nooses from my flyers, (don't ask; it seemed like a good idea at the time).

Walking through the familiar streets this summer I felt a pang for that August, a time where I remember a real sense of anything being possible, of being at the start of an incredible experience, of being and doing exactly what I was meant to be. Walking down the Royal Mile this August, I was in truth feeling a little jaded. 15 years on, the prospect of 3000 shows now seemed exhausting rather than inspiring, people thrusting flyers at me felt intrusive rather than an invitation to an adventure. I had a real yearning to reconnect with the optimistic 18-year-old me

Then I met her, well sort of.

As I was walking down the Royal Mile, I bumped (literally) into Beth who was sporting a very fetching Z theatre company sweater; she was flyering for her show. Very over-excitedly, and in truth probably a little embarrassingly, I launched into a full speech about how I had started as a director with Z all those years ago and listened with delight as Beth told me she herself was currently doing the very same thing. I felt instantly connected to this young woman. It is a feeling I have had many times on discovering, in an audition or a meeting, that someone also studied Drama at Hull.

Throughout my career, successes (and failures), I have felt a huge debt to all that was instilled in me throughout, what was undoubtedly three of the best years of my life.

I have never forgotten how my mind was shaped by the dedication and passion of our lecturers or how my life was enriched, and continues to be so, by the amazing people I studied alongside.

I look forward to seeing what path Beth's journey will take, and I hope that in 15 years time when she is feeling a bit too old for a festival she will bump into her 18-year-old self and be reminded what a great adventure it has all been so far.

Poacher turned Gamekeeper

Richard Tall. Single Honours Drama, 1998
Production and Stage-Management Tutor and Supervisor (HUDD)

I have been one of the few graduates lucky enough not only to have had the experience of being a student in the Department, but also the privilege of being paid to work in our magnificent Gulbenkian Centre. The same place, but two very different times in my life which, whilst distinctly separate, are full of wonderful memories and recollections, some of high drama (on and off the stage), some sad and happy moments, many successes and many failures.

But always the wonderful ethos and charm present in the culture that has been passed down through the years from student and staff member to student and staff member. This ethos pervades not only everything we have done and continue to do in the Department, but also has had a profound effect on the changing nature of our cultural industries as our graduates have dispersed into the creative landscape.

As a student I think it's fair to say I was obsessed with production activity. It was something that I (and most of us) lived and breathed. Close to my heart will always be the productions of *Into the Woods*, *The Libertine* and *Henry V* as well as our second-year adventures in Edinburgh with Z Theatre Company which I still remember with hilarity and much fondness. 'And 'im – 'e 'ad a cone on his 'ead' – the only time I've ever been refused entry to anywhere.

I also 'grew up' during my student time in Hull and most of my best friends now are people who either graduated from Drama at Hull, or are people who are friends of people who I was friends with at Hull. I feel great affection for that time. There is something about Hull that attracts thoroughly decent people who, whether they go on to great acclaim or not, always seem to end up working hard and offering all they can to their chosen career. I think we can be safe in claiming that Hull University Drama students have given a great deal to the world, and especially the theatre, partly, perhaps, because we all know that there are other people 'just like us' – a shared generosity of spirit.

As a member of staff of the Department I've now seen something like a thousand students come and go through the Gulbenkian front doors and I can honestly say it never gets easier to see them leave. One of the wonderful things about working in the Drama Department is you get to see the development of individuals, a kind of evolution of talent and skill. A student comes into the Department wanting to be an actor and may leave with a completely different set of skills and a different career path entirely, having been lured to the 'dark side' of areas such as stage-management. But one thing graduates always leave with is a drive, determination and confidence that, I think (and others who are perhaps more objective have told me), is unique to our Department and our courses.

As we go beyond the 50 years, my hope is to continue to promote the same opportunities and experiences to new generations of students in the same way they were offered and so freely given to me. Whatever the future may hold for higher education, it surely can only be one where the University of Hull Drama Department will thrive, prosper and continue to produce graduates who know, feel and care.

The Hull Mafia

Ruth Gibson. Single Honours Drama, 1999
Actress

I think it's probably fair to say that studying Drama at Hull University changed my life. I understand that many students talk of their university days as the best years of their life, the lasting friendships they have made and how it may have affected their choice of career. And I can claim all these things; I am still very close to my Drama Department mates, sharing a flat with one of them for many years after we had graduated. I'm also an actress, so it had impact on that too. However, it was a party hosted by Hull Drama Department alumni that really made a difference, as it was there I met my husband, Guy Bass.

Guy also studied Drama at Hull, but graduated before I started. It was a pretty quick courtship; first dates go swimmingly when you can reminisce about tutors, studio weeks and how we both embarrassed ourselves in HUDDLEs. After you realise this one may be 'the one' you have the dreaded introduction to the parents. This, in my case, wasn't so threatening as my father, Peter Gibson, is also a Hull Drama Department alumnus (1966-9). At family gatherings we sit around a table where the majority of people have an anecdote about Michael Walton – I'm not sure many Christmases can claim that. My sister also went to Hull University, but studied Sociology, so she's not quite in the gang.

So the Drama Department permeates my personal and professional life. My agent once said that my going to Hull was the best thing I ever did for my career as so many directors, casting people etc. are alumni. We are known in the industry as 'The Hull Mafia' and, trust me, we are everywhere. I remember checking my biog for a program during one show and a fellow-actor asked why I included my years at Hull in my biography. As I was about to explain Malcolm Sinclair (the current Equity President) walked through the door exclaiming 'Ruth, I didn't know you're Hull! I'm Hull!' at which point our Tony Award-winning sound designer [*Paul Arditti*] added, 'I'm Hull too!" 'That's why', I replied.

Thank you, Hull Drama Department, for giving me a great 3 years, a great start to my career and a great husband.

The First Time I Got Lucky

Laura Maclean (Townshend). Single Honours Drama, 1999
Senior Copywriter (and Resting Actress)

I don't consider myself to be a very lucky person. In fact, I'm rather accident-prone and will invariably lose a coin toss. For some people University was the first time they 'got lucky'. For me, the same was also (kind of) true, as the day a place came up through clearing to study Drama at the University of Hull was one of the luckiest days of my life.

Having never been to Hull before, I'd not experienced that unique collaborative aroma of fish, leather-tanning and chocolate, but I loved the place and knew it was the University for me. Despite having to live in temporary accommodation to begin with (which was not the best start to my university experience, as I don't tend to travel light), I landed on my feet again, finding a lovely room-mate, who also happened to be on my Drama course, in a house on the famous student road, Cranbrook Avenue.

There were plenty of opportunities to get involved in various different productions at The Gulbenkian Centre and I adored working on shows constantly. It was the first (perhaps only) time that 'work' didn't feel like work. Even now, I dust off my old VCR to watch videos of Main House productions and Studio Week shorts to relive those memories.

The Drama Department had a nurturing environment; it felt like an extended family. Students became very close, even when friendships were seriously put to the test by living together, working together and socialising together.

I am so grateful to the University of Hull Drama Department for not only providing me with a great basis for my working life, an extensive knowledge of drama, which helped enormously in preparing me for drama school (which I attended a few years afterwards), but also a fantastic group of very dear, hopefully lifelong, friends. 15 years after meeting them, I'm proud to say my university friends are still a big part of my life and have shared landmark moments with me. It might be a cliché, but I can say, hand on heart, that those Uni days really were some of the best of my life. Thank you Lady Luck.

The Class of 2000 – The Millennium People

Richard Spencer. Single Honours Drama, 2000
Vice-Principal, Impington Village College

Sometimes it takes a few years to realise what you've been given. We've all played the 's/he went to Hull' game while scanning the programme at the theatre, or smiled with pleasure as we see the likes of Sam Spruell, Sam Troughton, Sam Roukin (if I have a son I'm naming him Sam) or Tom Brooke flash across our screens in another TV or film triumph. We bask in their successes and are happy to have been there with them at the start.

They are wonderful examples of what a great performance training-ground Hull has proven for so many of us who were there around the turn of the century. And there are so many others making a fantastically successful career, some in the public eye, others behind the scenes or behind masks/puppets/screens. Hell, every time I pick up my voicemail I'm greeted by a Hull graduate (Ruth Gibson – the voice of 'Orange'). We are all over the telly, the big screen and the radio and we are so very, very proud of them.

But beyond the more visible successes, what always surprises me is the staggering range of professions and vocations we happy few have ended up in. It is a testimony to the truly 'transferable' skills we sucked up, soaked up and swotted up over those three sparkling years that the class of 2000 boasts: book-sellers, managing directors, IT magazine editors, press officers, social workers, marketing executives, film producers, script editors, teachers, journalists, salesmen, stage-managers, writers, costume-designers, musicians and even the editor of a mobile phone magazine.

The Olympic opening ceremony was moving enough, but I'm not ashamed to say that my eyes moistened all the more knowing that two of the class of 2000 were heavily involved in helping Danny Boyle prepare that triumph [*Laura Cubitt – Movement; Sally Christopher – Props*].

We've gone in so many different directions, but are all unified by what we were given: the right in those critical years to try something bold and fail; the challenge to succeed while exploring what we were best at in a creatively nurturing space; and the tenacity, work ethic and good humour that owning the Gulbenkian for a period of time gifted us. I recall Sarah-Jane telling us on day one that we should view the building as our 'playground'. She was right, but it was more than that; it was the making of us.

The class of 2000 were my friends and colleagues, but many of them now feel like family. We are now all at that point in life where things like marriages, babies and burgeoning careers mean we meet less frequently, but there remains a special and knowing bond. Paradoxically, you get to really know someone when you've seen them in a mask or measured them for a costume.

Thank you Hull University Drama Department. Thank you to all the staff, so many of whom live fondly in our hearts and our memories. Thank you class of 2000 – we had a blast and we're still just warming up.

Finding my voice

Tomm Coles. Single Honours Drama, 2001
Actor

When I first sat down to write about my experience at Hull I was completely stumped for anything interesting to say. On the surface, my time at Hull seems distinctly 'normal'. I attended all my lectures; I submitted my assignments on time; I didn't drink very much; I partied a little bit; I made some great friends, but on the whole I had quite an uneventful three years.

It's only when I delve into those memories that I realise quite how much my time at Hull shaped the person I am today.

I started at Hull doing a Joint Honours Drama degree with French. I never had the confidence to throw myself completely into Drama full-time, so I thought it best to keep on with my languages as a fall-back. It wasn't long, during my first year, in fact, before I developed the confidence to throw myself into Drama full time and the Department supported me in my decision to convert to Single Honours Drama.

Soon after, a production of the musical *Cabaret* was being cast. This was predominantly a third-year production, but keen to embrace my new Single Honours status, I put myself up for one of the leading roles: Cliff Bradshaw.

That production changed my life in so many ways. It's hard to believe that we only performed for a few nights, yet in that short time my whole trajectory shifted track. I hadn't sung in public since I was 11, after puberty wreaked havoc on my vocal folds. Having been told that I would be unlikely to sing again and ceremoniously dropped from the school choir, I spent much of my school years secretly training my voice, determined to get it back on track to sing again in public.

It was at my audition for *Cabaret* that I decided to road-test my vocal folds. I never told anyone how big a deal that was for me, and in the countless auditions I have had since as a professional actor, nothing comes close to the nerves I felt that day. I was suitably chuffed when I got the part.

When I stepped out on opening night I felt such an overwhelming support from my tutors and classmates that a confidence was born within me; my lifelong dream of performing in musicals was reignited.

I was taught throughout my time at Hull to value the text of all drama, be it Greek, Shakespearean or more modern plays. I was further encouraged to apply that respect to libretti and to the text of musicals, a genre that is all too frequently accused of being superficial.

When I was auditioning for drama schools for life after Hull I was thus drawn towards the classical drama rather than those specialising in musical theatre. I attended the Royal Welsh College, where it was no coincidence that clearly the best tutor of all was also a Hull alumnus (the ridiculously-inspiring Marilyn Le Conte).

I have now been performing as an actor primarily in musical theatre for over 10 years, a career which has taken me onto the West End stage and around the world on several occasions and which continues to bring me an incredible amount of joy.

That moment when I found my voice remains one of the highlights of my life to date. I pride myself that I have always addressed musical theatre as a legitimate art form despite numerous contradictions from others. I thank Hull University Drama Department for building the foundations on which that approach and respect was built.

Drama of The Golden Age

Tom Frankland. Single Honours Drama, 2001
Theatre Maker

My younger brother is currently applying for university courses and has asked my advice on where to go. It is a difficult question to answer, as what I really want to recommend is that he go back in time to the Hull University Drama Department that I went to. I think I experienced a golden age at Hull (although I suspect everyone feels that), but the combination of the staff, students and general vibe of the university, made it a very special place to be.

From my first visit I knew I wanted to study there. Despite the 14-hour journey from my home town, I was inspired by the Donald Roy Theatre and excited that we would not only get to perform on the stage, but would make the performances happen: design, direct, costume and (sometimes) write the content – of none of which I had any experience at the time.

I arrived as someone who considered himself an 'actor' and, like many of my companions, was introduced to not only the wide scope of opportunities that the industry contains, but respect for all aspects and angles of it. This, for me, was the ethos of the course – everyone working together. It is this that still governs my working practice and has inspired me to create and produce work in addition to playing a part in the work of others.

There was an incredibly close bond forged between the people that I met and studied with during my three years in the Department. I met my wife, my closest collaborator of 12 years, the person I share an allotment with and many of my professional contemporaries and friends 12 years on. Much is talked about the 'Hull Mafia', but if I am in a new company, it is a good bet that someone will have, or will know somebody who, studied at Hull. It is always a good recommendation.

So I have been advising my little brother to get the Flux Capacitor working and figure out how to power it to 1.21 giggawatts, because I can't imagine having a fuller and more rounded experience in any time or place... plus, he could maybe get back in time to stop Ali falling through that glass table.

From East Coast to East Coast

Sam Roukin. Single Honours Drama, 2001
Actor

The city of Kingston Upon Hull was contributing nothing to the sales pitch of Hull University Drama Department on the day I arrived for my interview in 1998. The city was enveloped by a blanket of rain, rendering the Humber Bridge barely visible. The sickly chocolate-refuse aroma from the various factories was in full effect and added to this, it was freezing. In other words, the conditions were perfect. If you can be lured into a three-year commitment anywhere under these circumstances, it has to be somewhere impressive.

I knew of the Department's reputation and the prominent alumni, but in the end I trusted instinct over reputation. It was simply the soul of the place. The moment you walk into The Gulbenkian you are aware of the building's energy. It oozes creativity. Fanciful? Maybe, but I think there is some architectural factor too. The building has no dead ends. On each floor, you can walk all the way round. It encourages a flow of ideas and provides the opportunity to bump into someone every minute. I felt creative in the building immediately and, more importantly, I felt at home, a feeling which grew the more time I spent there. The Department has a parenting system where finalists nurture freshers. My 'Daughter' Alice still calls me her Dad.

It is only when looking back, that I realise how much the time spent there formed future experience, particularly in the business. One of the great things is how the tutors, most of them expert practitioners in their own right, lead by example. In our first term, Nike Imoru, a heroine of mine, played the title role in *Medea*. She led our very first acting class which culminated in Tom Brooke and I having a slow motion boxing match, topless (we have been firm friends ever since). Then to see her three weeks later putting her money where her mouth was and laying her acting guts out on stage in front of us, garnered maximum respect. Many of the tutors were involved in projects along the way and it gave an inspiring context to their work and ours.

Nike encouraged so many of us to forge ahead even if we were destined for some sort of creative failure. This was a triumph in her eyes. Failure is a crucial part of any rehearsal process; the permission to get it wrong and I learned it from her. I know many other people who have similar stories, not just about her but other members of staff. Most students had their 'person', the tutor that lit their creative fire in whatever discipline it happened to be and encouraged risk-taking. The Department itself upheld this philosophy via daily HUDDLEs. A £5 budget, a performance space for 30 minutes any lunch-time and the promise of an audience. Anything goes. Some great theatre never to be seen again came from these performances; some artists were born.

There were so many great artistic experiences during my time in Hull that have weirdly come full circle in the future. I remember being humiliated during a workshop with the great classical actress, Jane Lapotaire. I understood what she wanted me to do intellectually, but was unable to put it into action at that point and in front of an audience too. I was frustrated and bruised by the experience. Two years later she came and did a similar workshop at Bristol Old Vic Theatre School where I was training and this time I was able to hit the ground running. One of the greatest things about the Hull Department and its facilities was the option to try out every aspect of professional theatre practice. During my Drama degree course I acted, sang, directed, stage-managed, learned set design, sound design, carpentry (badly) and then some. Graduates leave Hull with a respect for every aspect of theatre. It seemed so basic at the time to have an interest in everything, but as soon as you are working professionally, you realise how rare that is.

People do talk in the theatre and media world of 'The Hull Mafia'. Wherever you are in the business, whatever you are doing, there is a high probability that you will find a Hull University Drama Department graduate. I was never more aware of it than in my most recent theatre gig, *The Kitchen* at The National Theatre. Tom Brooke played Peter, I played Paul, Ruth Gibson played Gwen and Anna Cole, whom I'd never met before, was an ASM. It was such a joy to experience this full circle. It turned out to be the last English job I did prior to moving to the US. As Tom and I walked down to the front of The Olivier Stage on opening night to take our joint curtain call, I said in his ear 'Who knew?' Hull had kick-started a friendship and two career paths that went in separate directions, only to join up again on the stage where we had together watched our acting heroes inspire us.

Hull did that.

The Joe Davies Rule

Zoe Bickerton. Single Honours, Drama, 2002
Television Production Manager

It's a really tricky task, trying to sum up three entertaining, exhausting, exhilarating and excellent years in just a couple of paragraphs and I'm not sure I can even begin to do justice to my time spent in the Department. The legendary staff, students and, of course, our good friends in the union – Chico Mendez and Johnny Mac [*both Bars. Ed.*] – helped me grow up and decide where I was going in life. I hope I might have supported others in the same way too.

What the Department gave us all was a chance to learn from our own mistakes in the most phenomenal theatre and creative environment. Some of the skills I learnt in Hull are with me every day, whether trying to balance a budget or wrangling with 'challenging' directors.

The specific challenges of scheduling 30 show rehearsals for Studio Week still offer me a platform for working on production and shoot schedules. The introduction of 'The Joe Davies rule', whereby actors could only do three shows per Studio Week – both to give less well-known members of the Department more of a chance to shine and also, immediately, to prevent an excel-induced nightmare – is the type of light-bulb moment I still often hope will strike when looking at an impossible schedule. The budgets are bigger now and the schedules more densely packed, but core skills were learnt in Hull, with staff there for support when necessary, while giving us breathing-space to find our own way.

Aside from the practical skills and academic lessons learnt, those three years were just an abundance of fun and great memories. At times it was ridiculous and we were knackered and emotional, but every day really seemed to count.

Some of those memories will be with me for life:

30 of us first-years dancing our hearts out one Studio Week with five of our members dressed as canned pineapple;

261

Mark Ravenhill being the lone voice supporting our production of *Roberto Zucco* at the NSDF;

fiercely competitive fancy-dress at the Christmas parties;

mortifyingly asking Donald Roy if he was 'a Friend of the Donald Roy', during a box-office stint;

the elation at hearing the words 'hellur, five ur' when booking a taxi.

Above all, the one thing I will always appreciate about my time at Hull is that it's where I met the people who are to this day my best friends. While we no longer live in each others' pockets, they remain a vital part of my life and I'm eternally grateful that, one bleak September morning in the last century, we all found ourselves in Hull.

No More Nails

Joe Davies. Single Honours Drama, 2002
Writer and Teacher

The thick snow fell and settled, camouflaging the uniquely white telephone boxes, as I made my way towards the Gulbenkian Centre. It was the day of the interview.

I was not alone. My Mum had thought I would gain additional confidence from the presence of my Godfather, a former student of Hull's Drama Department, a member of the original intake. My Godfather will not mind me saying that he was, and is, outrageously camp, and whilst this is all well and good, enjoyable even at certain moments, it was, on this somewhat nerve-racking occasion, an ungodly nightmare in a hopeless world. Dressed in a florescent blue vinyl jacket (him not me) and obscenely tight leather trousers, my Godfather squealed and screeched his way around the foyer performing for the other prospective students as I attempted to impress them by crawling inside myself; no mean feat.

As I reflect on this ghoulish beginning to my Hull history, I wonder if perhaps his embarrassingly flamboyant behaviour numbed my nerves for the upcoming day, the bleak and yawning universe screaming out to me that *things couldn't get any worse*. I have no memory of the interview but somehow I managed to get in. If I hadn't got in, I wouldn't be writing this. The car battery was flat when we got back to it as if the city too screamed at me 'Kingston-upon-Hull – you'll never leave'.

The second time that I approached the doors of the Gulbenkian Centre was the first day of my course. The big glass front doors were locked. There was a Department meeting in there for us at 10 o'clock, but the doors were locked. I was so anxious about everything that this minor glitch was enough to send me off in the opposite direction, away from the building, thinking that I would probably have to call my Dad and tell him it had all been a terrible mistake. If it hadn't been for Kat Joyce, who first appeared to me as a blurry vision of black puffer jacket and roller blades wheeled towards me at speed, that could well have been it for me. Fortunately, Kat (who is one of those people that just seems to know what you're meant to do as if she was being guided by the spirits of long since dead Drama students), took me in through the shadowy smokers' door at the side and that was that.

Three wonderful years. Three years that lasted forever, and were over in an instant. Three years that, more than anything else, taught me how to think for myself. The Drama degree at Hull seems to me the way that Drama should be taught. Professional schools might look to Hull for a model rather than a more out-dated syllabus which emphasises only limited aspects of a broad and ever-more complex discipline.

I spent three years creating fantastic theatre and rubbish theatre with a group of people who remain the most important friends I will ever have. We got the chance to have a go at anything (within the confines of what the law will allow). It was this genuine freedom that allowed us to explore what it was we were truly capable of and has led us to become writers, actors, booksellers, directors, teachers, illustrators, filmmakers, curators, lecturers, publicists and all manner of other tangential things.

Other than that stuff (and chips, cheese, mayonnaise and chip spice), my time spent in the workshop, building and designing sets was of huge personal significance. No longer could my parents know me as manually incompetent, a boy incapable of anything DIY, the boy who once tried to glue a nail into a wall. No, that boy had become a man; a man who could chop things up, hammer things together and countersink a screw as soon as look at it. As a final comment, and in reference to the nail I tried to glue, it is important to note the robustly healthy sales of a product called *No More Nails*. If anything, you see, I was ahead of my time when I glued that nail in. I was sitting on the top of the DIY bell curve, waiting for everyone else to catch up.

'On Second Thoughts ...'

Kate Mackonochie. Single Honours Drama, 2002
Producer

I remember arriving at that big black door of the Hull University Drama Department convinced – as I had been from a very early age – that I wanted to be an actor. This was my first step towards achieving this dream.

It took one audition for a Department show to realise that acting wasn't going to be the answer. I had been a big fish in a little pond; now I was swimming with more talent and commitment to acting than I had.

So there I was stuck in a Drama degree having absolutely no idea what I was doing there. I very strongly considered swapping to some other degree course. After an anxious discussion with my tutor and only a little soul searching (it's astounding now to look back at the flippancy of youth), I was persuaded (thank you Brian Parsons) to stay until the end of the first term, to see how it went.

And I am grateful, to both him and to the Department, for leading me to realise what I really wanted to do with myself. The fantastic thing about the Department – something that I have only truly appreciated since undertaking a career – is the opportunity to try things out. While we were helped and supported along the way, there were real budgets, real audiences, difficult deadlines, tricky artists, hours spent getting a show together, predictable panics and a lot of angst-ridden conversations by the big black door. There was also an impressive level of hard work and commitment. Of the productions during those three years two really stick with me. John Gardner's *The Crucible* is still the best I've seen and Zoe Stephens' production of *Arabian Nights* the most magical piece of theatre storytelling.

Combining the productions with theoretical courses was ideal too, 'Gender and Identity' giving a whole new vocabulary and way of viewing the world.

I now work as a Producer and I know that HUDD is very well thought of by others in the industry. I feel immensely proud and privileged to be a part of the Hull alumni – albeit not quite as I had originally planned.

Some Things Change

Amy Simpson (Skinner). Single Honours Drama, 2002; Ph.D. 2008
Hull Drama Department Lecturer

On reflection, what stands out about Drama at Hull is how our graduates never quite leave. I am, perhaps, one of the most literal examples of this: Hull Drama undergraduate, postgraduate, administrative staff and, most recently, Lecturer. But there are others too and each year I am struck by how generous our graduates are with their time and talent, returning to run workshops, tutorials or question-and-answer sessions for current students. There's something about these sessions, connecting undergraduates to the 'real world', through people who have once been in their shoes, which makes them unique experiences, however many times they take place.

There's also something about the quintessential Hull Drama student. I might occasionally joke about 'student recycling' ('doesn't that new first-year remind you of so-and-so who graduated ten years ago?'), but in reality Hull Drama students don't change that much. I think of the energy, focus, determination of my own graduating class and see it mirrored in our current third-years. There is always something strangely familiar about a Gulbenkian technical rehearsal, whoever is running it. I put it down to the sense of community which is apparent from day one when, as a trembling first-year, you meet your Drama Parents (yes, they still do that), and are initiated into the ways of Gulbenkian.

Some things do change – it's the Sanctuary now, not the Rez – and I like how current students are fascinated by my time as an undergraduate. There is always a stream of questions about what's different now: this year alone, I've explained the Z Ball, the fancy-dress Christmas party and the Studio Week Meal (denounced as a ridiculous idea by events reps dealing with the organisation of 300 students). Games of Killer, graduates of the class of 2002 will be pleased to hear, still take place on an annual basis. When I'm asked if it's 'weird' to be still here, 10 years after my own graduation, I hesitate, but the truth is, it's not weird at all – in fact, it's a great privilege. Hull Drama Department has given me an education and a career and, as I begin the supervision of my first Hull graduate-turned-Ph.D. student, I hope that this will be the case for many others as well.

A Dangerous Liaison

Sarah Talbot. Single Honours Drama, 2002
Head of Drama, Jerudong International School, Brunei

I went along to *Les Liaisons Dangereuses* auditions because Annabelle Murphy told me she fancied giving it a go, but wouldn't unless I did. We were in first year and felt pretty gauche; neither of us expected anything to come of it. After all, this was a Main House. Third-years were cast in Main House Productions.

Directors Sarah O'Meara and Katy Schutte never got the memo. They cast a second-year *Joint Honours* student in the lead role (Amanda Walker gave a wicked Merteuil), and I got Cécile. Less surprisingly, George Dalton was to play Valmont to Laura Cubitt's Madame du Tourvel.

It seems ridiculous now, but I remember reading the cast list with disbelief, feeling quite overwhelmed. Sarah Cauldwell did nothing to allay my fears; did I know I had a sex scene with George Dalton? No.

I remember looking at the gym mat lying in the middle of the Rehearsal Room opposite Paula's office and listening to Sarah O'Meara explaining the ambiguities surrounding Valmont and Cécile's first encounter. Does she really not want him to, or does she really not want to want him to? Is Valmont a rapist or a master seducer playing out 'every woman's fantasy'? I remember being unconvinced by this suggestion at the time. 12 years on, the jury's out.

George's decision to substitute breast for stomach was a stroke of genius. Not only did it establish a business-like approach to the first rehearsal, when we barely knew each other, but as time went on, I lost sight of the target. On the opening night, when he grabbed my breast for the first time, I remember my eyes popping involuntarily as I suppressed the urge to slap him across the face.

Time passed and I started to enjoy myself. We were play-fighting. I'd trained with the Hull University Women's Rugby team earlier in the year and grown up with two brothers, both of whom loved to practice-tackle. This was like being at home, or out on the field. George was close behind me, kneeling with his knees spread, when Sarah asked me to move away. Assuming we were working towards a Valmont – Predator, Cécile – Victim approach I propelled myself forward, one foot on the mat, the other somewhere else, somewhere soft. I remember there was a lot of give. Sarah's horrified expression prompted me to look over my shoulder. George was doubled over, his eyes tightly closed, his mouth wide open. Very calmly, Sarah indicated I leave the room. I remember suggesting George might like a drink (for some reason, I thought lemonade would ease the pain). George shook his head and Sarah said, 'Just go. We'll pick up where we left off another time. That's enough for now'.

George was very good about it. I wouldn't go so far as to say we became friends. A mutual respect flourished. With a lot of help from Sarah, we found our way through the scene and I think she was pleased with the outcome.

About a year ago, I attended a readthrough of the play elsewhere. Merteuil and Valmont locked horns, each grimly determined to subdue the other, Madame du T wafted and drowned in a miserable mixture of love and loathing. Indeed, the play seemed far crueller than I remembered. As Christopher Hampton praised the acidic nature of the performance, I wondered whether he would have approved of a 19-year-old Cécile who, in a desperate attempt at emancipation, inflicts searing pain on an unsuspecting Valmont.

To avoid an insincere conclusion, I offer a sincere, if belated, apology.

Sorry, George.

James Graham. Single Honours Drama, 2003
Playwright

It's the sound of the doors closing for me. In the corridors. That little 'fffth' as they swing back and forth. The smell of the radio studio. The echo of your feet on the Front-of-House floor tiles. These are what I remember – what I'm reminded of when I go back. That *feeling* of working late in the paint shop to get a set built for a show, dark outside, in winter. An early morning weekend call in the studio to rehearse a HUDDLE, or whatever.

I couldn't really *see* Hull on my Open Day because it was covered in snow, which on reflection was a bit of a cheat. It all looked very picture postcard. Don't get me wrong, Hull is one of my favourite places on the planet, it's where my best memories come from, but entering the city centre from Clive Sullivan Way, up Beverley Road – I'm not saying it's not pretty, but ... you know. It's no bad thing you couldn't see it under the snow, that's all I'm saying. I'm grateful. It made me say 'Yes'. And thank God I said 'Yes'.

We, the intake of 2000, were the first 'big year'. During the Green Room Club drinks on Bev Road somewhere (where your 'mums' and 'dads' look after you, introducing you around), the second- and third-years', who numbered perhaps 30 to 40 each – were visibly shaken to see all 80-odd of us swan in. What to do with us all?

About a fortnight in I found myself standing in the living room of a third-year in just my boxer shorts having my picture taken, thinking blimey, this isn't what I'd imagined. Tomm Coles was taking my photo for a poster. A poster that still hangs in the foyer today. Rather precociously for a newly-arrived first-year, I'd been cast as the main part in GRC President Andy Kelly's new play *The Wife and Times of Armitage Shanks*: the title-character inspired by the toilet manufacturer, of course. In fact, during a Saturday night *Twisted* in the Union, some friends ran over excited while I danced to Chesney Hawkes. In one of the girls' toilets, above the 'Armitage Shanks' label, someone had scrawled 'James Graham *is...* I know it was only graffiti in a toilet bowl, but I'd never felt so famous.

Apart from the learning, the reading, the writing, the performing, some of the biggest dilemmas were in deciding where to drink and dance on what night. This seems to have changed through the generations. For our year group, it was (often but not always) Waterfront on a Monday; Tuesday was the Fez, though later on Position; Wednesday I can't remember, maybe we stayed in, though I doubt it; Thursday *always* LA's; Friday evolved into the Piper, but there was always Welly and Spiders to contend with.

I recall my seminars with Mike Walton in his office (the one with the scary traffic-light buzzer – green for 'enter', amber for 'wait', red for 'turn-around-and-go-back-the-way-you-came-right-now'). I'd never seen so many books as in his office. I asked if he'd read them all. He smiled and said 'Well, I did write one or two of them'. On close inspection of the spines I realised it. was true. I was delighted to see his name as editor of Methuen classical playtexts. It's my greatest pride to have since had plays published under the Methuen banner. I like the idea that mine might soon be on those shelves too.

I wrote my first ever play, *A Pleasant Rhyme*, in Hull; it was staged in the Gulbenkian, now the Minghella Studio. I became a writer, there. One of the most extraordinary days and the most memorable encounters, amongst a raft of extraordinary days and memorable encounters, was meeting Anthony Minghella, hearing him talk about his own writing, his own days walking the corridors, with the doors that go 'fffth'.

Standing on the shoulders of giants, and all that.

HUDD, A Fortunate Accident

Felix Scott. Single Honours Drama, 2003
Actor

I looked around Hull University because my Mum told me to. I had no intention of going there as I had grand plans of attending a bigger, more fashionable city, like Manchester or Bristol. All I knew about Hull was that it had a football team and was near Leeds. I had no idea of the small, perfectly-formed Department waiting for me.

A fully-functioning theatre, studio theatre, radio studio, design office and workshop? This place was not like any other Drama Department I'd seen and within a half-hour of being there on my Interview Day, Hull had moved from an outside wildcard to my top choice.

Main House productions, HUDDLEs, HUDDEEs [*HUDD Evening Events*], Studio Week, the GAFTAs, the Green Room Club etc.: HUDD was a world of its own and an inspiring one at that. While most of my mates were popping into their university once or twice a week, we were in every day, whether to build sets or work on some kind of performance. The Donald Roy theatre (with it's distinctive musky smell) and the amazing range of plays I witnessed there all helped to mould and train me in acting. You learn most in front of an audience and the opportunity to perform to the public taught me so much in the discipline of being an actor.

Hull benefitted hugely from the integration and socialising of all three years. I still am in contact with numerous people and have even had the pleasure of working with old Hullites on professional jobs. There is always a warm and knowing conversation to be had reminiscing about the Department. The teaching was brilliant and I have particular fond memories of Keith Peacock and Brian Parsons.

I would not be an actor today if it had not been for Hull. I owe the Department a huge thank you for helping to guide me towards my chosen profession.

Long may the Department continue.

The Workings of Fate

Duška Radosavljević. Ph D Drama, 2003
Dramaturg, Lecturer

In the autumn of 1998 I was presented with a tough dilemma: to accept a Graduate Teaching Assistantship at the University of Hull or to go and work as John Barton's Personal Assistant at the RSC. I had spent most of the last year of my undergraduate degree looking for funding opportunities to enrol for a Ph D. Then the two interviews came together and, having successfully attended the Hull interview first, I went to John Barton to seek his counsel. Most of all he wanted to know whether I was a 'political animal', but he was very generous and empathetic about my predicament – he took the time to list pros and cons about both options and then asked me to let him know what I had decided. Eventually, I wrote him a letter explaining that I was not Antigone – I am not exactly sure what I tried to say with that, but I think it was something to do with feeling that I needed to accept my fate of staying in academia.

I had a good time in Hull, even though a couple of months into it, in 1999, the NATO bombing of Serbia started, triggering off all of my dormant and not so dormant political sentiments. Of several productions I was involved with at the Drama Department, I most vividly remember working with the then already retired Professor Don Roy on a new Serbian play called *The Props-Master*. The playwright Ugljesa Sajtinac had written the play about his grandfather, a former theatre Props-Master, using verbatim anecdotes and recollections, but he also managed to make it come across as a powerful commentary on the changing times in Serbia. I made a first draft of the translation of the play and brought a young Serbian director Vladimir Popadic over so that we could work with the British actors to arrive at a more colloquial final version.

Don Roy played the Serbian theatre man with great gusto, taught us the technical terms such as 'combinations' (a 19th century male undergarment), and filled in our gaps in the general history of drama. The final production got as far as the Festival of Contemporary European Plays in Huddersfield. We managed to get the playwright Ugljesa Sajtinac out of Serbia for the first time in his life so that he could see his play, and this eventually led to a play called

Huddersfield, which premiered at the West Yorkshire Playhouse in 2004. It was the first Serbian play to be produced professionally in the UK. In Serbia it was made into a blockbuster film, following a successful run of its Belgrade production.

My time at Hull did help me discover my calling. After submitting my Ph D on Yugoslav Metadrama in the autumn of 2002, I was employed as Dramaturg at Northern Stage and Newcastle University. In a strange twist of fate I did end up working at the RSC. I was interviewed by the Education Department for a new post of a Higher Education practitioner. It had transpired in the course of my interview that I was not available to attend the workshop element of my 'audition' due to a pre-existing clash of dates, so I was asked to provide names of colleagues who could comment on my teaching.

Unbeknown to me, a former student from Hull, whom I had taught in his first year, Gareth Collins, already worked in the Education Department at the time. It so happened that it was he who actually provided my first reference, convincing the bosses that I was the right person for the job.

Furtherance and Fulfilment

Kat Oliver. Single Honours Drama, 2004
Theatrical Agent

My years within the Department were truly 'formative' and I am quite certain that I owe my current career to my time at Hull. From the moment I stepped onto the campus my gut told me that the Drama Department at Hull was where I was meant to study. I am so glad I trusted my instincts. The teaching was first-rate and there was always a great sense of support between the staff and students. The thing that stays with me most, however, was the encouragement we had to pursue our own projects – we were given a virtually free reign over an incredible space and some of the best facilities available. This more than anything nurtured the students in my opinion, and fuelled whatever passion was already within us.

As a result the sense of community between classmates was strong throughout and the bond stretches far and beyond the five year-groups I had direct contact with from '01 to '05. Even now I meet people with whom there is an instant bond based on the Hull Drama connection. My friend Hannah Chissick, who was some years before me, gave me my first break into casting for which I am eternally grateful.

Another wonderful alumna closely followed, Hannah Miller, who, after my spell with her at the RSC Casting Department, recommended me to the agency Conway van Gelder Grant.

I have been with CVGG for seven years now and began taking on my own clients last year. It is a highly respected agency and I could not wish to be anywhere better. I don't think that there is any chance that I would be in the position I am without Hull behind me, so I have a lot to thank the Department for. The people that I met have become my very best friends and the encouragement of the alumni has led me to my ideal vocation.

I hope that HUDD continues to thrive and that I will be in a position to help young alumni myself some day.

Simply the Best!

Peter ORourke. Single Honours Drama, 2004
Academic

I can vividly recall Matt Hartley, GRC President, sitting at the bar of the Haworth welcoming us freshers to the Drama welcome party. That evening was the first of countless drunken gatherings over my three years at Hull, which saw me waking from a stupor to do press-ups for Brendan Hughes, get stuck in a football net at a GAFTAS after-party and impersonate Tina Turner on more than one occasion.

Many of those evenings and early mornings are hazy memories now; more distinct however are the much more fulfilling hours spent within the walls of the Gulbenkian:

painting endless boards of MDF to appear as solid pine for *The Crucible*; squeezing into leather pants for Louisa Lewis's Z show *Sex Cells: the DNA of Dating*;

being an outrageous Berkoffian sycophant in *Dahling, You Were Marvellous*;

traipsing around Hull in search of autumnal leaves for Alex Evans's version of Schwartz's *Little Red Riding Hood*;

sporting a canary-yellow pilot's jacket matching Kate Skelding's air hostess garb in Rob Cheesmond's production of *Camino Real*;

ordering a heart-shaped gobo for my pink lighting state for Sam Grayston's production of *Assassins* (needless to say Jim Lambert wasn't convinced);

and playing a doctor in a mostly collaborative adaptation of *The Pumpkin Eater*, directed by Matt Pereira.

Presenting the GAFTAS with Frankie Dixie was a pleasure, especially thanks to the cooperation of jazz band *par excellence*, the Blue Parrots, with the dulcet tones of singer Heidi Smith.

Another highlight was my third-year research project inspired by Louise Peacock's Playback Theatre option, which saw Claire Medd (of head-stuck-in-parcan-attached-to-flybar-fame), Nia Roberts, Kat Oliver, Beth Lower and I researching into the effectiveness of Playback on the radio – it was most fun, with a range of results. Getting voted onto the GRC as Secretary was also great, after my campaign speech in which I stated my expertise in 'student bodies'.

In spite of all the production work and socialising we also miraculously managed to get a degree: the academic work was stimulating and inspiring. In particular I recall Mike Walton's Greek lectures; Rob Cheesmond's lectures on Appia and Craig; 'German Theatre of the Golden Age' with Tony Meech; and 'Drama and History' with Keith Peacock. Brian Parsons made us all obsess over *The Shining*; Terry Hale belly-danced to illustrate orientalism and Sarah-Jane Dickenson provided us with an exclusive sneak preview of Minghella's screenplay for *Cold Mountain*. Indeed, Minghella's visit to the Department was most memorable, as were the 40th anniversary celebrations.

Carole-Anne Upton's supervision and encouragement when writing my dissertation on Irish theatre was later to inspire a return to academia; something I never dreamt of pursuing on graduating in 2004. Thus far in my experience of the academic world I have had unerring support from the Drama Department and it has been great to be able to see my old lecturers as helpful colleagues. Furthermore, there are many academics with Hull degrees 'on the circuit', so the old Gulbenkian links die hard.

The University of Hull changed my life trajectory (I'm now married to the girl I met on my first day in the city) and studying in the Drama Department provided me with opportunities I could never have anticipated. I count my Drama peers among the closest of my friends. The inter-year bond and shared experience mean that I feel part of the Hull Drama Department family.

In Tina's words, Hull Drama Department *'Simply the Best!'*

Everyone Remembers a Good Teacher

Sophie Bush. Single Honours Drama, 2005
Lecturer in Performance, Sheffield Hallam University

I have taught in four separate university Drama Departments over the last three years. All of them have had their merits, but none of them seemed to have what really made my time at Hull so memorable: the extent of its extra-curricular performance culture.

Perhaps my current students are too busy worrying about assessed performances and the part-time jobs they need to pay their higher fees, but I miss the vibrancy, the buzz of Events Week, the knowledge that if you didn't have anything to do that lunchtime, there was probably a HUDDLE to drop in on.

Watching Richard (Reg) Howlett play *Scaramouche Jones* under the expert direction of Chris Holliday remains one of the finest hours I have ever spent in the theatre.

Sleepily rigging lights with Dan Cheyne at one o'clock in the morning in an otherwise deserted studio seems implausible by today's Health and Safety standards, but we lived to tell the tale and walk home with the urban foxes.

As I progressed from HUDDLE, to HUDDEE, to Main House, I learnt many of the skills I use today, as a director, teacher and facilitator, whilst collaborating with a wealth of talented practitioners, including the indispensable Anna Cole, who now stage-manages for the National Theatre, the Donmar or the Young Vic, rather than for me.

Of course the Department had its frustrations as well. As one of the 50-odd girls in my year fighting tooth and claw for any part going and watching the 10 or so men waltz merrily into anything they liked, I became more aware of the gender politics of the profession I was hoping to enter. This was discussed at length amongst my peers. It seemed fairly inevitable that the numbers game benefited the boys in terms of casting, but other questions were less simple.

Why, for example, considering the glut of women in the Department, were so many Main House productions directed by men? Why was every President of the GRC during our time male? [*It wasn't always so. Ed.*]

None of us could really believe that anyone involved in the selection or election of these opportunities and positions was being actively sexist, so something subtler and self-perpetuating had to be at work. After much thought, the theory some of us developed was that the men were, from the moment they arrived, celebrated and endorsed by the myriad opportunities flung their way. It was universally acknowledged that even the less talented actors among them could enjoy a number of decent parts during their degree, and the really gifted were destined for departmental stardom. Their female counterparts, however, even those who were exceptional actresses, were met by disappointment after disappointment, as they competed with their friends for the few available roles, each defeat bringing another dent to their confidence. Was it, therefore, surprising that the men, believing themselves invincible, went on to lead both the performance and the social culture of the Department?

The antidote to these realisations was the strong female role-models we had, both within the student body itself and amongst the staff: Sarah-Jane Dickenson, Helen Iball, Louise Peacock, Pauline Chambers. Their support and encouragement not only helped and inspired me and countless others through our degrees at Hull, but also set many of us on the paths to our future careers. I remember my surprise at Sarah-Jane's suggestion, at the end of one 'Dramaturgy for Stage and Screen' seminar, that I might consider post-graduate study.

Being strong-willed and curious about the world outside education, I did not immediately follow up this recommendation, but, two years after graduating, SJD was still happy to provide the information and advice that I needed to make my return to academia. I don't remember whether she has ever said she told me so, but everything about my doctorate and the teaching I now do myself has confirmed to me that *this* is what I want to do. If I can make half the difference in someone's life that she and the other people cited here made in mine, I will consider myself a good teacher.

Getting There

Kitty White. Single Honours Drama, 2006
Administrator at TSYS International Payment Solutions

My time at the University of Hull studying Drama holds very dear memories. I would like to share how I managed to secure my place to join the Drama Department in September 2003, as well as to show my appreciation.

I knew the Hull Drama Department was for me the moment I walked through those doors into the Gulbenkian. Here I joined various other interviewees on a March morning in 2002. I was extremely nervous, but was put at ease by various lecturers. Interestingly, when I visited the second time in January 2003, for the same process, I felt the same, but was even more sure the place was for me. On both visits we were taken on a brief tour around the building, participated in a drama practical with Louise Peacock and had an interview, my first with Keith Peacock, the second, with Brian Parsons which had lasted 10 minutes when he recognised who I was.

My story – I had wanted to join the Hull University Drama Department in September 2002, but I became ill that year with glandular fever. I recall my conversation with Brian Parsons in August 2002, a couple of days before my 18th birthday. I had been offered a place conditional on Bs in Drama and English, a C in History. I hadn't met the grade in English. Brian's advice was to take a year out, get better and re-apply for the following year. How right he was. I took his advice, re-enrolled at the sixth form college and re-took my exams in January 2002. Again, I missed out on my grade by a couple of marks finding out my results in Bryon Bay, Australia at 10pm in the evening.

I knew I should ring the Drama Department straight away and explain how much I wanted to come to Hull. Paula Lambert picked up the phone, listened to my tale and asked my UCAS number, which I didn't have. My mum phoned it through to Louise Peacock who informed her that I had definitely secured a place, In September 2003, I joined the Drama Department. In a practical session in the first week Louise came up to me as she was walking around meeting and greeting the students. She *had* remembered who I was.

continued from page 107 (1976)

Let's Get One Thing Straight!

Penny Greenland, MBE. Single Honours Drama, 1976
Director. JABADAO – Movement Play company

Let's get one thing straight.

Neither I nor my daughter Abbi meant to do this family thing. Neither of us meant to go to Hull. Just as our mother/grandmother (History, 1946) never meant to go; and our cousin (Psychology, 2012.) never meant to go either. We all had other first choices, but something sucks the women in our family towards Hull. Good job. We have had the best of times.

Penny (1976)

Dance was a really significant element of the course during my three years. Down south, London Contemporary Dance Theatre was just beginning to make its mark and the first regional residency (now commonplace for dance companies, but unheard of then) took place in Hull. Doing master classes with the very scary Robert Cohan, watching company rehearsals and performances and hanging out with the dancers inspired a group of us. We fell in love with Graham technique, with our physicality, with figuring out how to make dance theatre. Viv Bridson offered to teach class twice each day (8.00 am and 1.00 pm), a stalwart and generous offer.

A group of us became obsessed with how high we could lift our legs, how high we could lift each other, how to create moving images that spoke deeply. As each of us in turn tried out our choreographic skills, the others became their dancers. Our focus, for a while, was all on training our bodies and finding out what we could do with them. Writing an essay, or revising, acquired a strange primary purpose – how to lengthen our tendons, work the lowest vertebrae – sitting on the floor, legs wide, lying down between, moving the paper further and further forward to extend our reach. Ouch! We loved it when we ached; when a bit of our body we hadn't felt before yelped. We experienced it as a small triumph – a new muscle/tendon/ligament lengthening, strengthening.

Other people in the Department, intrigued, joined us from time to time, putting on tights and lumbering about with us in the lunchtime class. (Is that mean? There was a fair amount of lumbering. And giggling.) We dancers were definitely an oddity. You must remember that there were no small dance companies in the UK at this time. Being a dancer wasn't an option unless you'd been to ballet school since the age of four. But there was a great energy around – and generous amusement, interest and support for our passion from everyone else in the Department.

The course included some academic study around Dance. It was brief and featured a lecture which I didn't understand at the time, introducing the concept of dance and phenomenology. I remember doing a lot of poo-pooing. But if I want to look at the subsequent 36 years with a neat, rounding-up frame of mind, working out what that lecture was about has been a throughline. I went to Hull to learn about theatre. I came away passionate about human physicality, the experience of being a body and the directness and depth of communication through the body. It has never dimmed.

Abbi (2009)

Abbi Greenland. Single Honours Drama, 2009
Theatre Maker - RashDash

UCAS requires you to have six university choices. I had five, so I needed one more. I didn't even look at the prospectus before shoving down Hull, knowing they must offer Drama because Pen had done it.

Hull was the first to offer me an interview – I thought I'd use it as practice. But after seeing the theatres, after meeting the then current Drama students, after meeting the staff – I didn't go to another interview, didn't look at another Uni. I knew where I wanted to be.

There's something about the warmth and the rough-and-ready – the freedom that the space and the course offers. No ego. Just give it a go. Have an idea, tell someone about it, make something, show it to people. That's what the space offered, and that's what I spent my three years doing.

And that's what I still do now I think.

It was by doing this that I met Helen Goalen, who runs RashDash with me. She didn't mean to come to Hull either. She ticked a box she didn't mean to tick whilst filling out UCAS forms in Thailand. I'm so glad she did. Whilst in Edinburgh with the first show we made together (it was so terrible, I can't even say its name – 'laughably pretentious' 1 star, *The Scotsman*), we saw a Russian company called Do-Theatre's show *Hangman*. The show had no words, just 'images that spoke deeply' to quote Pen, above. And it was this show that woke us up to a whole world of theatre we hadn't really explored … yet.

After that we spent all our spare time in the dance studio, not seeing how high we could lift our legs or each other (although there was a fair amount of that too), but playing with how movement and dance can articulate feelings, thoughts, ideas, experiences in a way that words can't. Trying to tug at how to express the felt experience, and – as Pen calls it – 'the experience of being a body and the directness and depth of communication through the body'.

But let's get one thing straight. I didn't mean to do the family thing either. I didn't mean to copy/follow Pen.

I meant to work out how to go about making theatre. And this is the special thing about Drama at Hull – what I found was that making theatre is all about being a community, a company. No matter what your role or your skills, we are all in this together and we are all going to make something together. Something that speaks of the people we are, the things we can do and the things we can say about the world. This community, this ensemble, this kind of collaboration is why we started RashDash and it's how we make work. It's how we value everyone involved. And Hull gave us that.

Hull also gave us the steel deck for our set for *The Ugly Sisters*. We dropped it back last week [*Sep. 2012*] after our run in Edinburgh. Thanks for that too.

HUDDLE Guests (apart from our own graduates) have included

Mike Bradwell
Simon Cadell
Ian Carmichael
Harry H. Corbett
Michael Denison and Dulcie Gray
Robert Eddison
Jimmy Edwards
John Franklyn-Robbins
John Godber
Susan Hampshire
Victor Henry
Nat Jackley
Veronica Lake
Mike Leigh
Sylvestra Le Touzel
John McGrath
Michéal McLiammóir
Sir Ian McKellen
Andrew Manley
Frank Marlborough
Michael Pennington
Edward Petherbridge
Alan Plater
Sir Anthony Quayle
Sir Donald Sinden
Eric Sykes
Sylvia Syms
Vera Vlasova
Denis Waterman
Auberon Waugh
Sir Donald Wolfit
Susannah York

Index of contributors, identified by their surname as students